Praise for the first *Financial Times Essential Guide to Writing a Business Plan*

'Vaughan Evans provides a thorough yet practical guide to writing a business plan. I particularly like his emphasis on market demand and competitive analysis because often we entrepreneurs tend to go with our gut feel rather than proper analysis. Miscalculate these two critical areas and you will probably enter the wrong business. I have been there before and no matter how good your team or execution is, it will be an uphill battle to convince investors if those two areas aren't compelling. Evans gets the priorities behind business planning right.'

Anthony Karibian, co-founder, Euroffice Ltd and XLN Telecom Ltd (both sold September 2010) and latest start-up, B. Online

'Raising capital is rarely straightforward. Evans' excellent book shines a light on what suppliers of capital expect in a business plan and why. It is an invaluable resource for all managers and budding entrepreneurs.'

Hugh Lenon, Managing Partner, Phoenix Equity Partners, and Chairman of the British Venture Capital Association, 2010

'Evans has nailed it! Clear, readable, no-nonsense thinking about the fundamentals every business plan must address. If writing a business plan is your next step, this book's for you.'

John W. Mullins, Associate Professor of Management and Chair in Entrepreneurship, London Business School, and author of *The New Business Road Test* and *Getting to Plan B*

'This guide cuts to the heart of what needs to go into a business plan – in any number of different scenarios. It is admirably clear and cleverly illustrated by real-life examples. It ought to be required reading for anyone contemplating any form of investment, even if they think they know it all already.'

James Brocklebank, Managing Director, Advent International

'At last! A book that explains how to write the kind of business plan that investors and lenders actually want to read. A clear and concise book – I haven't seen one that approaches the subject so straightforwardly. Evans uses his vast experience in advising real companies and financiers to make this guide authoritative and authentic, yet also practical and easy to follow.'

James Courtenay, Global Head, Project and Export Finance, Standard Chartered Bank

'Where was this book when I was producing business plans? With his extensive experience and unique style Vaughan Evans has produced a comprehensive, clear guide which unravels the mystique of business planning. Peppered with good examples it is an essential reference for those contemplating a start-up as well as existing businesses moving to their next phase of growth.'

Grahame Hughes, co-founder, Haven Power Ltd (exited 2010)

'Many investors say they back people, not businesses. Yes and no. People matter, of course. But so too do the markets the company addresses, the nature of the competition that's waiting around the corner, the value proposition the company brings to market . . . That is what a business plan should focus on and that is what is set out so lucidly in this book. It is written for managers and entrepreneurs to present to investors by someone who knows only too well what investors need to know.'

David Williamson, Managing Director, Nova Capital Management

'Vaughan Evans's considerable experience in creating business plans and evaluating them on behalf of investors is very much in evidence in this eminently readable book. From my private equity perspective, a plan submitted along these guidelines will stand out from the rest. It will speak the language of potential investors.'

James Pitt, Partner, Lexington Partners

'The fact that most new businesses fail is well known. The distinctive feature of *Writing a Business Plan* is the recognition that most businesses fail even before they are launched – they fail to attract financial backing. Vaughan Evans's emphasis on rigorous strategy analysis as the foundation for any business plan is based in practicality. His emphasis on understanding customers, recognising competition and appraising resources is relevant to all the critical phases of new enterprise creation: attracting backers, launching the business and developing it into a self-sustaining enterprise. This book offers a robust, realistic and readable framework for successful business planning.'

Robert M. Grant, Eni Professor of Strategic Management, Bocconi University, Milan, and author of *Contemporary Strategy Analysis*

'We engage advisers like Vaughan Evans to forensically examine the business proposition of a potential investee company. Evans himself has been doing this for years and focuses in his book on analysing those issues which are most critical to driving enterprise value – market growth, competition and a robust, distinctive strategy. Follow his advice, tackle those issues head on in your business plan and you'll be taking your first step towards getting funding.'

Ken Lawrence, Partner, Gresham Private Equity

'A good business plan does not get you the backing, it gives you an opportunity. It raises the right issues, which later you need to address with your backer. With a bad business plan, you are dead on arrival. Follow Evans's book and you'll get a good one.'

Jose Maria Maldonado, Partner, Bridgepoint Capital (Spain)

'Vaughan Evans knows the way an investor's mind works – the deliberations of risk and return over major issues – and here he introduces the reader to this mindset. The result will be a business plan that will have pre-empted all the key questions likely to be demanded by investors. Now they are in print. This is an invaluable guide for a private equity backed growth company such as ours.'

Stephen Lawrence, Chief Executive, Protocol Education Ltd

'Whether a start-up, early stage or mature business, this book provides essential and in-depth guidance on how to prepare a compelling business plan. With an emphasis on achieving credibility with the various readers of the plan, the guide offers more than just a template for producing a business plan. It brings together valuable real life examples as well as some priceless advice on strategic and operational issues. It should prove an invaluable tool for any company, large or small, that needs to produce a credible business plan.'

Vince O'Brien, Director, Montagu Private Equity and Chairman of the British Venture Capital Association, 2005

' "You can get it if you really want", but only if you have a good plan to get you there. Writing a business plan is one of the most important jobs anyone in business has to do at some point in their working lives. And yet in almost twenty years of reading business plans as an investor I only rarely come across a good one. In this well-written book Vaughan Evans has produced an insightful and practical guide to writing a business plan, born from a wealth of experience. Follow it and you stand a much better chance of getting "what you really, really want".'

Andrew Ferguson, Managing Director, Baird Capital Partners Europe Ltd

'Business planning in large organisations is sometimes done by rote, an extension of the budgeting process. Evans is right. It should be done properly or not at all. Properly means in-depth analysis of markets and the business proposition. This succinct, punchy book shows managers how to do it properly.'

Christine Harvey, former Director of Business Analysis and Planning, GlaxoSmithKline R&D

'We receive dozens of business plans a year from SMEs. If entrepreneurs invest the time to read this book, it will make our life simpler and their chances of obtaining finance so much higher.'

Peter Wright, Investment Director, Finance Wales

'This book provides an essential toolkit for anyone needing to assemble a business plan, with their ideas presented in a concise, no-nonsense way. Lively, contemporary case studies and essential tips, coupled with easy to follow writing, make it a perfect read for all levels of experience.'

Bill Priestley, Managing Director, LGV Capital Ltd

'The first question I always ask when looking at a business concept is "do they have a well thought out plan?". If not, then it's normally "decision made". Getting backing for your business is about selling a well-thought-through concept and ensuring you provide the reader with the information and analysis needed in a clear and convincing manner. This book is written from the viewpoint of the potential backer, targeting his/her key questions. It provides a no-nonsense, easy-to-follow guide that will ensure you deliver a persuasive plan.'

Robert Samuelson, Executive Director Group Strategy, Virgin Media

'As a private equity investor we see many business plans that fail to meet the "Seven Cs" outlined in Vaughan Evans' excellent book. If you are seeking financial backing, this step-by-step guide is the place to start.'

Paul Gough, Partner, STAR Capital Partners Ltd

'Over the years there have been many guides to *what* you should put in a business plan. The crucial difference with Evans' book is that it tells you *why* and *how* as well. It does so in crystal clear, jargon-free language, from an author whose experience in sifting the strategic wheat from the chaff on behalf of top investors is second-to-none. Not only will putting his advice into practice enhance your funding prospects – it will help you think more incisively about your business as well.'

Richard Kemp, Managing Partner, Sephton Capital

'Let's get real: the majority of so-called business plans we see are built of straw. They can be toppled over by an investor's puff. Build a business plan with bricks, one that can withstand the hurricane of investor analysis, and you may get funding. Evans shows you how to build.'

Jonathan Derry-Evans, Partner, Manfield Partners

'I have not met many entrepreneurs who actually enjoy taking out the time needed to put a proper business plan in place. After all, we could use that time to make some sales calls, think up some new ideas . . . and the list goes on. However, Vaughan Evans has shown in this excellent book that business planning is not only essential for success but it can also be a whole lot of fun – especially when you succeed in raising the capital you need to start or grow your business. This book will prove useful for both new and experienced entrepreneurs.'

Loxley McKenzie, Managing Director, Colordarcy Investment Ltd

'Well, we've seen them on TV – those aspiring entrepreneurs, long on passion but short on next year's forecast sales and profit figures. Sometimes even last year's performance is rendered vague and unquantified. But, as Vaughan Evans points out in this excellent guide to creating a business plan, backers need evidence as well as passion before they sign up to an investment. That's the strength of this book – it is slanted towards the initial market for the business plan – the backer – and once that perspective is established, the criteria and priorities follow. The book will help transform what can be an intimidating challenge into a well-informed, skilful task that might just make the difference in attracting a backer.'

Greg Spiro, Managing Director, SpiroNicholson

'Just as when you sell your product or service, you have to differentiate yourself AND your business in the minds of investors to raise finance. Simply having a great product or service is not sufficient. This insightful book – rare in its genre – walks you through how to do just this. This is a book that's well worth reading and having on your shelf even if your business idea is an early dream at this stage.'

Mike Price, Managing Director, Better Strategy Ltd

'Evans provides detailed and hugely practical techniques, templates and focused case studies to enable entrepreneurs and developers to prepare materials and documentation that for many would otherwise be sourced from high-priced hired hands. Written in a cheery and non-patronising style that generates enthusiasm for the task. Evans' light touch mitigates the drudgery of accounting and forecasting methodologies without any sacrifice to rigor and focus. His approach to demand forecasting is succinct and masterly. No less so his differentiation between advertising and marketing. The guide's positive spirit should feed through to the business plan itself and thus to the ultimate objective of raising support from internal and external backers.'

Stephen Uhlig, Managing Director, Colinette Partners

'I enjoyed this book immensely. As someone who has written business plans, indeed advised others on how to do so, this book provides new perspectives on the challenge. It's full of practical tips and detailed guidance. For those more financially challenged, the chapter on Financials and Forecasts provides the most straightforward explanation of the critical terms, their meaning and how to calculate them that I have seen.'

Andy Tomkins, Managing Director, Atomki

'Over the years I have written a few business plans for my own start-up businesses, however a year ago I needed to write one for a successful company which was poised for expansion and decided I needed some external, low cost assistance. I scoured the (online) shelves and bought a market leading book as a guide. I ended up with a reasonable plan, but it was a struggle. The book was long-winded and complex, as concerned with the minutiae and financials as the business rationale. Business planners today have it easy. This book is exceptional. Short and sharp, it goes straight to the meat – what we need to get right to meet the demands of the investor. It is lively to read, full of insightful guidance – based on Evans's years of experience of what works and what doesn't. It is dotted with great examples, from Levi Roots to LoveFilm, and deals with the financials succinctly and sufficiently. This book is a must and will save SME owners, both those starting up and those wishing to inject some strategic direction into their businesses, not just their hair but tens of thousands of pounds in consulting fees. It should result in what we all want – a great business model, saleable to investors!'

Amanda Hills, CEO, Hills Balfour Ltd

'This book is very useful and well written. Comprehensive yet concise and written in a chatty yet credible style. Very enjoyable as well as instructive. Excellent.'

Ian Lang, CEO, Higher Level Systems Ltd

Aux tombés de 7 Janvier 2015, qui ont préférés 'mourir debout que vivre à genoux'. Je suis Charlie.

The Financial Times Essential Guide to Writing a Business Plan

How to win backing to start up or grow your business

Second edition

Vaughan Evans

Harlow, England • London • New York • Boston • San Francisco • Toronto • Sydney
Auckland • Singapore • Hong Kong • Tokyo • Seoul • Taipei • New Delhi
Cape Town • São Paulo • Mexico City • Madrid • Amsterdam • Munich • Paris • Milan

PEARSON EDUCATION LIMITED

Edinburgh Gate
Harlow CM20 2JE
Tel: +44 (0)1279 623623
Fax: +44 (0)1279 431059
Website: www.pearson.com/uk

First published 2011 (print and electronic)
Second edition published 2016 (print and electronic)

The Financial Times. With a worldwide network of highly respected journalists, The
Financial Times provides global business news, insightful opinion and expert analysis
of business, finance and politics. With over 500 journalists reporting from 50 countries
worldwide, our in-depth coverage of international news is objectively reported and analysed
from an independent, global perspective. To find out more, visit www.ft.com/pearsonoffer.

ISBN: 978-1-292-08514-2 (print)
       978-1-292-08515-9 (PDF)
       978-1-292-08517-3 (eText)
       978-1-292-08516-6 (ePub)

British Library Cataloguing-in-Publication Data
A catalogue record for the print edition is available from the British Library

Library of Congress Cataloging-in-Publication Data
A catalog record for the print edition is available from the Library of Congress

10 9 8 7 6 5 4 3 2 1
19 18 17 16 15

Cover image © Garry Gay, Getty Images

Print edition typeset in 8.75 / 12pt by 71
Printed by Ashford Colour Press Ltd, Gosport

NOTE THAT ANY PAGE CROSS REFERENCES REFER TO THE PRINT EDITION

Contents

Publisher's acknowledgements

We are grateful to the following for permission to reproduce copyright material:

Figure 4.1 reprinted with the permission of The Free Press, a division of Simon & Schuster, Inc from *Competitive Strategy: Techniques for Analyzing Industries and Competitors* by Michael E. Porter. Copyright © 1980 by The Free Press. All rights reserved. Articles from *Financial Times* in Appendix C: Bounds, A. 'Low rates and QE push angels of the north to invest into start-ups' *Financial Times,* 7 May 2015, © The Financial Times Limited 2015; all rights reserved. Hazlehurst, J. 'The search for seed capital' *Financial Times,* 8 May 2015, © The Financial Times Limited 2015; all rights reserved. Dunkley, E. 'New sources of funding bring difficult choices' *Financial Times,* 3 January 2015, © The Financial Times Limited 2015; all rights reserved. Evans, J. 'Peer-to-peer investors to get savings tax break' *Financial Times,* 19 March 2015, © The Financial Times Limited 2015; all rights reserved. Bounds, A. 'State lender says banks need further help' *Financial Times,* 9 February 2015, © The Financial Times Limited 2015; all rights reserved.

In some instances we have been unable to trace the owners of copyright material, and we would appreciate any information that would enable us to do so.

About the author

Vaughan Evans is well placed to be your guide in business planning. He has been advising financiers on whether to back businesses for 30 years and, on the other side of the table, has written many successful business plans tailored to meeting the concerns of backers.

He is an independent consultant specialising in business strategy and planning for SMEs and in strategic due diligence for private equity having worked for many years at management consultants Arthur D. Little and investment bankers Bankers Trust Co.

He is the author of many successful business books, including the sister book to this, *The FT Essential Guide to Developing a Business Strategy* (2013) and the innovative and highly acclaimed *Key Strategy Tools* (2012).

An economics graduate of Cambridge University and a Sloan Fellow with distinction of London Business School, Vaughan is an entertaining speaker and seminar leader. His recent book, *Stand, Speak, Deliver!* (2015), is a pithy, witty guide on how to survive – and thrive – in public speaking and presenting.

Preface

You need a backer for your business? You need a business plan.

Don't know where to start? Congrats, you've come to the right place. Let this book be your guide in crafting a plan that will meet your backer's concerns.

This is the second edition of this book. The first, launched in 2011, met with a gratifying response – from entrepreneurs, managers, employees, consultants, academics and students.

They liked the style, the approach, the tools and the case studies. But, most of all, they liked the perspective.

This book is written from the perspective of the backer. It guides you all the way through to addressing the issues that are likely to concern your backer.

It urges you to tailor every word, every number, every fact, every assertion in your plan to the needs of your backer.

The reason behind this emphasis is simple. The vast majority of business plans received by a financier end up in the bin.

Put yourself in their shoes. They see SO many business plans, dozens and dozens of them, every month, that unless it is evident that the plan writer has done the homework and taken the trouble to address their likely concerns, in the bin it goes – even if the business proposition contains elements of (unproven) promise.

This book will show you how to design, craft and shape a plan to the needs of your backer.

Readers' feedback also included a number of most useful recommendations on how the book could be improved, which I have happily taken on board for this edition. Here are the main changes:

- Further drawing out of the specific challenges faced by start-ups – particularly on pinning down your perceived market niche and your perceived competitive advantage
- A new chapter, by specific request, on pitching the plan – an art as much as a science, but an area I have great pleasure in including, having 25 years' worth of tips on public speaking and presenting to impart!
- A new chapter on performing against plan, taking in key performance indicators and milestones
- A new appendix on alternative sources of finance
- A new appendix showing an example business plan in its entirety, from start to finish
- A new appendix on what to read next.

The main aim of this book, as in the first edition, is to help you write a winning business plan. But the secondary aim has always been to give you a good read.

Enjoy – and best of luck with your launch or expansion plans!

Vaughan Evans

PS Need a hand in writing a winning business plan? Or an independent critique before you pitch your plan to financiers? Let me know at: ve@vaughanevansandpartners.com

Introduction

You've got it! You've got a great idea for a new business. Everyone you talk to thinks it's terrific. 'A sure-fire winner!' they say.

But words are cheap. What you need is cash. You don't have enough in the bank to take this on, nor does your family, nor your friends. You need a backer – an angel investor, perhaps, or a venture capitalist.

To land that backer, you need a business plan.

Or maybe you run your own company and need to expand. You could just about finance it from your balance sheet or through your existing bank facilities, but you could do with some extra cushion. You need a backer, most likely your bank.

You too need a plan.

And what if you are planning serious expansion, possibly acquisition? You'll need equity backing from a development capitalist.

You need a serious plan.

Or maybe you're planning a management buyout. Boy, do you need a plan! It will have to be robust, nay, rock solid, because your private equity backers will hold you accountable to it once the deal goes through.

Or you're a middle manager and one Monday morning the big boss collars you at the water cooler with: 'Charlie, the board needs a business plan. Can I leave it with you?' You're pretty good at your job in sales or marketing or finance. But you've never written a business plan. Where do you start?

To make matters worse, as the boss heads off with his plastic cup of water, he turns and chirps: 'Oh, one other thing, Charlie, can you let me have the first draft by close of play Friday? Thanks!' And off he trots.

You gulp. You need a plan.

In all these cases, let this book be your guide to writing a winning business plan. It is written from the perspective of a backer, whether a banker, an investor or a board director.

Every word on every page is designed to help your business achieve the backing you seek.

You don't need an encyclopaedia for a business plan. And you don't need an encyclopaedic guide to help you write one.

Indeed, your backer would walk out of the room if presented with one. He or she wants the meat, and having to chew through the fat will make them back off, not back you.

It's the message that counts, not the detail. Size is not important.

You need a plan that is clear and concise, and easy for your backer to read and understand. You need a plan that is coherent, consistent and convincing, furnishing your backer with the evidence and the argument needed for go-ahead.

You need the *essentials* of a business plan.

This is the book for you. It is tailored to meet the needs of your backer. Many business planning guides lead you through the process from the perspective of what you as a manager or entrepreneur would wish to say about your business.

Not this guide. It is customer-driven, not supplier-driven. It works backwards from the backer to the planner – from what your backer needs to know about your business to what you need to research and analyse to address their needs.

And who is this book for, who is this 'planner'? You are someone who has been tasked with producing a *backable* business plan. As described above, you may be a manager in a medium-sized business handed the task by the managing director. Or you may be the owner of a smaller business – and you have delegated the task . . . to yourself.

You may even be a manager in a large company who wants to cut to the chase and draw up a short, sharp, backable plan, an essential plan, rather than a long-winded, interminable tome complete with pages of spreadsheets that will be out of date by the time the report lands on the boss's desk.

Or you may be an entrepreneur starting out on a new venture. Again, this is the guide for you, one which helps you spell out the very essence of your backable proposition.

The book is set out in three parts:

1. Preparing your plan
2. Writing your plan
3. Using your plan.

Part 1 is about what you need to do before you get going on your business plan, in terms of purpose, research and organisation.

Part 2 is the meat of the book and is laid out in a format designed carefully to help you write a backable business plan. The chapters in this part have exactly the same titles – and numbers – as the chapters that your business plan will have.

For example, Chapter 3 in this book is on market demand. Chapter 3 of your plan will also be on market demand. Likewise Chapter 4 will be on competition, in both this book and your plan.

Chapter 1 of your plan will be an executive summary, with the final one, Chapter 9, a conclusion (as indeed for Chapter 9 of this book).

Part 3 of this book is on using your plan. Its first use will be in the pitch and Chapter 10 shows you how best to pitch to your prospective backer – how you should tailor your plan to the requirements of your backer, how you should structure your presentation and how best you should deliver it.

But your plan's usefulness won't end at the pitch. You can use it to set targets against which the performance of the business and its managers can be assessed. These targets are described in terms of key performance indicators and milestones in Chapter 11.

Ultimately, writing a business plan is the easy bit. The hard bit is doing it, performing to plan. Chapter 12 discusses how you should monitor progress against plan on a regular basis and at some stage in the future, possibly three or four years down the line, evaluate it.

This book also contains highly practical appendices on how to derive your competitive position (A) and how to undertake structured interviewing of customers (B).

Appendix C discusses the alternatives sources of finance now available to entrepreneurs.

Appendix D sets out in slide format an exemplary business plan case study, namely the Dart Valley Guest House and Oriental Spa, which features as the central case study through every chapter of this book.

The book concludes with a selection of books for further reading (Appendix E).

The appendices in your business plan will of course differ from those of this book. No two business plans will have the same sets of appendices, but most should contain further detail on your products/services, the market segments they serve, the competition they face, your company's competitive positioning, customers, marketing, management, facilities, IT, etc.

It is up to each planner/writer to assess what elements of further detail should best be placed in an appendix – with the sole and specific purpose of furnishing further supporting evidence and comfort to the backer, as required.

Finally, and importantly, remember that your business plan will have every chance of winning the backing it merits if it is coherent, consistent and credible. You need to get all your ducks in a row (see Figure 0.1).

figure 0.1   Your backer wants to see your ducks in a row

figure 0.2 If they are all over the place, you have no backer!

If your ducks are all over the place (Figure 0.2), if they are incoherent, inconsistent and incredible, your backer, as he or she has done on hundreds of previous such occasions, will show you the door.

This book shows you how to get your ducks in a row, how to write a business plan that will wow your backers and win you the funding you need for your business to succeed.

part

1

Preparing your plan

1

Essential preparation

> The only thing we know about the future is that it will
> be different.
>
> *Peter Drucker*

In this chapter

- Result
  - An established business
  - A start-up business

- Need
- Preparation
  - Research
  - Organisation

- A plan for SMEs

Let's start with the output: what should a good business plan look like? We'll get that firmly planted in the brain before we delve into detail. Then we'll consider in more depth what the plan is for and for whom it is written. Finally, we'll look at what you need to prepare prior to kicking off on your winning business plan, in terms of research undertaken and organisation put into effect.

Result

Where do we need to get to? What is the end result of this process? What does a good, winning plan look like and how would that differ from a bad, losing plan?

In short, what is the *essential* outcome?

We'll look at the outcomes under two scenarios:

- A plan for an established business
- A plan for a start-up business.

Let's start with the established business, because it's easier. The business has a track record, both operational and financial, achieved within a historical, recorded context of market demand, industry competition, strategic positioning and resource deployment. Forecasts will be based as much on fact as on judgement.

If you are planning for a start-up, you should still read this section. This is where you're aiming to be in a few years' time, when your start-up has established itself and is poised to attain the next level.

An established business

What does a successful business plan look like for an established business?

We'll take a fictional case study and use it throughout this book. Hopefully it will be a case you can relate to – I'm sure we have all felt the urge now and again to flee the rat race and set up our own business on some idyllic patch of this earth.

This particular piece of British paradise is in Devon, on the gently rolling slopes atop the valley of the river Dart, about 10 miles upriver from Dartmouth. The Dart Valley Guest House and Oriental Spa is owned and run by Dick and Kay Jones, he a former management consultant and she a stress management counsellor of Anglo-Thai heritage.

The business has been operating for three years and has just started to turn a profit. Dick and Kay have secured planning permission to build a 16-bedroom extension and swimming pool – an investment they believe will transform the profitability of the business. But they have run down their personal funds over the past few years and need a further injection of external finance.

In short, they need a backer. So they need a plan. Here's their executive summary (itself précised for the purposes of this book), where, in the equivalent of a mere one and a bit pages of A4, most of the key questions a backer needs to know can be satisfactorily addressed.

Essential case study
The Dart Valley Guest House and Oriental Spa business plan, 2015

Chapter 1: Executive summary

The Dart Valley Guest House and Oriental Spa ('Dart Valley') is a destination with a difference. It is set overlooking a spectacularly beautiful valley in South Devon and yet offers visitors a touch of the Orient in its rooms, cuisine and spa. It has 17 rooms for hire, with spa and restaurant facilities also open to day visitors. It turned over £513,000 in 2014, having grown by 36% per year since 2012, and operating margin is expected to top 20% in 2015. Further investment of £1.05 million in a 16-room extension and a swimming pool is forecast to double sales by 2019 and boost operating margin to 34%. Opportunities to exploit a proven concept outshine risks of cost overrun or slower build-up of occupancy.

Dart Valley has three main business segments – rooms, catering and the spa. Room revenues have been growing fastest, at 45% per year, with spa revenues (20% of total) slower (at 18% per year) due to buoyant custom from non-resident visitors from the start and subsequent capacity limitations, to be eased with the planned Phase II development.

The market for West Country tourism was worth £225 million in 2014 (Source: VisitBritain). Key long-term drivers are the growth in UK population and per capita incomes and the propensity for people to take multiple holidays each year. The main short-term driver since 2008 was the boost to domestic tourism caused by the financial crisis – the so-called staycation effect. This reversed in 2013–14 with

▶

the recovery in the economy and overseas holidays, and the market can be expected to remain flat over the next few years.

There are many excellent hotels, guest houses and B&Bs throughout Devon and the West Country. The industry is competitive, with low barriers to entry, with occupancy rates, depending on size and location, improving over time and with the most highly differentiated businesses thriving and enjoying repeat custom. Spa facilities are less widespread in rural Devon than in a big city like Plymouth, but there are good spas to be found in neighbouring Torquay and Totnes. Restaurants offering oriental cuisine, namely Chinese, Thai, Japanese and Vietnamese, can also be found in either one or both towns.

The Dart Valley Guest House is distinctive in two main ways: it enjoys a spectacular location atop one of the most beautiful valleys in England; and it has an oriental theme. The theme is understated, with a hint of the Orient applied to the bedroom decor and oriental treatments available, in addition to standard ones, at the spa. Oriental cuisine is offered in the restaurant, but so too is European fare. The customer is given the choice. In the three years since opening in December 2011, occupancy rates at the Dart Valley have grown from 39% to 56% to 71% and are budgeted conservatively for 75% this year. Restaurant take-up by overnight visitors has risen to 35% of visitor nights and spa occupancy to 26%, both above budget.

Dick and Kay Jones bought the freehold to the premises in 2010 for £715,000, against which they took on a mortgage of £500,000, and spent a further £280,000 of their own funds on renovation. The owners work full-time in the business and employ a staff of three full-time equivalents, with part-time help added as appropriate. Spa professionals are contracted as required.

The business broke even at the operating profit level during 2013, the second year of operations, and achieved a profit before tax of 11% in 2014, budgeted to rise to 15% this year. The owners believe that profitability will be greatly boosted with the planned Phase II expansion, costing £1.05 million for a new building with 16 rooms and an outdoor, heated swimming pool. Overheads, other than financing costs, will rise by 50%, but revenues, once occupancy rates return to today's levels by (conservatively) 2019, will have almost doubled. Operating margin, assuming no change in directors' remuneration, is forecast to reach 34% by 2019 and profit before tax 24%. The speed of growth will continue to yield challenges of cash flow, and the owners will look to their backer to provide the necessary flexibility of finance.

The key risks to this plan are a slower build-up of occupancy, whether caused by a further drop in staycation tourism as economic recovery gathers pace, the opening of direct competition, a peaking of interest in the offering or insufficient awareness, slippage in construction works and the health of the owners – all of which are examined in depth in the plan and found to be containable.

Upside opportunities lie in raising occupancy rates higher than in the plan through marketing focused on exploiting a proven concept, the introduction of new, complementary services or products, lift-off in the spa segment profitability and the acquisition of another site (Phase III), like one identified in the Fal Valley, to replicate the oriental spa concept in Cornwall.

In conclusion, the Dart Valley has established itself as a serious player in the West Country tourism industry, offering visitors something very special. It is now poised, through this expansion, to become the leading player in spa services in South Devon and make healthy profits. Its owners seek a financial partner who shares this vision.

So what makes this a good business plan? First, it is clear and concise. Second, it is coherent and consistent – the storyline hangs together well. Third, it tackles risk. As you will see in Part 2 of this book, a backer is primarily concerned with four areas of risk, all of which seem to be covered adequately in the plan:

- Market demand risk (see Chapter 3) – demand is resilient, having grown counter-cyclically during the most severe economic recession since the 1930s, and now stabilised.
- Competition risk (see Chapter 4) – industry competition is tough, but less so when the offering is distinctive.

- Strategic risk (see Chapters 5 and 6) – Dart Valley has gained share through its distinctive offering and seems well placed to gain further share through this strategically sound expansion.

- Financial risk (see Chapter 7) – the forecast numbers seem consistent with the market, competitive and strategic context.

That's it, then. Dart Valley looks backable, subject, of course, to due diligence.

Essential tip

Your business plan journey should traverse the Seven Cs: a good plan is clear, crisp, concise, consistent, coherent and credible. But above all it is convincing, particularly in its assessment of risk. Its raison d'être is to convince your backer. Remember all Seven Cs, but especially the last.

So what does a bad plan look like? Even a bad plan for a good company?

Suppose Dart Valley's business plan had been drawn up not by Dick Jones, BA, MBA, a former management consultant, proficient not just in managing a business but in strategic and financial analysis too, but by someone dismissive of the need for such a plan.

Here goes.

Essential case study
The Dart Valley Guest House and Oriental Spa business plan, 2015

Chapter 1: A bad executive summary

The Dart Valley Guest House and Oriental Spa is a top location in the West Country for visitors and spa seekers. Revenues are growing fast and the business is profitable.

Devon is one of the major tourist destinations in the UK and the Dart Valley Guest House is the best place to stay.

It is owned by the Joneses and they employ some help around the guest house, spa and gardens.

The owners plan to build an extension and a pool, which will make the business even more profitable. There are no serious risks to this plan, but plenty of opportunities to replicate this model at similar locations in the West Country.

In conclusion, this is your chance to back the Dart Valley and make some easy money.

Convinced? I suspect not. But why not? Have a go yourself at applying some red ink to the 'plan'. I could list scores of things wrong with it, but let's stick to seven, which happen to reflect the headings of each chapter in the business plan, as set out in Part 2 of this book:

■ There are no key numbers on sales, growth, sales by segment, margin, market size, market share, etc. Sure, this atrocious executive summary exaggerates to make the point, for most of its ilk have some numbers on sales, profit, etc., but you'd be surprised how many business plans offer no numbers at all on sales by segment (see Chapter 2), let alone on market size or share.

■ There is no discussion on market demand drivers, which should underpin any discussion on market demand growth (see Chapter 3).

■ Competitors are dismissed, treated as an irrelevance. Not just many, but *most* business plans fail to address convincingly the capabilities of competitors, and very, very few analyse the dynamics of competitive intensity (see Chapter 4).

■ 'Dart Valley is the best.' You may be surprised, perhaps horrified, but such broad-brush, unjustified, pub-talk claims are surprisingly commonplace in business plans (see Chapter 5).

■ So there are some employees, great, thanks, but how many? (See Chapter 6.)

■ How much will the extension project cost, and what will be the subsequent uplift in profitability? (See Chapter 7.)

■ What, no risk?! (See Chapter 8.)

That's how not to do it. We'll return to what it is you should be doing in Part 2, but first let's check on what the result should look like in a start-up.

A start-up business

What is the difference in a start-up business plan, compared with that for an established business?

Not much, in truth. The structure of the plan remains the same – an introduction to the business (proposition), market demand, competition, strategic position, resources, financials, risk, and so on – except that it will be set largely in the *future tense*.

What changes most is the level of uncertainty throughout, and in particular in the reception in the marketplace to your business proposition. In a start-up, this market reception is largely unknown. However, it can be researched, assessed and estimated in advance, as you will see in some detail (in Chapter 3).

Let's suppose that Dick and Kay Jones needed to raise external finance for their Dart Valley start-up in 2010, rather than finance the investment through the sale of their London home and a mortgage. Suppose they had to draw up a business plan at the time. Here it is.

Essential case study
The Dart Valley Guest House and Oriental Spa business plan at start-up

Chapter 1: Executive summary

The Dart Valley Guest House and Oriental Spa ('Dart Valley') will be a destination with a difference. It will be set overlooking a spectacularly beautiful valley in South Devon and yet offer visitors a touch of the Orient in its rooms, cuisine and spa. It will have 17 rooms for hire, with spa and restaurant facilities also open to day visitors.

The market for West Country tourism was worth £200 million in 2009 (Source: VisitBritain) and is currently experiencing a 'staycation' boom caused by the deep economic recession. Key long-term drivers are the growth in population and per capita incomes and the propensity for people to take multiple holidays each year.

There are many excellent hotels, guest houses and B&Bs throughout Devon and the West Country. The industry is competitive, with low barriers to entry, but with the most highly differentiated businesses thriving and enjoying repeat custom and high occupancy rates. Spa facilities are less widespread in rural Devon than in a big city like Plymouth, but there are good spas to be found in neighbouring Torquay. Restaurants offering Chinese and Thai cuisine can also be found in both Torquay and Totnes.

The Dart Valley will be distinctive in two main ways: it enjoys a spectacular location atop one of the most beautiful valleys in England; and it will have an oriental theme. The theme will be understated, with a hint of the Orient applied to the bedroom decor and oriental treatments available, in addition to standard treatments, at the spa. Oriental cuisine will be offered in the restaurant, but so too will European fare. The customer will have the choice. We expect the guest house to open in late 2011 and conservatively forecast occupancy rates to grow from 25 to 30% in 2012 to 60% in 2014. Restaurant take-up is forecast to rise to 25% of visitor nights and spa occupancy to 20% in this period.

These forecasts are underpinned by substantial market research and some test marketing. We have compiled a report on the location, offering and resources of a dozen competing three- and four-star hotels in the region and an inventory of competing spa facilities. We have also visited and enjoyably experienced the facilities of two similar 'oriental spas' in the UK, one in London and one in Durham. And we spent two days talking to visitors in the Torbay area, armed with a clipboard and questionnaire, and found that 82% of those currently staying in similarly positioned and priced accommodation would be happy (and 37% 'very happy') to give a concept like Dart Valley a try.

We have an offer to purchase the freehold to the premises for £715,000 and plan to spend £240,000 on conversion and renovation to 17 bedrooms with en-suite bathrooms, a new kitchen and spa facilities – including an outdoor spa tub, a sauna/steam massage shower, two treatment rooms and a meditation room. We shall work full-time in the business and employ a staff of three full-time equivalents, with part-time help added as appropriate. Spa professionals will be contracted as required.

▶

We plan to keep a tight control on operating costs, such that operating profit breakeven can be achieved at 40% occupancy and net profit breakeven at 55%. We forecast that the latter should be achieved by 2014, with net profit rising to 5–10% beyond that. The speed of growth will yield challenges of cash flow, and we shall look to our backer to provide the necessary flexibility of finance.

The key risks to this plan are insufficient custom, with occupancy falling below even the 40% breakeven, slippage and/or cost escalation in renovation works, the opening of direct competition and the health of the owners – all of which are examined in depth in the plan and found to be containable.

The main upside opportunity lies in raising the scale of this venture in a Phase II. If we can gain planning permission, the construction of 12–16 extra rooms in a purpose-built extension, along with an aesthetically harmonious outdoor swimming pool, would permit a greater contribution to site overheads and result in much higher profitability. We plan to commence the planning application as soon as the Phase I renovation work is underway.

In conclusion, the Dart Valley can become a serious, profitable player in the West Country tourism industry, offering visitors something very special. We seek a financial partner who shares this vision.

Apart from the future tense, what's the main difference? You spotted it. It's the additional paragraph 5, where you have to convince your backer that this is not just a punt, but an investment grounded on some *painstaking and rigorous market research.*

We'll return to the market research you need for a start-up later (see Chapter 3).

Need

What is the purpose of a business plan? Why do you need it? Who's it for?

Some guides devote pages to all the possible permutations in answer to those questions. That's a waste of time. The *essential* answers are straightforward:

You need a business plan to obtain backing. It is written for your backer.

It's as simple as that. If you are in need of backing, for whatever reason, a business plan is essential. And you'll craft that plan to address all the key issues likely to be raised by that backer.

You may need backing because you are launching a start-up. Or your company is set for a lift-off in growth. Or it is facing rough times and needs a cash injection.

In each case you need backing, so you'll need a business plan. Of course it can be more complicated than that, but only a little. Here are some purposes worthy of special mention:

- For a start-up
- For raising equity finance
- For raising debt finance
- For board approval
- For a joint venture partner
- For the sale of the business
- For differentiating from a project plan
- For use as a managerial tool.

Let's look briefly at each of these purposes in turn.

A business plan for a start-up

This is not essentially different from a business plan for an established business seeking growth finance. The chapter headings will be the same, but, as you will see in Part 2, special additional questions will need to be addressed – for example, the identification of prospective customers, the crafting of a distinctive value proposition, a pilot survey and the assessment of competitive response.

The business plan for a start-up will be tailored according to whether you are seeking equity or debt finance, but that is the same for an established business (see below).

A business plan for raising equity finance

Your backer is an investor. They look for a return on their investment – as high a return as possible with as little risk as possible. Investors place as much emphasis on opportunity to exceed plan as the risk of falling short of plan. Each chapter of your plan will be written with that in mind, exploring upsides creatively but realistically.

A business plan for raising debt finance

Your backer is a banker. They look to earn fees on the transaction and interest on the loan extended. They want assurance that your business will generate sufficient cash to cover interest payments. And bankers want some form of guarantee, some security, that they will get their money back, all in one piece, at the end of the loan period.

And remember this: your banker may not make the decision. That may be for the bank's credit committee members and they won't meet you. They won't have the benefit of hearing your upbeat version of the future.

They will just examine a cold document, your business plan. So you had better address all the downsides and convincingly dismiss them. The credit committee won't be remotely interested in the upside – that won't benefit them one penny. They only want to know what could go wrong, with what likelihood, and what you will be able to do to mitigate the damage once things have gone wrong.

The whole tenor of a business plan for a banker will be different from a plan written for an equity investor. You will be conservative, cautious and risk averse. Forecasts must be readily achievable. Risks to such unambitious forecasts must be extremely unlikely.

I worked in an investment bank for a number of years and had many a memorable session with credit officers. One thing never ceased to amaze me. No matter how conservative you are in your downside case, the credit officer will always go a shade or two more conservative – no matter how unlikely. So be prepared, and well-armed with the counterargument.

A business plan for board approval

The majority of business plans fall into this category. You can imagine the scene in the boardroom a month or two beforehand, with the chairman expostulating: 'Good grief, Charlie, you and your team have so many exciting ideas for moving this wonderful company of ours forward – but, you know, I'm a bit confused. Where are we going to aim first? Where are our best bets? Which is the more risky? What could go wrong? What could go horribly wrong? Will we have enough cash to fund all this expansion? We need a plan!'

The circumstances may differ, but the business plan itself, when written for board approval, should be no different from a plan written for an external investor. The board is effectively an investor, albeit of internal cash resources, and should be treated as such.

A business plan for a joint venture partner

I have advised on many joint ventures over the years. They are like any relationship – their success rests entirely on both parties continuing to benefit from it. If one party obtains a seemingly unfair advantage over the other upon formation of the alliance, it will not last and the break-up will be painful on both sides.

Thus the initial success of a joint venture depends on the terms agreed at the outset – and these in turn depend on both parties drawing up and exchanging robust business plans. These will be written as if for an investor, for in effect your partner is investing in your business and you are investing in theirs.

A business plan for the sale of the business

Most business plans I have scrutinised over the years have been for the sale of a business, and too many have read as if written purely for an equity investor. That's fine if the buyer is a 'trade buyer' (that is, another company in the same or related line of business), a joint venture partner or a venture capitalist.

However, that's not so good if there is a broad range of prospective buyers, some of which are private equity houses. The latter will want to structure the transaction with as little equity as they can get away with, and with as much debt as can be achieved without endangering the financial stability of the company.

This means that the financing will require the approval not just of the investment committee at the private equity house, but also the credit committee at the bank – and maybe also the credit committee at the mezzanine provider (i.e. a financier of high-yield unsecured debt with an equity kicker).

That means that the business plan should be written to address both upside for the investor and downside for the banker. It needs to be cleverly balanced.

A business plan for differentiating from a project plan

A project plan is similar to but differs from a business plan. A project plan makes the business case for a specific investment project. It isolates revenue streams and costs directly attributable to the project and recommends go or no-go decisions accordingly. The decision is typically taken at board level and is hived off for external finance only rarely and on very large projects.

A business plan considers the future of the whole business. That business may be a division or subsidiary of a much larger company, but it has its own profit and loss (P&L) account and will be forecast in full.

Business planning for use as a managerial tool

My publisher may not approve of me saying this, for fear that a prospective buyer may now shove this book back on the shelf. But the truth is that annual business planning, while typically a useful discipline in large, multi-divisional, multi-country organisations, is largely a waste of time for small and medium-sized enterprises (SMEs).

In theory, it is a great idea. Every year the managing director appoints a capable manager to review last year's three-year plan and prepare this year's plan. Lessons are learnt and steps taken to improve performance.

In practice, insufficient time and effort will be invested in the market research and strategy development parts of the annual plan, rendering the three-year forecasts unsubstantiated, often wildly optimistic and potentially misleading. The only part of the plan for which managers will be accountable, and typically reflected in their pay package, will be the next year's budget numbers. So why invest hours or even days every September producing robust three-year forecasts against which you are not going to be monitored?

I have seen medium-sized businesses that turn over £150 million presenting rolling annual business plans that are meaningless. No manager believes in them, not even the managing director, but some adviser some time ago told them that they were a useful discipline. They are not, unless they are done properly.

And doing them properly means investing time and effort – resources that are in short supply in a thriving SME and generally better directed towards serving customers and improving performance.

The time for a SME to do a business plan properly is when there is a specific need – when the board demands one, when an investor seeks one, when the bank needs one, when the business is for sale. Otherwise, management time is better focused elsewhere.

For whichever of these purposes you are writing a business plan, this book will be your essential guide. It is a guide designed to address the needs of different types of backer.

Preparation

There are things you need to do in advance, before you put pen to paper and write your business plan. In essence, they can be split into two areas:

- Research
- Organisation.

Let's take them one at a time.

Research

You might think you know your business, but how much do you know about what's driving your customers' behaviour? And what are your competitors up to?

If there are gaps in your knowledge, you might find yourself making 'soft' assumptions in the business plan. Just wait until you face cross-examination from your backer!

There are three areas of research you should either undertake, or feel confident that you and your colleagues know enough about already, before starting your plan. Each of these areas will be covered in detail in the relevant chapters, but in brief they are as follows:

- Data on market demand, size, drivers and growth trends (see Chapter 3)
- Data on competitors – their size, location, number of employees, turnover and profitability (if available, best estimates if not), positioning, competitive advantage, strategy and plans for the future (see Chapter 4)
- A customer survey, whether actual customers if yours is an established business or prospective customers in a start-up, to find out what customers expect from your business, and from your competitors, both now and in the future (see Chapter 5).

Essential tip

A business plan with little research behind it is a flimsy affair. At best it might be clear, crisp, concise, consistent and coherent. But it is unlikely to satisfy the sixth C and be credible – let alone the

▶

seventh C and be convincing. Your backer will ask questions like, 'How did you arrive at that market growth estimate?' and 'How are your competitors responding to that?' and 'What makes you think customers would pay for that?' You had better have credible answers rooted in research or you will have no backer.

Allow yourself a month or so to gather all this information. Hopefully much of it will be at hand already, squirrelled away in some filing cabinet, real or virtual, in the marketing department. But filling in the data gaps can be time consuming.

Most time consuming tends to be the customer survey. You should allow two to three weeks for this, to put together a questionnaire, call them up and assemble the results. For details on questions to be asked, see Chapter 5 or Appendix B.

Organisation

There are various organisational items that are best sorted out in advance, specifically:

- The planning team
- The timetable
- The tools
- The contents
- The appendices
- The length
- The drafting process.

Here are some tips on each of the above.

The planning team

It goes without saying that one person must be tasked with full responsibility for leading the planning team. Not a team of two or three with equal responsibility, but one manager, backed up by an email from the managing director delegating responsibility to that person.

In a small business or start-up, of course, that 'manager' will be the owner, you!

One person must take charge, not only for purposes of assembling all the data and analysis to be fed into each chapter, but also for establishing a consistent, coherent style and message throughout the main document. Only the appendices can get away with giving the appearance that they have been written by another hand.

Think of the user – the investor, the banker. They want something as readable as this book – written by one hand, edited perhaps by another.

In a small company or a start-up, one hand is typically all that will be involved in the business plan – yours will write the whole thing.

In a somewhat larger business, the team leader may need two or three complementary team members, depending on the complexity of the business. One, possibly the leader, should come from the sales and marketing team and take responsibility for market and competitor analysis and the customer survey. Another could come from operations and be assigned to compile all the technical information needed on the company's assets, people, systems and processes. A third could come from finance to take charge of the financial forecasts.

For a medium-sized business, say with revenues of around £25 million, the team leader should expect to devote at least 50% of his or her time over a one-month period. Combined inputs of the others in the team could well come to two to three person-months, again depending on the complexity of the business.

The timetable

If your boss says they want a business plan done by the end of the week, so be it. It can be done and I have done it – but the boss can't expect a properly researched, genuinely robust plan. There will certainly be no time for a customer survey. All that can reasonably be done in a week is to summarise what you already know about the business and where it is headed and to create some forecasts around that.

A business-plan-in-a-week may be no bad thing if the boss just needs something to float across the bows of a putative backer. But remember this: once in print it inherits an authority that may be out of proportion to the effort put in. Once those forecasts are set out on paper, they may become engrained in the backer's brain – and it may take much time and persuasion to shift those perceptions at a later stage.

Worse still is when a business plan is rushed out, PDF-ed and sent out by email to the prospective backer. Once in cyberspace, that plan could theoretically, notwithstanding any non-disclosure agreement, make its way to any financier, customer, supplier or, worst, competitor anywhere in the world – on the click of a mouse.

By all means, rattle off a business-plan-in-a-week, but superimpose every page in huge letters with DRAFT PRELIMINARY, place a disclaimer footnote on every page and only let your would-be backer have one hard copy – with an understanding that it may not be photocopied.

A robust business plan takes a month to prepare. Fine, strategy consultants can be engaged, expensively, I must confess, and they can do the job expertly in two or three weeks, but if you are to do it in-house it will take some time. If you have never done anything like this before, and nor have your colleagues, allow for six to eight weeks – the iterations as the draft circulates among the team will be many.

I advised on one recently which took us three months. But that was because we decided to go back to square one and develop a business strategy bought into by the whole management team – and that required a series of carefully constructed workshops. Once the strategy had been agreed, we were able to move at a faster pace to build a plan around it.

The tools

There is some clever software available these days, offered by leading banks or independent providers like Business Plan Pro. These packages provide a business plan structure, guide you through the process and ensure that your P&L, balance sheet and cash flow forecasts (see Chapter 7) are in harmony with each other. Try an internet search on the three words *'business plan software'* and see what catches the eye.

I have every respect for these software entrepreneurs and hope they do well. But I am assuming that by reading this book you, like me, would prefer to follow a written guide, rather than a pre-programmed (and often expensive) electronic process.

Above all, I suspect there is no software available on writing a business plan from this book's perspective of addressing the needs of a backer. Nor would any such software include the innovative tools on demand forecasting or assessing risk introduced in Chapters 3, 7 and 8 of this book.

The only tools you need to write your essential business plan are off-the-shelf word processing and spreadsheet applications, such as Microsoft Word and Excel, and possibly a presentation application, such as PowerPoint. And this book.

The contents

I have seen guides on business planning that suggest that the contents of a plan should be tailored to the specifics of the business.

This is not so. The contents should be tailored to the needs of *the backer*. And the backer wants risks and opportunities to be assessed in an orderly and predictable way, as follows:

- Your business – which segments drive the most profit, now and going forward?
- Market demand – what is driving demand for the buyers of a product such as yours?
- Competition – how intense is industry competition among you and fellow suppliers of your product and will it intensify?
- Your strategy – how well placed is your company and what is your strategy for improving its position?
- Your resources – what resources will you deploy in implementing your strategy?
- Your financials and forecasts – do your forecasts realistically reflect both external market trends and internal competitiveness?
- Risk and sensitivity – what are the main risks and opportunities around the forecasts? What is the likelihood and impact of each? And how sensitive are the financial forecasts to adverse circumstance?

It's as simple as that. That is what your backer needs to know. All else is detail.

These seven areas of analysis form the bedrock of a business plan and are covered in detail in Chapters 2–8.

Here, then, are what should be the contents of any business plan, with chapter names and numbers (after Chapter 1) arranged to be just as in the contents of this book:

1 Executive summary
2 The business
3 Market demand
4 Competition
5 Strategy
6 Resources

7 Financials and forecasts

8 Risk, opportunity and sensitivity

9 Conclusion

Appendices

Many, if not most, business plans have no chapter on competition, merely offering a token two-paragraph section in the chapter on the market. That will make a backer highly suspicious. What's the betting that the financials later on will show exponentially rising forecasts with no competitive response?!

Some plans discuss the company's strategy and resources before the market and competition. This is dangerous thinking. A company exists to serve a market, not the other way round.

Other plans have separate chapters on manufacturing facilities, sales and marketing, IT, employees, management, and so on, rather than just one on resources. This tends to bulk up the plan with data. Again this is dangerous. The backer needs to know if the storyline is worth backing. They don't want to get lost in wads of information and data. Details on resources are best relocated to the appendices.

Even other business plan guides fall into this trap. One has more pages devoted to suggested layout than to market demand. Another gives a whole chapter to marketing, more than to market demand, which gets a backer's prime concerns the wrong way round. A backer knows that marketing issues can be fixed. Market issues cannot. Yet another guide offers no chapter on competition, just one on competitive advantage. No wonder the business planner is confused.

I repeat. This book suggests a business plan tailored for a backer. I have spent almost 30 years advising backers on whether they should back business plans. This is what they are looking for, this is what they need.

The appendices

Hurrah for the appendices! This is where the heavy stuff can be shunted, without swamping the reader of the main report. All the detail needed to justify the conclusions of the main report can be gathered here – product descriptions and images, data on market size and growth by segment, details on competitors' sales, employees and strategic focus, the nitty-gritty of your company's facilities (along with photographs and site layouts), operations, employees, management biographies, organisational structure, sales and marketing teams, advertising campaigns, and so on.

But don't load the appendices with superfluous junk. Only stick in the extra detail if it is going to lend further evidence for your business case and extend further comfort to your backer.

The appendices don't have to be read. Your backer need only dip into those bits as needed. Everything contained in the appendices will be summarised in the main report.

The length

The main document should be 25–30 pages of A4, 35 pages maximum. The main chapters on market demand, competition and strategy should be three–four pages each; those on resources and financials/forecasts perhaps a bit longer at four–six pages each. The flanking chapters, 2 and 8, should be just two pages each, while the conclusion should be a masterfully written, upbeat half a page.

The appendices can be the same number of pages again, depending on what further information or evidence you feel is necessary to include to convince your backer.

An alternative to the standard A4 business plan is the PowerPoint presentation. The overwhelming advantage of PowerPoint, when done properly, is that it forces the writer to be concise and adhere to a visible storyline. The main disadvantage is that many entrepreneurs and SME managers will not be sufficiently familiar with either business plans or PowerPoint to present a convincing case in that format to the backer.

If you were to hire strategy consultants, PowerPoint would be their format of choice – it certainly is mine. But I've had decades of experience crafting PowerPoint presentations – it's what I do for a living!

My advice is to stick to what you and your backers are accustomed to. And if your business plan is to head in the direction of a banker, it had better be on A4.

The drafting process

Beware the perils of team drafting. You have just spent a morning putting the final touches to the chapter on forecasts and you receive an email from your colleague with detailed amendments to an *earlier* draft of that same chapter on forecasts. Your mood darkens at the thought of having to re-input all those changes onto the latest draft.

This can be avoided by the team leader always keeping control of the master draft and by rigorous file naming. Each draft issued by the team leader should have a number and a date – since there could be two or three drafts of the same chapter made on one day. Each draft reviewed by a team member should be initialled.

A typical chapter draft issued by the team leader could then be: bizplan.ch7.v4.18Sep15. This could be subsequently reviewed late in the evening by a team member, Joe Bloggs, with: bizplan.ch7.v4.18Sep15.jb, whereupon the team leader would review and issue a new draft the following morning with: bizplan.ch7.v5.19Sep15.

A touch bureaucratic, perhaps, but a naming system helps to avoid drafting mix-ups that can be hair-tearingly infuriating as the deadline looms.

A plan for SMEs

I had a number of queries from the first edition of this book about whether a plan for a small or medium-sized business should look like that for a large business, or indeed for a start-up.

The answer is simple. Yes.

Whatever the stage of evolution of the business, whatever its size, whether the current turnover is £1,000, £100,000 or £100,000,000, the structure of the plan should be as set out above.

Your backer wants to know in which segments the profits reside, where market demand is headed, what your competitors are up to, what your competitive advantage is, what resources you will deploy, including management and marketing, what your financial prospects are and what are the risks, opportunities and sensitivities around those forecasts.

Your backer wants to know the answers to all these questions irrespective of the size of your business. So your plan should follow the recommended structure.

I am perhaps oversimplifying to make the point. In truth a larger company will have a more complex job to do in preparing a crisp, concise, clear business plan.

The larger company may well consist of a number of separate businesses, each with their own P&Ls. Each of these businesses may have a substantial turnover. Each business will serve a number of different product/market segments, some more profitable than others.

The challenge for the plan writer of a large company will be to zero in on those businesses and/or segments within businesses that matter to the backer – and to relegate those that do not matter as much to appendix status.

A business currently turning over £100,000 and forecast to reach £275,000 in three years' time is ripe for an upbeat business plan and backers may be queuing up to get involved.

But if that business is part of a large company with a turnover of £100 million, it may well reside in the appendix. Backers, and especially bankers, will be far more concerned with the prospects of those businesses within the company currently turning over £99.9 million.

You've done your essential research, you've sorted out the organisational aspects of the process, you're well prepared. Earlier, you established what the purpose of writing your plan was and you learnt what the result ought to look like.

You understand that your business plan is first and foremost written for your backer – and that both structure and content will be drawn up bearing in mind your backer's needs at all times. It's time to get stuck in to the plan itself.

part

2

Writing your plan

2

The business

" Vision is not enough, it must be combined with venture.
It is not enough to stare up the steps, we must step up
the stairs.

Vaclav Havel

In this chapter

- Background
- Business mix by segment
- Segmentation in a start-up

T he plan starts here. In this chapter you set the scene. You brief your backer on the bare essentials of the business – what it does, for whom, why, where, with whom, with what and how it got to where it is.

If yours is an established business, you'll also set out briefly how well the business has done so far. If yours is a start-up, you'll briefly set out why the business is poised to enjoy a sustainable competitive advantage.

The rest of this chapter will be about segmentation. You'll introduce the reader to the product/market segments that matter in your business. Each segment will be analysed in some depth in the forthcoming chapters, so it is important to get the segmentation right at the very start.

This chapter, Chapter 2 of your business plan, is where you introduce more detail on the background to your business than you will have set out in your Chapter 1, the executive summary (discussed in Chapter 9 of this book). But don't put in too much background. Remember that your plan is to be a short, sharp, punchy document aimed at hooking your backer. There is no place for waffle.

Background

This is where the backer is introduced to the business, where you set out clearly and concisely what makes the business tick. We'll discuss this under five headings:

- The opener
- Goals and objectives
- Strategy
- Resources
- Basic financials.

The opener

Here, in one paragraph, should be the essence of your business. Or your business proposition, if it is a start-up.

It will form the first paragraph of Chapter 2 of your plan, but the reader will have seen it before. It will be reproduced, word for word, as the first paragraph of the executive summary in Chapter 1 of your plan.

This is because all the essential bits of information will be in that paragraph. It will include:

- who you are – the name (or code name, if yours is a confidential plan) of your business
- what products or services it focuses on
- which main customer groups your business serves
- where it is based, where else it has operations and where it sells
- with what success, in terms of revenues and operating margin (operating profit divided by sales), and by which year.

Let's look again at the opening paragraph of the executive summary for the Dart Valley Guest House and Oriental Spa:

> *The Dart Valley Guest House and Oriental Spa ('Dart Valley') is a destination with a difference. It is set overlooking a spectacularly beautiful valley in South Devon and yet offers visitors a touch of the Orient in its rooms, cuisine and spa. It has 17 rooms for hire, with spa and restaurant facilities also open to day visitors. It turned over £513,000 in 2014, having grown by 36% per year since 2012, and operating margin is expected to top 20% in 2015. Further investment of £1.05 million in a 16-room extension and a swimming pool is forecast to double sales by 2019 and boost operating margin to 34%. Opportunities to exploit a proven concept outshine risks of cost overrun or slower build-up of occupancy.*

That's all you need at this stage – an elevator-speech type of introduction to the business and the plan.

Next you set out briefly how the business has evolved over time in terms of its goals and objectives, strategy, resources and financials. There is no need for a separate section on history, but rather all these sections should track key historical developments inasmuch as they are relevant to the company's situation today.

Goals and objectives

We could debate endlessly on how a company should articulate with pure strategic clarity its vision, mission, aims, purposes, goals, objectives, values, beliefs, principles, and so on.

Fine in theory, but in practice by the time you have grappled with all the definitional nuances, by the time you will have split a salon full of hairs, the business plan will be out of date!

This is an essential guide; 99% of small and medium-sized enterprises (SMEs) won't be bothered with this kerfuffle.

So here is what you should use: goals and objectives, full stop.

A goal is something your business aims to be, as described in words. An objective is a target that helps to measure whether that goal has been achieved, and is typically set out in numbers.

One of your goals may be for your business to be the most customer-centric supplier of your services in the North of England. Objectives to back up that goal could be the achievement of a 'highly satisfied' rating of 30% from your annual customer survey by 2018 and 35% by 2019, with 80% 'satisfied' or better by 2020.

Or you may aim for your business to be the UK market leader in a key segment, with measurable supporting objectives being 40% market share by 2018 and 45% by 2020.

Goals are directional, objectives are specific. You may have come across the useful acronym SMART for setting objectives, which stands for Specific, Measurable, Attainable, Relevant and Time-limited.

The best objectives are indeed SMART – as exemplified above: Specific (a market share target in that segment); Measurable (market research to which you subscribe will reveal whether the 40% is met); Attainable (you are at 33% now and your new product range has been well received); Relevant (market share is a good indicator of strategic progress); and Time-limited (2018).

So what about all these other terms, you may ask, shouldn't they also slot into the plan? Suppose your backer wants to know, for instance, what your company's mission is (unlikely, but possible)? Here's how to allow for them in essence:

- Mission – in theory, what sets your business apart from the rest of the competition; in practice, you can treat this as a goal.
- Vision – in theory, where your business aims to go or become; again, you can treat this as a goal.
- Aims – they can be taken as roughly synonymous with goals.
- Purposes – ditto.
- Values – in theory, a set of beliefs and principles that guide how your business should respond when there are moral, ethical, safety, health, environmental or other value-related demands on the business that may conflict with the goal of shareholder value maximisation; in practice, this tends to be obvious in most SMEs and should only form part of the business plan if there is a serious conflict – and then its resolution can be identified as a separate goal.

What were the goals and objectives of your business when it started? Were they met? How have they evolved over time to what they are today? This is what you should describe here briefly, particularly if these goals and objectives are still of relevance to the issues in the business plan of today.

If your business is a start-up, what are your goals? What SMART objectives have you set towards the achievement of those goals?

Essential tip

Your backer is looking for smart goals and SMART objectives.

Strategy

This is where you set out your company's competitive advantage and what strategy you deploy to sustain and enhance it. We'll go into strategy and its definitions in more detail later (see Chapter 5) but for the time being just set out here, in summary, how the company has maintained its competitiveness over time, including in response to any adverse circumstances.

If your business is a new venture, what is your strategy for creating a sustainable competitive advantage in the marketplace you are targeting?

Resources

You will describe in detail the resources deployed by your company in Chapter 6 of your plan. Here, in just three or four paragraphs, you will distil the essence.

How have the resources deployed developed over time? This is where a timeline chart can be most useful to the reader. Many are the times that I have skipped the words in this section to focus just on the timeline chart, which should highlight neatly the main resource impactful events in the company's history.

Resources covered in the timeline chart could include the following:

- Location and scale of main business infrastructure, e.g. office headquarters, manufacturing facilities, distribution depots, IT centres
- Notable landmarks, such as the one hundredth employee hired, French agent engaged, US subsidiary launched, patents applied for or approved
- Acquisitions – of key people, companies.

If you are starting a new venture, address the basics: Where will it be based? What space will you require, what physical assets, how many employees, what systems? Who will manage?

You should include one paragraph on the management team. It is a truism that investors back people, not businesses. Your backer will want to know what credentials the people heading operations, sales and marketing and finance possess – as well as yours as managing director. They will also want to know how any changes in management over time have impacted on performance in the past few years.

If it is just you in the business at present, as a sole trader, what do you bring to the table in promoting this venture? Will you be contributing transferable experience and capabilities in addition to coming up with the business concept?

Finally, this is where you should add a sentence or two on how the ownership and governance of the business has evolved. A summary is fine for the time being – if ownership and governance are complex, they will be dealt with further in Chapter 6.

Basic financials

In the opening paragraph, you have already set out the turnover and operating margin of the business for the latest financial year. Here is your chance to summarise recent financial history, showing the financial impact of key developments at the company or in its markets over time.

Again, at this stage aggregate numbers from the profit and loss account, preferably just sales and operating margin, are the only level of detail needed. Balance sheet and cash flow data can be left for the detail of Chapter 7. There is one exception to this: if a significant item of capital expenditure has influenced performance in recent years, you should highlight it here.

If yours is a start-up business, you will have no sales history to set out here. But you will surely have incurred some costs, probably self-financed, and this is a good place to summarise them – as well as specify how much time you and your partners have invested thus far.

Business mix by segment

What is your business mix? What products or services does your business offer and to which customer groups? Which count for most in your business?

Your backers don't like wasting precious time. They want to focus their thoughts on considering those chunks of your business that are most important. There is little point in them pondering the merits of a product you offer to a customer group that only contributes to 1% of your sales. They want to know about the 80%.

Essential tip

Focus on the segments most relevant to the backing decision. These are the ones that make the greatest contribution to your operating profit forecasts over the plan period – the segments that matter to your backer.

Businesses seldom offer just the one product (or service, henceforth just 'product') to one customer group. Most businesses offer a number of distinct products to a number of distinct customer groups.

A product tends to be distinctive if the competition differs from one product to another. Some competitors may offer all your services; others may specialise in one or two of them. Others still may offer just the one as a spin-off to a largely unrelated business.

A customer group is distinctive if the customers have distinct buying characteristics and are typically reachable through distinct marketing routes.

Thus a customer group can be defined by who they are (e.g. leisure or business visitor, young or old, well or less educated), what sector they are in (especially for business-to-business ventures), where they are located (e.g. town or suburbs, region, country) or in other ways where different marketing approaches will be needed to reach them.

Each distinct product offered to a distinct customer group is a segment, called, in rather ungainly business-speak, a 'product/market segment' or, more simply, a 'business segment'.

If your business offers two products to one customer group, you have two business segments. If you stick with the same two products but develop a new customer group, you'll have four segments. Introduce a third product and sell it to both customer groups and you have six segments.

How many products does your business offer? To how many customer groups? Multiply the two numbers together and that's how many business segments you serve.

Now consider which two, three or four segments are the most important. Which contribute most to operating profit (or, more simply, sales, if each segment has a similar cost profile)?

And will these same segments be the main contributors to operating profit over the next few years?

Essential example

Tinopolis's business mix

A Llanelli-based supplier of Welsh language television programmes largely for the Welsh television channel S4C, Tinopolis rose in the 2000s and early 2010s to become the largest UK-based independent television production house. The growth of Tinopolis was largely through acquisition – of companies such as Mentorn (producer of BBC TV's Question Time), Sunset + Vine (a sports TV producer of, for example, BBC TV's Grand National coverage and the Glasgow Commonwealth Games in 2014), Video Arts (the interactive corporate training firm founded by John Cleese), Pioneer (a factual producer with a track record in the US market) and the prominent US production houses A. Smith & Co and BASE. The company also expanded organically into e-learning and other interactive digital content, as well as into animation.

Tinopolis's revenues topped £200 million in 2014, with profit before tax of £30 million – up an impressive fifteenfold in seven years. One challenge in drawing up a business plan would be to ensure that analytical attention is focused not just on those segments likely to prosper most over the next three to five years, but also on the stalwart segments, like the Welsh current affairs and sports programmes, without which there would have been no foundation for growth.

This is what you need to set out succinctly in Chapter 2 of your plan. In too many plans this information is not provided. Sometimes, if lucky, a plan will reveal at this stage a pie chart of sales by main product, or even sales by region or country, but what is typically left out is:

- sales by product/market segment – that is, sales of a specific product to a specific customer group
- that same information over time, say over the last three years.

Let's take a simple example. Your company makes widgets, small, medium and large, which you sell to three sectors, manufacturing, engineering and construction, in each of two countries, the UK and France. You operate in 3 × 3 × 2 = 18 product/market segments.

By far your biggest segment is large widgets to UK engineering, which account for 40% of sales. This is followed by medium-sized widgets to UK engineering at 25% of sales and large widgets to French manufacturing at 15% of sales. Together these three segments account for 80% of sales. The remaining 15 segments account for just 20% of sales.

In 9 out of 10 business plans, what would be set out here would be a pie chart showing a breakdown of sales by widget size, alongside another pie chart showing sales by country. This is useful information and your backer will be thankful to see it.

But what would be *more* useful would be a pie chart showing the real product/market segmentation as set out above. It would show one segment alone accounting for 40% of sales and another for 25%.

Your backer would register that throughout the 25–30 pages of this plan, they should be most attentive to market demand, competition and company strategy trends in *one* particular segment – large widgets to UK engineering. Not large widgets in general, not medium widgets, not the UK as a whole, not France as a whole country, not European engineering in general, not construction in the UK, but specifically . . . large widgets to UK engineering.

Engineering customers will have different demand influences from construction customers. The UK may be at a different stage in the economic cycle from France. French engineering companies may have different solutions favouring medium over large widgets. Small widget producers may be more numerous and have more flexible, short-run production facilities than large widget producers.

For any or all of these reasons, your backer would benefit from knowing that one product/market segment – large widgets to UK engineering – matters most to your business.

And what of the future? Perhaps you are set to launch an extra large widget tailored to the UK aerospace sector, which, if all goes to plan, could account for 20% of sales in three years' time.

So let's have a second pie chart alongside the first showing forecast sales by main product/market segment in three years' time.

Your backers will then know that as they read the rest of the plan, they will have to keep an eye out for the argument on why UK aerospace would benefit from extra large widgets.

In summary, what we need in this business background section is a breakdown of what matters most in your business mix, now and in the near future. Which product/market segments will make or break your business?

Essential example

Nokia's business mix

From making galoshes to becoming the biggest mobile telephone producer in the world, Nokia's evolution has been astonishing. And ongoing. Having fallen behind in the smartphone race to Apple's iPhone and Google's Android platform, Nokia sold its mobile telephone business to Microsoft in 2013 and now focuses on telephony infrastructure.

Nokia's nineteenth-century heritage was in the pulp industry, later moving into rubber manufacture and cables. After the Second World War, the group diversified further, with business units ranging from paper to consumer electronics, tyres to communications equipment. You can imagine being tasked to draw up a business plan for Nokia in the early 1970s – the product/market segmentation alone would have been a challenge, let alone the subsequent market analysis in each segment. But one thing is for sure. The tiny business of making chunky 'car radio phones' would not have featured prominently. It would have been lumped into an 'other businesses' category in the financial forecasts. The bulk of the plan would have focused on key issues in paper, tyres, military communications, and so on.

By the late 1980s and the launch of a relatively light, hand-held phone, this business may still have been considered a niche market, affordable only for yuppies. By the end of the 2000s, Nokia was the world's major producer of mobile phones, with all other business units long since divested. Segmentation would have been done by product group, customer type and geographical market, all for mobile phones. Now all such segmentation is history.

Segmentation is a moveable feast – rely on a static analysis of today's contribution from each segment at your peril. Things change – and nowhere as dramatically as at that former pulp company based in Espoo, Finland.

Segmentation in a start-up

The need for segmentation applies likewise to a start-up. If your plans are to launch just the one product (or service) to one group of customers, fine, you won't need to segment any further. But are you sure you'll only have one product? One customer group?

Try categorising your products. And your customers. Is further segmentation meaningful? If so, use it. If not, don't waste time just for the sake of seeming serious. Stick to the one product for the one customer group – that is, one business segment.

But there is one big difference. No matter how you segment, no matter how many customer groups you identify, they are all, at present, gleams in the eye.

You have no customers. Yet.

And no matter how attractive the product or service sounds, without customers it will be of no interest to your backer.

Your product must be couched in terms of its *benefits* to the customer. That is the *business proposition*.

Not the way in which your product or service can do this, do that, at this price. But in the way in which your product or service can *benefit* the target customer. That is the language your backer wants to hear. Who is the target customer? In which way will they benefit from your offering?

And that is just in the one segment. Are there others?

Segmentation may lie at the very heart of your business proposition. It may have been in the very act of segmentation that you unearthed a niche where only your offering can yield the customer benefit. And you have since tailored your offering to address that very niche, that customer benefit.

Here is a slightly different way of looking at it. Does your offering address some 'unmet need' in the marketplace? Does it fill a gap in a target customer's needs? This is one of the secrets to a new venture's success highlighted by William Bridges in his book, *Creating You & Co* (Perseus Books, 1997). He suggests that an 'unmet need' could be uncovered by spotting signs such as a missing piece in a pattern, an unrecognised opportunity, an underused resource, a signal event, an unacknowledged change, a supposedly impossible situation, a non-existent but needed service, a new or emerging problem, a bottleneck, an interface or other similar signs.

However you define the customer benefit, whether in terms of unmet needs or in a way more meaningful to your particular offering, your backer will need evidence of its existence. They'll want as close as they can get to proof.

They won't get it – no investment is risk-free – but they can reasonably expect you to undertake some basic research to dig up whatever evidence you can glean of customer benefit. We will return to this in the next chapter on market demand prospects.

Essential case study
The Dart Valley Guest House and Oriental Spa business plan, 2015

Chapter 2: The business

The job of drafting a business plan for Dart Valley's Phase II development is delegated to co-owner Dick Jones. As a former management consultant, he knows his way around such plans. His wife, Kay, will act as reviewer and sense-checker.

Dick takes care with the opening paragraph, since he knows that it will also form the opening paragraph of the executive summary – which will be the last thing he writes in the plan.

Happy with his opener, as reproduced at the start of this chapter, Dick moves on to the rest of the background section. Here is his chance to set out in a bit more detail how Dart Valley got to where it is today:

■ *Goals and objectives.* These have not changed much, he thinks: the overriding goal was and still is to offer visitors a distinctive, memorable, special stay in glorious surroundings, brushed with a hint of the Orient; objectives were primarily occupancy related at the outset, now visitor return rate objectives have been added.

■ *Strategy.* The early strategy of maximising occupancy rates at the expense of average room price has given way to demand-related pricing over the last 12 months, as occupancy has reached a healthy level, but will need to be resumed after the Phase II extension is built and 16 further rooms have to be filled.

■ *Key dates.* Dick sets out on the timeline, with some nostalgia, dates such as the hiring of staff, going live with the new reservation system, the spa opening ceremony, the first day at 100% occupancy, the first major group booking (over 10 rooms taken) and the day of the burst water pipe in Room 15.

▪ *Financials.* Dick explains why the major renovation work in 2010–11 turned out to be 17% over budget and how Dart Valley's profit and loss account improved steadily and gratifyingly after the tense opening months.

Then there's the business mix, the segmentation. Dick knows he must be careful here. His is a small, young business, and over-elaborate segmentation could be meaningless.

Dart Valley operates in three product segments, with this current breakdown of revenues:

▪ Accommodation (64%)

▪ Catering (16%)

▪ Spa (20%).

Dick sees this as valid product segmentation – the business faces a different array of competitors in each segment.

But market segmentation is not so straightforward. There are various ways of categorising types of visitor – for example, by purpose (e.g. leisure, health, business), by duration (overnight, day) or possibly by nationality (in the last season the business attracted a large number of Dutch visitors).

If Dick is to choose to segment visitors by purpose, he will then have three product segments operating in three market segments, giving him nine product/market segments. If he opts for segmentation by duration or nationality, he will have six product/market segments.

Dick's reservation system gives him whatever data breakdown he needs for any of these visitor segmentation alternatives, but, Dick wonders, is there any point? Around 75% of visitors come for purposes of leisure, 85% of revenues are from overnight visitors and 80% of visitors are British.

Segmentation by product/market would therefore seem an unnecessary level of detail for his business. Dick resolves to stick to a simple segmentation by product for the time being, giving Dart Valley just the three segments.

Essential checklist on the business

Introduce the bare essentials of your business to your backer. Set the scene, under five headings:

- **The opener** – the first paragraph of your executive summary repeated
- **Goals and objectives** – remember to make them SMART
- **Strategy** – your sustainable competitive advantage
- **Resources** – a timeline on resource build-up may help
- **Basic financials** – recent performance in sales and operating margin.

Set out your business mix, now and over the next few years. Disclose to your backer which products or services sold to which customer groups – in other words, which 'product/market segments' – will make or break your business plan.

3

Market demand

> The only function of economic forecasting is to make astrology look respectable.
>
> *John Kenneth Galbraith*

In this chapter

- Market size
- Market growth
  - A web of information
  - The HOOF approach to demand forecasting
- Market demand for a start-up
  - Test marketing
  - Estimating your addressable market
- Market demand risks and opportunities

The analysis of market demand must come right up front in your business plan, whether yours is a start-up or an established business. It is the crux of the plan.

Your products or services address a marketplace that's also served by other producers or service providers. That market must be of sufficient size, now and in the future, to support at least your business, not to mention your competitors.

If there aren't enough buyers of the type of products or services you offer, at the right price, you won't meet your plan.

Your backer wants to know, before all else, who these buyers are, how much they are buying, how much they are paying, why they are buying, what has been influencing them, how those influences may change and how much they are likely to buy in the future.

And they want to know all this in each of your main business segments.

If you can make this chapter of your plan convincing, you may have a backer. If not, you won't.

I have seen so many business plans where analysis of market demand is hedged, sidelined or compressed into a couple of paragraphs in a chapter devoted to the company's oh-so stellar products (or services) and their market positioning.

Many of those plans were written for the sale of a company. Potential backers either walked away or made an offer at a much lower price.

Your backer wants the market demand situation laid out as it is, clearly and concisely. If market demand prospects are not great, be they flat or even mildly declining, tell it like it is. Don't try to obscure the reality.

If your backers have to find out for themselves that the reality differs from that presented in your business plan, you have no backer.

Of course, a backer would prefer to invest in a business that addresses a growing market. However, fortunes have also been made through backing winners in a declining but consolidating market.

Let's be clear. This chapter considers demand not just for your product or service, but for all providers of products or services with whom you compete. It looks at overall demand in the marketplace.

Any market is made up of demand and supply. When demand and supply are in balance, that's good news for all concerned. When demand outstrips supply, that's good for the suppliers – though usually only for a while, until more supplies and/or suppliers arrive. When demand falls and supply exceeds demand, that's bad news for suppliers. You're one of those suppliers.

We are going to apply those fundamentals to the market for your product or service. We will look at market supply in the next chapter, but we'll start with market demand in this one. We'll try to assess the size of market demand and forecast where it is headed over the next few years.

Your backer will also want to know what the risks are of things turning out worse than expected. And, conversely, what the opportunities are for things turning out better.

Market size

How big is the market your firm addresses?

If your business is called Tesco, you will subscribe to a market research organisation. You will feed it data at the end of each appropriate period and receive results promptly on the overall size of the UK grocery market, its growth since the previous period and whether your market share has gone up or down from around 30%.

And so it is with most large companies.

Yet many medium-sized companies enjoy a similar relationship with a niche market research house or industry association. I have worked in some obscure niches of the British economy over the years and it never ceases to amaze me how companies with a turnover of just a few million pounds still receive good, regular, informative market data from some enterprising independent research house serving that company and most of its competitors.

But for small companies this data may be punitively expensive to acquire, may not be directly relevant or may not exist.

Tough. Your backer needs an estimate of market size.

They want to know whether you are a big fish in a small pond, or vice versa. Suppose you are a mega fish in a tiny pond, but one that can be protected from other waters. Your backer would love to hear that.

You'll have to have a go, make an estimate yourself.

It is not that difficult. Many years ago I developed a bottom-up process for market sizing, which I termed *marketcrafting,* and have used it frequently with entrepreneurs or managers of smaller businesses over the years. Used with care, it works.

Marketcrafting is a doubly useful process. Not only does it give you the base data needed for market demand sizing and growth (Chapter 3 of your business plan) but for industry supply too (Chapter 4).

It is, however, all terribly approximate. Appreciate that, live with that and do it anyway – and you'll find that your backer will thank you for it.

There are seven main steps in marketcrafting:

1 Select your main competitors – those you pitch against regularly, those you exhibit alongside at trade shows – and don't forget the foreign competitors, especially those from lower cost countries.

2 Starting with competitor A, ask a series of questions: Do you think they are selling more or less than you into this market? If less, by how much less, *very roughly*? Are they selling half as much as you? Three-quarters? If they sell more than you, by how much more, roughly? Ten per cent more? One-third more? Is there any publicly available information that can guide your assessment? (Competitor A's sales to this market are unlikely to be available if it is a private company, but employment data can be indicative.) What do customers tell you? And suppliers?

3 Taking your current sales level as an index number of 100, assign the appropriate index number to competitor A. If you think they sell less than you in this market, but not that much less (say, 10% less), give them an index number of 90; if you think they sell a lot more than you, perhaps an extra half as much again, give them 150.

4 Repeat steps 2 and 3 for each of the competitors named in step 1.

5 Make an allowance for any other competitors you have not named; for example, those who are small or only appear now and again. This should also be an index number. If you think all these other competitors together sell about half what you sell to the market, give this 'Others' category an index number of 50.

6 Add up all the index numbers (including your own 100), divide the total by 100 and multiply by your level of sales; that is your preliminary estimate of market size.

7 Ask your sales director to complete the same exercise. Get her to talk to the guy on the sales team who used to work at competitor A and the woman in R&D whose former boyfriend now works at competitor B. Get their inputs. Then get inputs from your operations director and head of R&D. Wherever their views differ from yours, discuss and refine the numbers. You have now built a reasoned estimate of market size.

Marketcrafting is hardly an accurate process, nor can it be guaranteed that the final number will not be way off. But it is better than nothing, *much better,* because you can use the results to get indicative values of four parameters key to business strategy and planning:

■ *Market size* (as above, though admittedly highly approximate).

■ *Market share.* Once you 'know' market size, you also know your market share (i.e. your sales level divided by estimated market size); you also have an estimate of the market share of each of your competitors.

■ *Market growth.* Repeat the seven-step marketcrafting approach above to estimate your market size of three years ago. For example, did competitor A sell more or less than you to this market three years ago, before, for example, their new depot came into operation, and by how much? You now have two data points – market size of today and that of three years ago. Punch that data into your calculator and out will pop an average compound growth rate over the three years, which serves as a crude estimate of recent market growth.

■ *Market share change.* Best of all, since you now know your market share three years ago and today, you also have an estimate of your market share gain (or loss), as well as the gain/loss for each of your competitors. These estimates will be most useful in assessing both the competitive intensity of your market (next chapter) and the competitive position of your firm (Chapter 5).

All these estimates are crude, perhaps in the extreme, but, believe me, they are better than nothing. Your backer will be impressed that you have tried to create some information out of nothing. And it gives them some sort of basis upon which to work, to challenge you on your assumptions, to do some checking on the Web and over the phone.

Above all, it gives them the groundwork to come up with their own range of estimates, should they choose to do so.

One caveat. Make sure you identify the *relevant* market size. It has to be that of the particular segment you are addressing. If you run a deli grocery in an off-high street location in Bristol, putting down the size of the UK grocery market as your addressable market will not be helpful. It's fine for Tesco, not for you.

Finally, here's a simple example of the findings that can be deduced from the marketcrafting process, adapted from an engineering company I worked with a few years ago (see Table 3.1).

table 3.1	Marketcrafting: an example	
Competitor	**Estimated index number for sales (latest year)**	**Implied market share (%)**
The company	**= 100**	17%
Competitor A	120	21%
Competitor B	85	15%
Competitor group C	125	21%
Competitor group D	65	11%
Competitor E	30	5%
Competitor F	20	3%
Others	40	7%
Total	**585**	**100%**

The company's turnover in this segment was about £30 million, so the market size could be estimated at 585/100 × 30, or around £175 million. The company's market share emerged at 17% (100/585), rather lower than the 25% that management had quoted before the marketcrafting exercise. Likewise, the market share of its Far Eastern competitors (Group C), though significant and concerning at 21%, did not seem to be as high as the one-third quoted rather sensationally in the trade press.

When we repeated the exercise to estimate market size of three years earlier, we found that the market had contracted heavily during the post-credit crunch recession, falling by one-third, or roughly 10% per year. Meanwhile, Far Eastern competitors had grown share greatly from 9% to 21%, with corresponding share losses by the domestic players, including that of the company, from 20% to 17%.

These were important findings. The trends were of course known beforehand, but their quantification through the marketcrafting process, though very rough, put some of the wilder assertions into perspective and helped focus attention on the strategic challenge ahead.

One final word on marketcrafting: it can be used not just by small companies serving markets which are too small for market research companies to investigate. It can also be used by much larger companies when analysing the market for certain of their product/market segment niches. While the company as a whole may address a broad market, which will be well covered by market research companies, some of their niche segments may well not be – and here marketcrafting can be used to gauge estimates of market size.

Market growth

This is the big question. Is demand in each of your main business segments going to grow? Will it be bigger in a few years' time, or smaller? Or more or less the same?

It's not the only question, of course. Equally important, as we will see in the next two chapters, is the nature of the competition you're going to face and how you're placed to compete.

It's all a matter of odds. You have a better chance of prospering in a market that's growing than one that's shrinking.

As they say in the world of business: 'It's better to be in a market with the wind at your back than in your face'.

So how do you find out where market demand is headed? Weave your web . . .

A web of information

I've been advising clients on market trends for 35 years. In the old days, you used to have to call up trade associations, write to companies active in the market asking for their annual reports, visit reference libraries to wade through reams of trade magazines and journals, and so forth.

Or you might have to purchase an expensive market research report, one often only of tangential relevance to the market you were researching.

Now it's a breeze. All you have to do is switch on your laptop, click on your internet connection, pop into Google or Yahoo, and type in the name of your market alongside such words as *'market'*, *'growth'*, *'forecasts'* and *'trends'*.

You'll find that Google comes up with hundreds – maybe thousands – of websites to visit. Most of them will be irrelevant. One, two or more will be spot on. You'll begrudge having to waste time trawling through dozens of useless sites – but, hey, think of the hours and hours of effort you're saving compared to the old days.

You just need some patience and perseverance to systematically wade through the referred sites. Open up a Word file, and whenever you come across an article on a website that seems useful, copy it and drop it into your document.

You're weaving your own web of information on your market.

You may find that your search directs you to reports produced by specialist market research companies. These should be used as a last resort. Some can be quite good, reflecting the direct access they may have had to market participants and observers, but too many turn out to be bland. And expensive. Better to do your own digging around on the Web first.

Try the national or regional news sites, many of which you can access with ease, without having to register or subscribe. The BBC's website (**www.bbc.co.uk**) is a hugely informative, internationally focused resource and doesn't cost a penny. Similarly international in outlook, the website of *The Economist* (**www.economist.com**) offers a free search on articles less than a year old, but subscription is needed for older articles. The websites of the main broadsheet national and regional newspapers are also good sources, such as *The Guardian* (**www.guardianunlimited.co.uk**), which is free and requires no registration. There are also *The Times* (**www.timesonline.co.uk**), *Daily Telegraph* (**www.telegraph.co.uk**), *Independent* (**www.independent.co.uk**), *Western Mail* (**www.icwales.icnetwork.co.uk**), *Scotsman* (**www.scotsman.com**) and *Irish Times* (**www.irishtimes.com**), some of which require registration. The *Financial Times* website (**www.ft.com**) offers a wealth of financial, company and market information, but to search through back copies requires you to subscribe.

You can also find out much about the companies working in your market by tapping into their own websites. Smaller companies tend to use their websites just as product or service showcases, but some may provide snippets of information on where the market is heading, such as a press release summarising a recent speech by the CEO to a trade conference. Publicly quoted companies will attach their annual reports, in which you'll find the views of the chairman or CEO on market trends.

Another good source of market information on the Web is online trade magazines. Typically they will have at least some sections open to the public without having to subscribe, which can often be expensive. If you work in the automotive industry, for example, you could look up **www.automotivenews.com**. If you're in the wine business – lucky you – how about **www.wine-spirit.com**? Whatever sector you work in, there is sure to be an online trade magazine.

Essential example

Go Ape's market demand

The market for activity-based holidays has been growing steadily for two decades. Drivers of this growth have included: increased personal disposable income; the high income elasticity of vacationing, leading to the taking of multiple holidays a year; increasing concern with health and fitness in our increasingly sedentary and overweight society; and growing awareness of and participation in adrenaline-fuelled activities – themselves encouraged by the extreme action observed while playing the most sedentary of leisure pastimes, the video game.

The European market can be segmented into geographical location, facilities provided, age group targeted and intended length of stay. Leading operators include PGL, with their UK and continental activity holidays aimed at the one-week pre-teen or teenage resident, and Kingswood's Camp Beaumont or Supercamps, aimed at the youthful day visitor. One facility typically present at a PGL camp is the high zip wire, enabling the harnessed visitor to zoom down from a substantial height to the ground safely. But this tends to be just one of an array of enticing offerings, from a climbing wall to quad bikes, abseiling to mountain biking, kayaking to raft building.

Go Ape opened in Thetford Forest in 2002 and focused essentially on one such activity – the zip wire – and set it, or rather them, in a forest environment, connected by treetop wooden walkways, ladders, bridges, tunnels and landing nets. It was a quality, niche offering, targeted at the PGL-type customer base, and was an immediate award winner. There are now 28 Go Ape centres in the UK, with 7 more in the USA and a further 3 opening in spring 2015. Sales topped £15 million in 2013, having octupled since 2006. Go Ape addressed a growing market, found an untapped niche within it and exploited it with a top-quality, readily replicable offering.

The HOOF approach to demand forecasting

Many years ago I developed a simple process for translating market demand trends and drivers into forecasts. I called it the HOOF approach, largely because HDDF, the strict representation of the first letters in each of the four steps, would be an unattractive, unmemorable acronym. With appropriate creative licence, the circular O can be borrowed as a lookalike to the semicircular D.

Also the name conjured up fond visions of the junior football team I coached for many years, where the youngsters would keep hoofing the ball down the pitch as hard as they could – with the ball following the perfect trajectory of the typical product life cycle . . .

The HOOF approach to demand forecasting is a four-step process. Get the process right and all falls logically into place. Get it out of step and you may end up with a misleading answer. You need to apply these steps for each of your main business segments. They are as follows:

1   **H**istoric growth – check how market demand has grown in the past.
2   **D**rivers past – identify what has been driving that growth in the past.
3   **D**rivers future – assess whether there will be any change in influence of these and other drivers in the future.
4   **F**orecast growth – forecast market demand growth, based on the influence of future drivers.

Let's look at each of these briefly, then at some examples.

Historic growth

To start with, get some facts and figures. It's surprising how the most straightforward of searches can reveal recent growth rates in the markets you're looking for.

Be careful not to fall into the trap of relying on one recent number. Just because demand for a service jumped by, say, 8% last year doesn't mean that trend growth in that market has been 8% each year. The latest year may have been an aberration. The previous year might have seen a dip in the market, followed by the 8% recovery.

You should try to get an average annual growth rate over a number of recent years, preferably at least the last three or four. As long as there haven't been serious annual ups and downs each year (and there may well have been for your firm during the difficult period of 2008–12), you can usually get a usable approximation of average annual growth by calculating the overall percentage change in, say, the last four years and then annualising it. If there have been ups and downs, you should smooth them out with three-year moving averages before calculating the percentage change.

If yours is such a niche market that there is little or no data to be found, that can't be helped. Useful information can still be uncovered. You just need to find out whether the market has been growing quickly, growing slowly, holding flat, declining slowly or declining quickly. We can define growing slowly as moving along at the same pace as the economy as a whole (gross domestic product or GDP in economics-speak), which is roughly 2–2.5% a year in the long run in Britain and most other large Western economies. That's in 'real' terms – in other words, in terms of tangible, wealth-creating growth.

On top of that sits inflation, typically around the same 2–2.5% a year over time, although it has been much higher in the past. Slow growth in terms of 'money of the day', or in 'nominal' terms, can therefore be taken as roughly 5% a year in the long run. Actual data on GDP growth can be extracted from government statistics if that is helpful.

Drivers past

Once you have uncovered some information on recent market demand growth, you need to find out what has been influencing that trend. Typical factors that influence demand in many consumer markets are as follows:

- Per capita income growth
- Population growth in general
- Population growth specific to a market (for example, of pensioners or baby boomers, or general population growth in a particular area)
- Some aspect of government policy
- Changing awareness, perhaps from high levels of promotion by competing providers
- Business structural shifts (such as towards outsourcing)
- Price change
- Fashion, even a craze
- Weather – seasonal variations, but maybe even the longer-term effects of climate change.

If yours is a B2B business, i.e. your customers are businesses rather than consumers, your demand drivers may well be none of the above and more specific to the business. If you sell, for example, to the health or education sectors, your main demand drivers may well be government policies and levels of public spending. If you sell personal financial services, one of your main drivers will be the level of complexity in personal finance. If you sell widgets to the engineering sector, a main driver will be the continuation of customers using the particular engineering solution which utilises your particular widget.

Drivers future

Now you need to assess how each of these drivers is going to develop over the next few years. Are things going to carry on more or less as before for a particular driver? Or are things going to change significantly for that driver?

Will, for instance, immigration continue to drive local population growth? Is the government likely to hike up a local tax? Could this market become less fashionable?

Will a new driver come into play, one that had no impact in the past, but could well influence demand in the future?

The most important driver is, of course, the economic cycle. If it seems that the economy is poised for a nosedive, that could have a serious impact on demand in your business over the next year or two – assuming your business is relatively sensitive (or 'elastic', in economics-speak) to the economic cycle. Or maybe your business is relatively inelastic, like, for example, the food industry. You need to think carefully about the timing of the economic cycle and the elasticity of your business.

Future growth

This is the fun bit. You've assembled all the information on past trends and drivers. Now you can weave it all together, sprinkle it with a large dose of judgement, and you have a forecast of market demand – not without risk, not without uncertainty, but a systematically derived forecast nevertheless.

Let's take a simple example of a business that offers a relatively new service to the elderly.

- Step 1 (H): you find that the market has been growing at around the range of 5–10% per year over the last few years.
- Step 2 (D): you identify the main drivers as (a) per capita income growth, (b) growth in the elderly population and (c) growing awareness of the service by elderly people.
- Step 3 (D): you believe income growth will continue as before, the elderly population will grow even faster in the future and that awareness can only get more widespread.
- Step 4 (F): you conclude that growth in your market will accelerate and could reach over 10% per year over the next few years.

You may find that the HOOF approach works best using a simple chart (see Table 3.2), where the balance of demand drivers and their changing influence on future demand for this service to the elderly is clearly illustrated.

table 3.2   The HOOF approach to demand forecasting: an example

Demand drivers for a new service to the elderly	Impact on demand growth			Comments
	Recent past	Now	Next few years	
Growth in incomes	–	o	+	▪ Economic recovery to be sustained in 2015–17, with GDP growth at 2.0–2.5% p.a. (OBR)
Growth in elderly population	+	+	++	▪ Proportion of population aged 65+ forecast to grow from 17% in 2010 to 23% by 2035 (ONS)
Increased awareness of service	++	++	+++	▪ Newspaper coverage, national and local, greater all the time
Overall impact	+	+	++	
Market growth rate	5 to 10%/yr	5 to 10%	Over 10%/yr	

H   O   O   F

Key to driver impact

+++	Very strong positive
++	Strong positive
+	Some positive
o	None
–	Some negative
––	Strong negative
–––	Very strong negative

And now here's an example of how not to do it. Many years ago I was doing some work with a crane manufacturer in the North of England and came across a draft business plan. In the section on market demand, its young author had stated that there was no data to be found anywhere on UK demand for cranes. So, for the purposes of the financial forecasts, he assessed real growth in the crane market to be the same as for UK engineering output as a whole, forecast by the OECD at 2.4% per year.

Oops! The mistake is one of exclusion. Yes, macro-economic demand was an important driver of demand in the crane market. But it was one driver only. There were three or four other drivers of equal importance, on which there was, admittedly, no hard and fast data but plenty of anecdotal evidence. They included evidence of destocking, a thriving second-hand market and, above all, an imminent downturn in high-rise construction activity.

None of these drivers bore any relation to engineering output as a whole and their combined impact served to translate a 2.4% per year crane market growth forecast into one of steep decline, possibly at 10% per year for two or three years.

The moral of this tale is to make sure that *all* drivers are taken into account, *irrespective of whether hard data can be found on them.* Use your judgement.

Essential tip

The HOOF approach to demand forecasting is very simple and rational. How has demand grown in the past? What influenced that growth? Will those influences change? So how will demand grow in the future? Get this process right, back it up with supporting evidence and sound judgement and you will leap over your backer's first credibility hurdle.

Essential example

LOVEFiLM's market demand

Video on Demand ('VoD') has been the Holy Grail of the media world since the 1990s – and LOVEFiLM came as close as any to it. VoD is when you can turn on your TV, laptop or smartphone, scroll down a library of dozens, hundreds or thousands of films and TV programmes, click on your choice and watch it, when you want to, for as often as you want to.

The BBC's iPlayer and commercial equivalents satisfy part of that demand, but if it was a database of movies you wanted, LOVEFiLM offered one solution. You didn't have to walk down to the video rental shop as of old. You didn't even have to fill in an order online and wait for a couple of days for the DVD to arrive, as was LOVE-FiLM's original core offering. You could stream the film directly onto your internet-connected TV or Sony PlayStation 3 console. LOVE-FiLM, like the much larger, US-based Netflix, served a potentially huge, latent market demand.

LOVEFiLM, then Online Rentals, started up in 2002 and, having attracted 1.6 million subscribers, was sold to Amazon in 2011 for close to £200 million. Its VoD product was merged into Amazon Prime Instant Video in 2014. It was a classic case of entrepreneurs spotting an unmet need in the marketplace and crafting a solution that met it.

Market demand for a start-up

This chapter of your plan may well be the most difficult of all to write for a start-up. Yours may be a new product or service designed to convey a customer benefit not previously realisable. In which case, how do you define the market? What is market demand for a product that has not previously existed? What is its size? What are its growth prospects?

On the other hand, your start-up may be in a market that's already well defined – like the Dart Valley Guest House and Oriental Spa, which will be unique and distinctive, but fits snugly into an already buoyant market for three- and four-star tourism in the West Country.

Or you may be opening a boutique selling designer childrenswear on the high street. Or you and a mate are setting up an independent plumbing business.

In each of these cases, your new venture is aiming at a definable, existing market. Your offering will be new, but the market won't be. Thus the market can be researched in the same way as set out in the previous sections.

But what if your product or service is indeed something that has not existed before? How can you convince your backer that there will be buyers for your offering, and at that price? How can you be sure that you are filling a need or a want that customers are prepared to pay for – and pay that much for? You need evidence.

In the previous chapter we talked about the possibility that your business may be meeting 'unmet needs'. You may have spotted a gap in the market.

But this leads us to the multi-million dollar question: **Is there a market in the gap?**

You need to show there is one. You need evidence.

You'll have to do some test marketing.

Test marketing

Which kind of test marketing you should do depends on whether yours is a business-to-business or a business-to-consumer proposition.

If yours is a business-to-business proposition, get on the phone and set up meetings with prospective corporate buyers. Accentuate briefly over the phone the benefits your offering will bestow and ask for the opportunity to tell them a little bit more face to face. This shouldn't be too tough. If your proposition is to have any legs at all, it should be worth at least 10 minutes of your prospective customer's time.

Start out the meeting by exploring the customer's needs, with you doing as little of the talking as possible. Then gently steer the discussion towards a perceived gap in the market, where the customer's needs are not being fully met. Again, try to nudge the customer to locate and describe the gap, rather than you having to point it out.

Now is your chance to pounce. Explain how your offering is designed to bridge that gap in the customer's needs. Set out how it will meet the customer's needs in ways that competitive offerings, whether direct or indirect, cannot do. And why at that price they will have a bargain!

Keep a record of these meetings and analyse the findings. Draw out key conclusions from the discussions, with each supported by bulleted evidence – using comments from named customers, backed up by comments from third parties quoted in the press or by further data dug up off the Web. Produce a short, sharp market research report, which will become Appendix A of your business plan. It will be the first appendix, because it will be the single most important item of evidence your backer will look for.

If yours is a business-to-consumer product or service, test it on the high street. Get out your clipboard, stand outside an Asda or a Waitrose, depending on your target customer, and talk to people. If you're offering a product, show them. If it's a service, explain lucidly but swiftly its benefits.

Again, collate the responses, analyse them, draw firm conclusions, support them with quotes and data, and stick the market research report in your Appendix A.

Estimating your addressable market

Having done your test marketing, you need to make an estimate of market size. Imagine perhaps that there are many suppliers of your product or service and the whole country is aware of its existence. What then would the market size be? How does that compare with the market size for products or services not that different from the ones you'll be offering? Does your estimate make sense?

That will give you an idea of the total available market. But when you launch it will just be you. No one will know you exist. You are invisible. It is unlikely that your available market will be the same as your addressable market – unless yours is an online business.

It is your addressable market that your backer needs to know about – the customers that you can realistically reach and try to sell your offering to in the first year or two following launch.

If you are opening a specialist sports injury physiotherapy clinic in East Sheen, South West London, is it likely that the whole of London will be your market? No. Possible? Yes, if yours develops a reputation as the best in the business, worth travelling an hour or more to get to. But that is impossible in the short term, unlikely in the medium term.

Your addressable catchment area is realistically a circle around East Sheen of a radius of around five miles, taking in Richmond, Kew, Barnes, Putney, Roehampton, possibly as far south as Wimbledon, east to Wandsworth, west to Twickenham and even stretching north of the river to Hammersmith, Fulham or Chiswick.

You can find population numbers for each of these London villages from the Web. You can also find London-wide average sports participation rates, broken down by sex, age group and type of sport. You can apply appropriate probabilities of receiving muscle, ligament, bone, etc. injuries in any one year, best again by sex, age group or type of sport, and that will give you a first estimate of your addressable market – the total number of people in your catchment area who might benefit from your physio treatment in each year.

But your very presence, and soon word of mouth, will attract physio patients with ailments not related to sports injuries – including many, like this author, whose physio requirements are as much age- as sports-related. You should make an estimate for this – perhaps as many as one non-sports patient for each sports injury within one half of the five-mile catchment radius for sports patients.

All a bit finger in the air, you might think. Perhaps, but you have made the effort. You will have shown your backer that you understand the concept and that you have been prepared to harness the best available data and analysis to narrow down the available market into an addressable one for your start-up.

You will have shown that you understand that your addressable market is not one of 8 million London residents, but more like 15,000 potential physio patients a year in your catchment area.*

I cannot stress this enough: your backer will respect your valiant attempt at demand analysis.

---

* Say, 8,000,000 London residents × 5% resident in catchment area × 50% participation in sport × 5% receiving injuries requiring physiotherapy × 1.5 for non-sports related patients = addressable market of 15,000.

And how about market demand growth? If your start-up is serving an existing market, you can use the same HOOF approach to demand forecasting that an established business would use.

If your start-up is for a new market, you may try the same HOOF process, but in reality this will not be the prime consideration of your backer, who will be more concerned with the existence of such a market in the first place. Any growth on top of discovering and serving a new market will be icing on the cake.

Essential tip

If your plan is for a start-up, test the market. Pick up the phone or get out and talk to people. Do some primary market research. Amass, digest and analyse pertinent data. Be armed for the inevitable grilling from your backer.

Market demand risks and opportunities

You have now come to a reasonable forecast of what's likely to happen to market demand in your key business segments over the next few years. However, your backer needs to know a little more than that. You've assessed what's *most likely* to happen. But what are the risks of something happening to market demand that could make things worse than that? What could happen to make things much worse? How likely are these risks to happen?

On the other hand, what could make things better than you have forecast? What could make things much better? How likely are these opportunities to happen?

Your backers are going to be very interested in these risks and opportunities. They are going to use your market demand forecasts to help assess whether your financial forecasts in Chapter 7 of your plan are reasonable. Then they will look at all the risks and opportunities around those forecasts in Chapter 8. And market demand issues will be the first set to be factored in.

Identify the main half a dozen risks that might affect your market demand forecasts, then assess them from two perspectives:

- How likely are they to take place – a low, medium or high likelihood?
- If they do occur, how big an impact will they have – a low, medium or large impact?

Now do the same for the opportunities you have identified.

Are any of these risks or opportunities *'big'* issues? We'll define a *'big'* risk (or opportunity) as one where:

- the likelihood of occurrence is medium (or high) *and* impact is high
- the likelihood of occurrence is high *and* impact is medium (or high).

Any big issues of market demand need to be set out clearly in your business plan. If it is a big risk, you must explain how you are going to address it and mitigate its impact. If it is a big opportunity, you must elucidate on how you plan to exploit it.

Essential case study
The Dart Valley Guest House and Oriental Spa business plan, 2015

Chapter 3: Market demand

As a former management consultant, Dick Jones knows his first port of call for data on tourism trends. He clicks onto the VisitBritain website, a veritable treasure trove for the statistical nerd, and soon digs up the following:

- Following the huge 17% jump in 2009, the so-called staycation effect caused by the financial crisis, total domestic tourism in Britain has since returned towards the *status quo ante,* tailing off 7% in 2010, bouncing back 7% in 2011, along with the double dip in the macro-economy, then dropping back a bit by 1% each year to 2013 – the level of which, at 57 million holiday trips, remained 14% above that of pre-crash 2008.

- 2014 saw a more severe levelling off, as overseas vacations made a belated recovery; in the 12 months ending September 2014, the latest data available to Dick when preparing his plan, the number of domestic holiday trips was down 8% in England – but somewhat less so at 7% in the West Country.

- Of 150 million holiday visitor nights (excluding those on business or visiting friends or relatives) taken by British residents in 2013, 48 million, or 32%, were in the West Country.

▶

- The visitors to the West Country spent £3.1 billion in nominal terms (2013 money) or £64 per person per night – up from an average £54 of two years earlier, an increase of 9%/year (which seems very high, reflecting perhaps the wide margin of error in such consumer surveys).

- There were a further 4.6 million business visitor nights to the West Country in 2013, with each spending an average of £91 per night.

- Taking total tourists as the indicator, due to definitional changes in 'holiday visitor' in the interim, the former stayed more or less flat to the West Country between 2011 (75.0 million nights) and 2013 (74.3 million).

- Devon is the second most popular county destination of domestic tourism, after Cornwall, attracting 13.4 million holiday nights (average 2011–13) or around 9% of the England total.

- The average length of stay on holiday trips in England was 2.9 nights in 2013.

Dick has found so much useful information on aggregate market demand that his problem will be keeping his appendix on the market to a manageable three to four pages.

But Dick has to delve a bit deeper. He needs to find visitor trends in Devon, not just in the West Country, and preferably in the Torbay area. He manages to find some interesting if outdated data from the Devon County Council website relating to 2007:

- Visitors spent 2.89 million nights in Torbay serviced accommodation (hotels, guest houses and B&Bs) or 35% of all Devon, with South Hams at 0.62 million nights and 7.5% respectively.

Now all Dick needs is some data on spa tourism, but that is hard to find. One problem lies in the definition of a spa – which can range from a facility offering a sauna adjacent to the fitness suite to the full works of multiple pools and treatment rooms. There are some market research reports available, but Dick is not convinced that the steep expense would be worth it.

Dick is ready for his Chapter 3 conclusions:

- Taking visitor nights in Torbay and South Hams serviced accommodation at 3.5 million, assuming conservatively no increase since 2007, having likely jumped in 2009 and levelled off somewhat since, and applying the 2013 West Country average spend per night of £64, addressed market size can be estimated at very roughly £225 million.

- Market demand growth in the West Country has been up, then down, in visitor nights, but with a strong increase in spend per visitor.

- Main long-term drivers have been per capita income growth, the growing propensity to take multiple short breaks and the steadily improving range of visitor facilities and attractions in Devon.

- The main short-term driver was the 'staycation' effect in 2009, which has since subsided with the 2014 pick-up of beach holidays in the Mediterranean.

- Dick therefore forecasts market growth over the next three years at flat in visitor nights and a conservative 2–3% per year in average spend.

- Larger and higher star hotels can be expected to fare better than the average during the bounce-back from recession as visitors reverse their former behaviour of trading down.

- Hotels offering special premium facilities such as spas should fare likewise.

- The main risk facing South Devon hoteliers was the staycation rebound, but that seems to have now worked its way through and further contraction in the market seems unlikely.

Given how market demand for Devon tourism was so buoyant during the 2007–11 economic downturn, Dick feels a backer will not have too many concerns over this chapter of his plan. But what of Dart Valley's competition for this £225 million market? That's for the next chapter.

Essential checklist on market demand

Set out for each of your main business segments, succinctly but convincingly, your assessments of the following:

- Market size – find a source or perhaps craft it yourself.
- Market demand forecasts – use the HOOF approach:
  - **H**istoric demand growth – again, find a source or craft it yourself.
  - **D**emand drivers past – what influences have shaped growth in the past?
  - **D**emand drivers future – how will these and other influences shape growth in the future?
  - **F**orecast demand – the logical output of 'hoofing' it!
- Market demand risks and opportunities – how likely and how big an impact?

This will all be done on three to four pages of A4. Supporting data – for example, tables showing market size by segment for each of the last three years and/or composition or trend data on key demand drivers – can be loaded into an appendix.

If your business is a start-up in a new market niche, concentrate in Chapter 3 on the rationale for the very existence of that niche. Test the market. Assess the size of the addressable market. Build up data and evidence and load your appendix.

4

Competition

In this chapter

- Your competitors
- Competitive intensity
- Competition in a start-up
  - Direct competition
  - Indirect competition
  - Competitive response
- Industry competition risks and opportunities

I t's a shame about competition. If your business were the only provider of your product or service, customers would be queuing round the block and you could charge them what you like, within reason.

But life isn't like that. There is always competition. And the more successful your business, the more likely it is that competitors will be eyeing your niche.

So why is competition frequently dismissed, almost as an irrelevance, in so many business plans? In 8 out of every 10 plans I have reviewed over the years, the analysis has been unconvincing. In half of those eight the analysis has been so cursory, so derisory, as to be misleading.

Why are managers and/or entrepreneurs so blindfolded when it comes to competition? Do they really believe that prospective backers will believe them when competitors are ignored or brushed aside?

And think of what happens if your backer, undertaking the most simple of due diligence tasks, picks up the phone and speaks to a customer who tells them that, sure, your firm is good, but such-and-such a competitor provides just as good a product but at a more competitive price. Hang on! Could this be the very same competitor dismissed in the business plan as producing poorly specced, unreliable products at such discounted prices that customers wouldn't take the risk of buying them?

Your backer will walk away. End of story. If they lose faith in your perceived commercial awareness, or, worse, your integrity, you will have no backer.

Tell it like it is. And at some length. Don't let the section on competition be one or two paragraphs squirrelled away in a chapter on your firm's strategy.

Give it respect. Make it a separate chapter. Face up to it. You know you're going to have to take the competition head on. Let your backer know just who you are up against.

Essential tip

Respect the competition. Give competitors the space they merit in your plan. Dismiss them and your backer will dismiss you.

Your competitors

With whom do you compete? A straightforward question, but not necessarily a straightforward answer.

There can be two areas of complexity in identifying your competitors: variation by segment and indirect competition.

You should expect competition to differ in some of your main business segments. If you recall the analysis of Chapter 2, the 'product' part of a product/market segment is itself typically defined by a product, or group of products, having a distinct set of competitors.

Think of Asda and its line-up of competitors. In clothing Asda takes on the likes of Primark, which sells no food. In DVDs it used to line up against Woolworths and Zavvi, among others, but they have fallen by the wayside. In food it competes not just with rivals Tesco and Sainsbury's, as well as the discounters Aldi and Lidl, but also with the local grocer, butcher and fishmonger. In ready-cooked food, Asda competes with local restaurants.

Then there is indirect competition. These are competitors not directly in your space but infringing on your space by offering an alternative solution to the customer. They are competing for your customer's pocket.

You could argue that the local grocer is an indirect competitor of Asda since it offers a different service – more personal, hands-on, quality assured, returns-friendly, neighbourly perhaps. An example of a truly indirect competitor would be iTunes, whose download solution for music reduces demand for CDs sold by Asda and its direct competitors.

Essential example

Pret A Manger's competition

In the mid-1980s, you might have thought that there were few more mature industries than the sandwich shop. The office worker typically unwrapped a self-prepared sandwich from a Tupperware container, or popped into Boots or Marks & Spencer for a ready-made sandwich or joined the queue at a sociable sandwich bar, where you struggled to make up your mind from an array of ingredients and some cheeky chappie behind the counter crafted a sandwich especially for you.

Not much scope for innovation there, you might have thought. One entrepreneur thought otherwise. He opened a sandwich shop in Victoria where sandwiches were made up on the premises in the early morning, packed and sold off-the-shelf as upmarket fast food at lunchtime. It was an instant success, boosted by a strong culture ('Pret behaviour'!) of staff joviality and lively communication on the healthiness of the offering.

The chain grew steadily and profitably. Today Pret turns over more than £450 million, with 335 outlets, all managed directly and none franchised, with a significant presence in New York, Hong Kong and Paris. But growth has not been without its setbacks. An investment by McDonald's in the early 2000s led to over-rapid expansion. It faced direct competition from a lookalike start-up EAT, but this served to further grow the market for them both. In the recession of 2009, it saw sales dip as the chain lost out to indirect competition – the resurgence of the Tupperware alternative, as consumers reacted cautiously to the uncertain economy. But by 2010 Pret was back on track and expanding steadily in the US, though was facing a new hurdle – American customers struggling with the French and referring to it as 'Pretty Manager'!

You need to find out all you can about your competitors. You should prepare summary profiles of them for an appendix, to be summarised here in your Chapter 4. The profiles should include the following:

- Sales – preferably by main segment. If the only data you can find is group sales or divisional sales encompassing a number of segments, only some of which you address, make a record of those actual sales but also attempt to estimate sales in each key segment – you're going to need those estimates for your market share calculations
- Sales growth over the last three years
- Operating and/or net profit margin – if available (unlikely if your competitor is a private company)
- Ownership – and an assessment of financial depth and backing
- Segments addressed – now and plans for the future (for example, new products in the pipeline, new markets/customer groups being targeted)

- Location of facilities and sales/service teams
- Physical assets deployed – for example, numbers and type of machinery
- Strategy – main focus, recent investments, growth plans (from, for example, press or trade show clippings, or even customer anecdotes)
- Positioning in market – unique sales pitch, pricing policy.

Only key extracts and conclusions from this appendix analysis should go into your Chapter 4. Which competitors play in which segments? What's their relative market share? How have they been performing? Have they been gaining or losing share? Why? What are they up to? What new products or new markets are they planning?

And let's have a couple of pie charts in this chapter. Show each main competitor's pie slice of market share in your main business segments. If illuminating, show a back projection of market share of, say, three years ago. If you've been the one who has gained share in this period, this is a must!

This is all background stuff. Important, necessary, but perhaps not very interesting. Much more interesting to your backer, and left out entirely in the vast majority of business plans, is a discussion of competitive intensity and how it has been evolving.

Competitive intensity

What your backer wants to know is how intense competition is in your main business segments and whether it is going to intensify. And why.

They want to get a sense of what is likely to happen to pricing in your market. Future pricing is critical in financial forecasting, more important even than market share gain, since every penny of a price rise falls straight to the bottom line.

Likewise, every penny of a price reduction is a direct hit to the bottom line. Your backer needs to know.

There's no better tool for assessing the competitiveness of an industry than Michael Porter's five forces model. It first appeared in his *Competitive Strategy: Techniques for Analyzing Industries and Competitors* in 1980.

Porter identified five main sets of forces that shape competitive intensity, as shown in Figure 4.1. Here's a quick word on each of them.

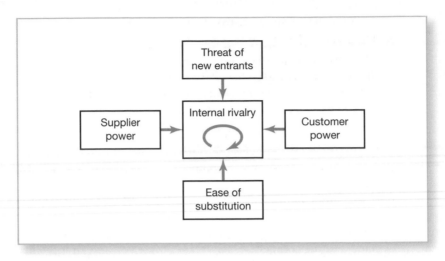

figure 4.1   **Five forces shaping competition**

Source: Adapted from Michael Porter, *Competitive Strategy: Techniques for Analyzing Industries and Competitors,* The Free Press, 1980

Internal rivalry

Internal rivalry is shaped by three main subforces: the number of players; market demand growth relative to supply; and external pressures.

The number of players

The more numerous the players, the tougher typically the competition. Are there many players in your marketplace?

Market demand growth

The slower growing the market, the tougher typically the competition.

But what of supply? Does your industry have a reasonable balance between demand and supply? If so, then internal rivalry may well be moderate.

If, however, your industry has indications of oversupply – where supply exceeds demand – that will increase internal rivalry. It will also place a dampener on prices. You and your competitors will have to fight more fiercely for custom, and any planned price increases to meet rising costs may have to be put on hold.

Do your customers have many suppliers they can choose from? Has this worsened in recent times? Are you and your fellow providers underutilised? Is industry pricing being squeezed? These are all signs of supply exceeding demand.

If, conversely, the industry is one of undersupply (or excess demand), where customers compete for relatively scarce supplies, that's good news for you. Internal rivalry will be modest and you and your competitors may be able to nudge up pricing above inflation.

How fast did you find your market to be growing in Chapter 3? And how is the market demand/supply balance?

External pressures

External bodies, in particular government and the trade unions, have great power to influence the nature of competition in many industries. Government regulation, taxation and subsidies can skew both market demand and the competitive landscape. Trade unions can influence competition in a number of ways – for example, through restrictive practices that serve to raise barriers to entry.

There are other factors influencing internal rivalry, which may be relevant in your industry. One is high barriers to exit, where providers have little choice but to continue competing when they should be withdrawing (for example, a restaurant with many employees, hence potentially high redundancy costs, or a service business with a long lease on office space that is difficult to offload). Another factor is seasonal or irregular overcapacity due to fluctuating levels of demand (for example, the fruit picking or ice cream industries).

Are there many providers in your marketplace? How fast is the market for your services growing (see Chapter 3)? What about the other factors? Put all these together and ask yourself how tough the internal rivalry is in your marketplace. High, low, medium? And in a few years' time? Why?

Threat of new entrants

The lower the barriers to entry to a market, the tougher typically the competition. Barriers to entry can be technology, operations, people or cost related, where a new entrant has to:

- develop or acquire a certain technology
- develop or acquire a certain operational process
- train or engage scarce personnel
- invest heavily in either capital assets or marketing to become a credible provider.

Then there are switching barriers: the higher the costs to the customer of switching from one supplier to another, the higher are the barriers. A drinks manufacturer may shift from one sugar supplier to another with relative ease, but it may require a complete redesign of its bottling plant in switching from one labelling solution to another.

How high are the entry barriers in your industry? How serious is the threat of new entrants? High, low, medium? Is the threat going to get more serious over the next few years, less serious, or stay more or less the same? Why?

Ease of substitution

The easier it is for customers to use a substitute product or service, the tougher typically the competition.

Think again of the impact of the likes of iTunes in the music industry. It was a substitute solution to the sale of CDs in the high street and a contributing factor, along with e-commerce and the supermarkets, to the demise of retailers such as Woolworths and Zavvi. In this case, the threat of substitution would be classified as high.

How big is the threat of you and your competitors losing share to substitutes? High, low, medium? Is the threat going to get bigger over time? Why?

Customer power

The more bargaining power your customers have over you, the tougher typically the competition. Ask any supplier to the supermarket chains, or to automotive manufacturers.

Often this is no more than a reflection of the number of providers in a marketplace, compared with the number of customers. The more choice of provider the customer has, the tougher the competition.

Customer power is also influenced by switching costs. If it's easy and relatively painless to switch supplier, competition is tougher. If switching costs are high, competition is less tough.

How much bargaining power do customers in your industry have over providers? High, low, medium? And in the future? Why?

Supplier power

The more bargaining power suppliers have over producers or service providers, the tougher typically the competition.

Again, it can often be just a function of numbers. There are, for example, numerous metal converters, but few (and increasingly fewer) metal producers (e.g. steel mills). When metal converters sell components to automotive manufacturers, they can find themselves in a vice-like squeeze – huge steel or aluminium suppliers at one end, auto giant customers at the other. But the best of them learn how to duck, dive and survive.

How much bargaining power do your suppliers have over providers of your kind of service? High, low, medium? And in the future? Why?

Essential tip

Beware of concluding that competitive intensity will ease off over the plan period. It may, but you had better have a watertight argument. Your backers will be wary of such a claim – especially if they are bankers.

Overall competitive intensity

These then are the five main forces shaping the degree of competition in a marketplace. Put them all together and you'll have a measure of how competitive your industry is.

How tough is internal rivalry? How serious is the threat of new entrants or substitutes? How much power do customers and suppliers have on you and your competitors?

In short, how intense is competition in your industry? High, low, medium?

And what of the future? Is industry competition set to intensify? Because however tough it is at the moment, it results in a certain level of industry-average operating margin achieved by you and your competitors.

What your backer wants to know is whether competitive forces will conspire to threaten that margin over the next few years. Or whether the industry competition of the past few years is unsustainable and likely to ease off in the future.

In other words, what will be the effect of competitive dynamics on pricing in your industry over the next few years?

Will competition intensify and put pressure on prices? Will it stay more or less as is and pricing move as it has been doing in recent times? Or will competition ease off, enabling players to nudge up prices and margins over the next few years?

Your backer needs to know. You should address this issue directly in this chapter or they may assume the worst.

Essential example

XLN Telecom

Scale is not everything. When the UK telecoms sector was deregulated in the early 2000s, a couple of entrepreneurs decided to take on the giant BT head on in the small business sector. Their former experience was in selling office products to small businesses. Now they built on their understanding of SME needs to sell them land lines, mobile and broadband telecoms, all based on a proprietary technology platform. XLN's pitch of high-quality, low-cost products with exceptional service struck a chord in the market. Sales had grown to over £50 million by 2010, all taken essentially off BT and achieved in direct competition with other similar start-ups. The founders monetised their capital gain in a buyout in late 2010.

Competition in a start-up

Too many start-up business plans are based on the premise that theirs is a new concept. Competition is non-existent, or irrelevant. In the vast majority of cases, this is at best only partially true.

There is always competition. Whatever your solution to the perceived needs of the customer, someone else somewhere else has another solution. Or will have. If they don't have a solution now, they may well do once they have seen yours.

Doug Richard, former Dragon on the BBC show *Dragons' Den* and founder of School for Startups, quips that you should know your competitors, love them, buy their products, send them back!

But his point is a serious one. You must find out all there is to know about them. Call up their sales or marketing people, tell them you are doing research on the market, which is true, and ask them their views on where the market is headed. Then ask them why their product or service is the best on the market – they'll talk about that for hours!

Finally, and crucially, ask them what their plans are for the future. What new products, new services, new distributors, new locations are in the pipeline? If it's confidential, they won't say, which is fair enough. If not, you need to know!

Let's look at three aspects of competition in a start-up:

- Direct competition
- Indirect competition
- Competitive response.

Direct competition

If your new venture is a business with a clearly defined existing marketplace, then your analysis for this chapter will be no different from that of an established business.

You'll identify the competitors, soon to be augmented by one, and assess competitive intensity, soon to be intensified perhaps by your firm's entry.

An example (as previously introduced in Chapter 3) would be a start-up boutique specialising in designer childrenswear on the high street. Your competitors would include other such boutiques, any boutiques focusing on adult clothes but also offering a selection for children, childrenswear chain stores, the childrenswear departments of department stores and all of these variants using different routes to market – for example, catalogue shopping or online e-tailing.

You will be entering a highly competitive market – retail can be an unforgivingly competitive arena – but hopefully with a distinctive edge that you will set out forcefully in Chapter 5 of your business plan.

Indirect competition

What if your idea is a new concept? Who are your competitors?

They are whoever was providing an alternative solution to the customer before your business existed, competing for a similar share of the customer's wallet as you are.

Suppose you invent an ingenious wooden rollerball back-massaging device that releases aromatherapy oils as you massage. It's new, it's unique, it's brilliant, it works!

But it has competition. The customer's need is relief from back tension or pain – and he is prepared to dip into his pocket to relieve that pain.

Customers have a range of alternative solutions – other wooden rollerball devices, plastic and metal versions, electrically powered massage devices, massage chairs. They can go to a masseur, even to an aromatherapist. They can purchase the oils and self-administer. They can take pills.

All these are competitors, even if only indirect competitive solutions. Your product will occupy a particular price positioning – above basic rollerball devices, below power-driven ones – but the customer has the option to trade up or down.

In your Chapter 5, you will set out the pros of alternative solutions from their perspective and the cons from yours. You'll make your case. But it's a case that must not be considered in isolation, but in relation to the alternative solution providers – and these competitors need to be described in this chapter and competitive intensity assessed.

Competitive response

Also frequently absent in business plans is the reaction of competitors if your venture turns out to be a success.

You cannot assume that they will stand idly by and cheer you on. Your backer won't. They will assume that your competitors will respond.

If your new concept is patent protected, that is great. Your backer will need to know full details. But there are ways for a competitor to negotiate a path around a patent, and legally. Offering a slight variant on the theme can often be enough.

How will you respond when, not if, your competitors respond to your market entry? Here is the place in your plan to say how.

Suppose your childrenswear boutique is successful. How will the department store down the road respond? Perhaps by cordoning off the childrenswear department, refitting the design, engaging a clown every Saturday afternoon. How would you respond to that response?

Suppose your oil-infused rollerball massaging device was successful. How will producers of basic devices respond? Will they copy the device if unpatented? If patented, could they offer their devices along with free-standing oils for self-administering at 15% below your price? How would you respond to that?

Consider competitive response. And prepare your return response.

Industry competition risks and opportunities

You have assessed competitive intensity in your industry, both now and over the next few years. What are the risks to that assessment? What could happen to intensify competition further?

What could happen to internal rivalry, to customer bargaining power or to any of the other forces to intensify competition?

What is the likelihood of those risks occurring? And what would be the impact if they did?

What are the *big* risks (as defined in Chapter 3) – those that are reasonably likely *and* with reasonable impact? How will you mitigate these big risks should they occur?

Conversely, what are the *big* opportunities to perhaps balance these risks? And how will you exploit them should they occur?

One or two paragraphs are all that is required on big competitive risks and opportunities in this chapter of your plan. But your backer will appreciate you addressing and tackling them up front.

Essential case study
The Dart Valley Guest House and Oriental Spa business plan, 2015

Chapter 4: Competition

In the last chapter, Dick Jones identified market demand for serviced accommodation in the Torbay and South Hams area at £225 million. Now he needs to assess how competitive the supply is to that demand in general, and more specifically in his addressed market niche of three- and four-star accommodation with spa facilities.

Again he raids the website of VisitBritain, finding out the following:

- Couples matter – average bedspace occupancy in England in 2014 was 52%, compared to bedroom occupancy of 69%.
- Region matters – West Country occupancy rates were somewhat below average at 49%, with London highest at 83%.
- Season matters – bedspace occupancy was lowest in January at 36%, highest during the summer at 62%.
- Location matters – bedspace occupancy rates were higher in large towns/cities at 57%, compared to small towns (46%), at the seaside (47%) or, more relevant to Dart Valley, in the countryside (45%).
- Size matters – hotels fared best at 54%, followed by guest houses (43%) and B&Bs (40%).

▶

- Size and time matter – occupancy rates were stable at guest houses over the period 2011–14, at around the 42–43% level, while B&Bs improved steadily from 37% to 40% over the period.

- Region and time matter – West Country occupancy rates rose steadily from 47% in 2011 to 49% in 2014.

From the Devon County Council website Dick finds out the following (for 2007):

- There were 18,460 serviced bedspaces in Torbay; 4,380 in South Hams.

- Bedspace availability fell to 82% in Torbay in January, which was the same as the Devon average, and 74% in South Hams, indicating how many hotels close their doors during the slow months.

- Average bedspace occupancy in Torbay was 43% (compared to all Devon's 41%), highest in August at 68% and lowest in January at 26% (of available beds at establishments open that month).

- Average bedspace occupancy for smaller hotels was lower than for larger hotels, with those with 21–50 bedspaces achieving 38% and those with 7–20 34%.

- For those with 21–50 bedspaces, December–March occupancy averaged just 23%.

Again, this is most useful information and will enable Dick to compare data on his own hotel's performance with local, regional or national trends in the next chapter of his plan.

But it also gives an indication of the supply/demand balance. Torbay average occupancy seems little different from that of all Devon or indeed of all England. If there is no indication of localised excess supply, in that demand and supply are in the same degree of balance as in the rest of the county and country, Dick's backer should not be overly concerned with pricing prospects.

Dick now focuses on direct competitors – those playing in the niche of three- and four-star accommodation with spa facilities. In the four years he has been studying, planning, developing and operating in this market, he has recognised this line-up:

- Seven hotels in Torquay and four in South Hams, mainly four-star, offering full spa facilities, including swimming pool, spa pool, sauna and treatment rooms.

- Two fitness clubs in Torquay offering full spa facilities.
- Five hotels (one of which is a five-star) and three fitness clubs offering limited spa facilities, typically just a treatment room or two.

He has met a number of their owners and managers, partly through the Torbay Hospitality Association, and has a good idea of how they have been faring during the post-financial crisis recession and tackling the issues that face them all.

Dick assesses competitive intensity in his niche as medium to high:

- Internal rivalry is medium to high, with many players – not just in South Devon but elsewhere in the West Country – but above-average demand growth in this niche.
- Barriers to entry are low, with many establishments setting up a treatment room and calling it a spa, but higher for full facility spas, due to the capital costs of set-up and operating costs of running the dedicated space. Nevertheless, there remains the risk that a directly competitive guest house-cum-spa operation in the Dart Valley mould could indeed be launched over the next five years; this could be seen as a threat to Dart Valley occupancy rates or as an opportunity, with the new competitor helping to spread the word about oriental spa vacationing in South Devon.
- The threat of substitutes always looms large – spa holidays themselves emerged as a substitute for other health-conscious holidays, like beach, swimming, walking or golf breaks, and will remain vulnerable to an extent to the advent of the 'next big thing'.
- The bargaining power of customers is high – they have plenty of options on where to allocate their health-holiday spend.
- The bargaining power of suppliers is low – there are a number of hot tub suppliers, for example, and labour is plentiful in Devon.

Dick doesn't envisage any significant competitive intensification over the next three years. The main risks remain those of a new entrant or, conversely, that the spa goes the way of a fad. In either scenario, the fallback position is that Dart Valley would still remain an attractive destination for the discerning visitor.

This brings the discussion neatly to the competitive positioning of Dart Valley, but that is for Chapter 5.

Essential checklist on competition

Your plan will stand apart from the majority of plans by dedicating a whole chapter to your competitors and competitive intensity. You will show you're unafraid of facing up to and tackling any beasts out there in the wild.

Put the details on the size, location, number of employees and so on of your competitors in an appendix, but summarise the most illuminating findings in Chapter 4 of your plan.

Assess how competitively intense your industry is and whether this is likely to intensify, by considering the following:

- **The forces of internal rivalry** – including the size and number of players, demand growth, external pressures, barriers to exit and possible overcapacity
- **The threat of new entrants** – describing barriers to entry
- **The threat of substitute products or services** – potentially disruptive
- **The bargaining power of customers** – often dependent on the relative numbers and scale of providers and customers
- **The bargaining power of suppliers** – likewise, but you are the customer.

Assess what is likely to happen to industry pricing should there be competitive intensification. Finally, point out the main risks and opportunities around industry competition over the next few years.

If your business is a start-up with a new concept, identify competitors that provide alternative solutions and analyse the industry accordingly. Consider how competitors may respond to your entry and how you in turn will respond to that.

This will all be done in two to three pages of A4. Any supporting data or evidence on industry competition should be placed in an appendix.

5

Strategy

> We shall either find a way or make one.

Hannibal

In this chapter

- Competitive position
- Strategy
  - Generic strategies
  - Strengthening competitive position
  - Boosting strategic position
- Strategy in a start-up
- Strategic risks and opportunities

Y ou have already set out the micro-economic backdrop to your business. In Chapter 3, you assessed prospects for market demand and in Chapter 4 for industry competition. Now it's time to slot your business into that context.

How competitive is your business in each of its main segments? What is your strategy for strengthening competitiveness in key segments? Or boosting the balance of your overall portfolio of segments? What risks may you face and what opportunities can you exploit? That's for this chapter – and then in Chapter 6 we will look at the resources you'll need to deploy to put that strategy into effect.

Your conclusions in this chapter will form an essential component of the justification of your sales and operating profit forecasts in Chapter 7 of your plan.

One caveat: as for Chapters 3 and 4, this chapter will set out conclusions from the extensive research and analysis you'll undertake before writing your plan – in this instance on your competitive position and strategy. Very little of the detailed analysis set out below will find its way into your plan. You would lose or bore your backer in no time. Only the conclusions go into the plan. Any further detail can be laid out in an appendix on competitive position.

But it will be hugely beneficial if you can convince your backer that your assertions have been pulled not from the top of your head, but from a foundation of solid research and analysis.

Your assertions will have depth, balance and relevance. In so many business plans, the writer waxes lyrical on the company's strengths – for example, how a product has a feature that is unique or by far the best in the market. That may have some truth, but let's have some perspective. Does the customer perceive a *significant* difference between your product and that of the closest competitor? Do they care? How important is that feature in an assessment of overall competitive position? Is it worth the price differential? Without that kind of rigorous analysis, your backer may remain unconvinced.

In this chapter of your plan, you must not overexaggerate your strong points, nor their importance to the buying decision, nor gloss over your weak points. You must place your firm's strengths and weaknesses in context – in terms of both the customer's buying decision and the capabilities of the competition. Imagine if a competitor stumbled across a stray copy of your business plan, left lying on a table at a conference (it does happen). Would they split their sides laughing at the one-sided hyperbole?

Your assertions must be sufficiently robust to withstand forensic examination. If they are not, your backers will pull out, having wasted your time and theirs.

Essential tip

You can always find something nice to say about somebody's character, appearance and skills, even though in reality you may think that person a rude, scruffy layabout. So too with companies. If you trumpet your firm's strengths without putting them in a competitive context, or without acknowledging your corresponding weaknesses, you invite your backer to be sceptical of your conclusions on your firm's competitiveness.

Competitive position

First you need to be clear about how your business stacks up against the competition. In each of your main business segments, how well placed are you? And how is that position likely to change over the next few years?

To answer that you should ideally go through three stages, for each of your main segments:

1 Identify and weight customer purchasing criteria (CPCs) – what customers need in each segment from their suppliers, which would be you and your competitors.

2 Identify and weight key success factors (KSFs) – what you and your competitors need to do to satisfy those CPCs and run a successful business.

3 Assess your competitive position – how you rate against those KSFs relative to your competitors.

Appendix A to this book shows you how to do just that. It sets out a systematic assessment of where your firm is currently placed relative to your main competitors, and how this is likely to develop over the next few years.

I strongly recommend that you follow the approach of Appendix A. It is comprehensive, rigorous and can be revelatory. It is not, however, *necessary* for your business plan. Indeed it will not form part of your business plan as delivered to your backer.

It will lie there in the background, forming a solid bedrock of research and analysis to underpin your forecasts in Chapter 7, ready to counter any clever cross-questioning from your backer.

The alternative, a shortcut, is to set out here your firm's strengths and weaknesses, as recommended in most business plan guides. I have three problems with this approach:

- Setting out strengths and weaknesses without weighting and rating them and deriving a reasoned, balanced conclusion, preferably a weighted average assessment of competitive position, can be misleading.

- This exercise is seldom done for each main business segment, where, virtually by definition of being a different segment, both the weighting and rating, and hence the overall competitive position, will differ.

- It is too often thrown in as part of a SWOT exercise (Strengths, Weaknesses, Opportunities, Threats), which is a dreadful, if ubiquitous, construct. SWOT typically shows just a jumble of items, ungraded for importance, relevance, probability or impact. It muddles up business opportunities with market opportunities, business risks with market risks, and comes to no conclusion whatsoever. It is a mess.

But by all means have a go at strengths and weaknesses if you would prefer not to go through the rigour (and, yes, time) of Appendix A. If so, please make sure you are as clear as possible when describing a strength or weakness to your backer by observing these tips:

- Give your backer some impression of the relevance of a strength or weakness in assessing a firm's competitiveness in your main business segments.

- Explain to what extent this is more important in some segments than others.

- Set it out relative to the competition – sure, your customer retention rates are admirably high, but are they higher than those of the market leader? And, if not, what plans do you have to raise them to the best in the business?

- Do not mix opportunities and threats with this assessment of your firm's strengths and weaknesses – market opportunities and threats have already been discussed (in Chapters 3 and 4); business opportunities and threats will be assessed below in this chapter.

Once you have set out your firm's competitive position in its main business segments (following the approach of Appendix A in this book), or taken a shortcut and listed your firm's strengths and weaknesses (as above), it is time to set out your plans for proactively strengthening your firm's competitiveness. That is your strategy, and it is covered in the next section.

Essential example

Lonely Planet's strategy

On my first trip to South East Asia in the late 1970s, a friend lent me his ragged copy of a small yellow guidebook, *South-East Asia on a Shoestring,* of which he said that 'this'll be your best mate on the trip'. He wasn't far wrong.

The market for travel guides must have seemed mature, even crowded, at the start of the 1970s. It was dominated by the Baedeker, Fodor and Michelin guides, differentiated mainly by colour, through their red, blue or green jacket covers. There were also the likes of Frommer's *Europe on $5 a Day* guides for the more budget conscious. More pertinently, there was (and remains to this day) the exceptional (and big) *South American Handbook,* which combines detailed historical and cultural context with practical advice at all levels of the travel market. But when Tony and Maureen Wheeler travelled 'in a beat-up old car' from London to Sydney for their year-long honeymoon in 1973, they found they had little to help them. They had to find where to stay, what to do and how to get there the old way, the hard way, by themselves. When they arrived in Sydney, 'flat broke', they were persuaded to write down their experiences for the benefit of other travellers, stapling random pages together at the kitchen table.

Across Asia on the Cheap sold 1,500 copies within a week of its appearance. The Wheelers had tapped into the traveller market, a derivative of the former hippie trail from London to Afghanistan of the late 1960s, but soon to mushroom through the insatiable appetite of young Australians for overland travel – saving up, travelling overland for a year towards Europe, working in a bar for a year in Earls Court, then taking another slow year to get home – the standard trail. And Lonely Planet was there to help them along the way.

▶

It did not have it all its own way though. In 1982, Mark Ellingham brought out a *Rough Guide to Greece* – full of historical and cultural context, along the lines of *the South American Handbook,* but targeting the traveller market as per Lonely Planet. That developed into a European series and the two soon started to compete head on, especially after Penguin bought Rough Guides in 1995. As with EAT challenging Pret A Manger (as we saw in Chapter 4) both players benefited from tougher competition. Lonely Planet's strategy had from the outset been one of differentiation – unafraid to take on the giants of Michelin and Fodor, the Wheelers identified a niche market, albeit one poised to grow rapidly, and tailored a product perfectly designed to that niche.

By the 2000s, as the printed product matured, Lonely Planet's strategy moved into product extension and new media. It developed thematic guides (e.g. on languages, food and walking), brought out its own travel magazine and moved into travel television production. It developed an online travel information and agency service inevitably more comprehensive than the books, threatening cannibalisation. Travellers can now access Lonely Planet information by sitting down in an internet café in La Paz, Lilongwe or Luang Prabang. Yet the books still sell well – travellers, it seems, like to peruse the book as much in the bar or in bed as on the laptop or smartphone.

Lonely Planet has been an astonishing success story – a veritable labour of love turned into a world-leading business. In 2007 it was bought for £130 million by BBC Worldwide (which offloaded it in 2013 to NC2 Media of the US at a loss to the UK licence payer of an extraordinary £80 million!), turning those one-time hippie trail travellers into deca-millionaires.

Strategy

There are myriad definitions of strategy, ranging from that of General Sun Tzu ('know your opponent') in the sixth century BC to Kenichi Ohmae's rather more recent interpretation ('in a word, competitive advantage').

I am an economist, so I believe that we should bring the word 'resources' into the definition. Just as economics can be defined as the optimal allocation of a nation's scarce resources, so we can define a company's strategy thus:

> *Strategy is how a company deploys its scarce resources to gain a sustainable advantage over the competition.*

What your backer needs to know is how you plan to allocate your company's resources over the business plan period to meet your goals. These resources are essentially your assets – your people, physical assets (for example, buildings, equipment and inventory) and cash (and borrowing capacity). How will you allocate – or invest – these resources to optimal effect?

More precisely, your backer needs to be convinced that your strategy will enhance your firm's competitive position in key business segments.

You have already set out your firm's competitive position in the section above. You even had a go at examining how that may change over time.

In this section you must show how you can *proactively* improve that position through deployment of a winning business strategy. That is how you will provide commercial underpinning to your forecasts in Chapter 7 of your plan. That is how you will convince your backer to back you.

What is your company's strategy? How will you deploy your scarce resources to gain a sustainable competitive advantage?

First, let's look at the generic strategies.

Generic strategies

There are again many definitions of generic strategies, with each business guru seeming to come up with their own. But, in essence, and in the vast majority of cases, a company needs to choose between two very different and easy-to-grasp generic strategies: low-cost or differentiation.

Either strategy can yield a sustainable competitive advantage. Either the company supplies a product (or service) that is at lower cost to its competitors or it supplies a product that is sufficiently differentiated from its competitors that customers are prepared to pay a premium price – where the incremental price charged adequately covers the incremental costs of supplying the differentiated product.

For a ready example of a successful low-cost strategy, think of easyJet or Ryanair, where relentless maximisation of load factor enables them to offer seats at scarcely credible prices, compared with those prevailing before they gate-crashed the market, and still produce a profit. Or think of IKEA's stylish but highly price-competitive furniture.

A classic example of the differentiation strategy would be Apple. Never the cheapest, whether in PCs, laptops or mobile phones, but always stylistically distinctive and feature-intensive. Or Pret A Manger in fresh, high-quality fast food. Or Lady Gaga with her outrageous flamboyance – a contemporary variant on Josephine Baker and her brazen banana costume.

One variant on these two generic strategies worth highlighting is the focus strategy, developed prominently by Michael Porter. While acknowledging that a firm can typically prosper in its industry by following either a low-cost or differentiation strategy, an alternative is not to address the whole industry but narrow the scope and focus on a slice of it, a single segment. Under these circumstances, a firm can achieve market leadership through focus and exceptional differentiation and thereby generate scale-driven low unit costs.

A classic example of a successful focus strategy would be Honda motorcycles, whose focus on product reliability over decades has yielded the global scale to enable its quality products to remain cost competitive.

Strengthening competitive position

Having clarified which generic strategy underpins your business, how are you planning to improve your competitive position over the plan period? How will you reinforce your competitive advantage?

The answer should lie in the analysis you have already done above when assessing your competitive position versus that of your competitors.

Against which key success factors did you rate less favourably than a key competitor? Is this an important, highly weighted KSF? Will it remain so in the future? Could it become even more important over time? Should this relative weakness be addressed?

Or should you instead be building on your strengths, widening an already existing gap between you and competitors in a particular KSF?

It is inadvisable to generalise, but in theory investment in building on strengths should offer a more favourable risk/reward profile than investing to address weaknesses.

If your generic strategy is one of low cost, what investments or programmes are you planning to reduce costs even further and so stay ahead of the competition? What major investments in plant, equipment, premises, staff, systems, training and/or partnering are you planning? What performance improvement programmes are underway or planned?

If your generic strategy is one of differentiation, what investments or programmes are you planning to reinforce that differentiation and make you stand out even more clearly than your competitors? What major investments in plant, equipment, premises, staff, systems, training, marketing and/or partnering are you planning? What strategic marketing programmes are underway or planned?

If your generic strategy is one of focus, what investments or programmes are you planning to reduce costs and/or reinforce your differentiation? What major investments, performance improvement or strategic marketing programmes are underway or planned?

How will these investments or programmes impact on your competitive position in key business segments? Your backer needs to know.

Essential tip

Whatever your firm's competitive position in a key business segment today, it probably won't be the same in three years' time. Markets evolve, competitors adapt. Your firm needs to take control over its future. Convince your backer that your firm is proactively improving its competitiveness.

Boosting strategic position

So far our analysis has been premised on the strengthening of your competitive position in your key product/market segments over the next few years.

But suppose you don't have the resources, whether in cash, time or manpower, to do all you would like to do. How should you prioritise between the segments? Which investments or programmes should you do first? Which should be dropped, possibly forever? Which segments should you get out of?

You may benefit from undertaking a portfolio analysis. This will identify how competitive you are in markets ranked by order of attractiveness. You should invest ideally in segments where you are strongest and/or which are the most attractive. And you should consider withdrawal from segments where you are weaker and/or where your competitive position is not that good.

And finally, should you be looking at entering another business segment (or segments) that is in *more* attractive markets than the ones you currently address? If so, do you have grounds for believing that you would be at least reasonably placed in this new segment, or that you could readily become reasonably placed?

This analysis will identify your *strategic position*. This is not to be confused with your competitive position, which relates to how competitive your company is in a particular product/market segment. Your strategic position relates to your balance of competitiveness across all segments, of varying degrees of attractiveness.

First, let's be clear on what we mean by an 'attractive' market. The degree of market attractiveness should be measured as a blend of four factors:

- Market size
- Market demand growth
- Competitive intensity
- Market risk.

The larger the market and the faster it is growing, the more attractive the market is, other things being equal. But be careful with the other two factors, where the converse applies. The greater the competitive intensity in a market and the greater its risk, the *less* attractive it is.

You will have to use your own judgement on the weighting you apply to each of these factors. Simplest would be to give each of the four an equal weighting, so a rating for overall attractiveness would be the simple average of the ratings for each factor.

You may, however, be risk averse and give a higher importance to the market risk factor. In this case, you would need to derive a weighted average of each of the four ratings.

An example may help. Suppose your company is in four product/market segments and you are contemplating getting into a fifth. You draw up a strategic position chart, where each segment is represented by a circle (see Figure 5.1).

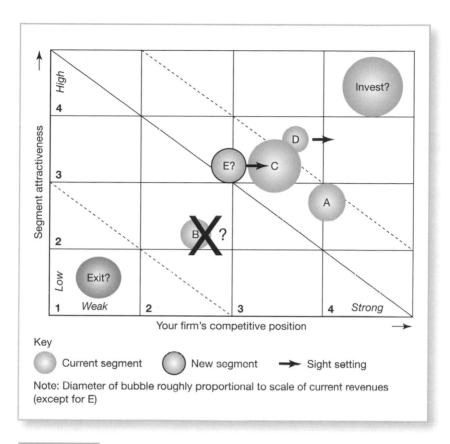

figure 5.1   **Strategic position: an example**

The segment's position in the chart will reflect both its competitive position (along the x-axis) and its market attractiveness (along the y-axis). The size of each bubble should be roughly proportional to the scale of revenues currently derived from the segment.

The closer your segment is positioned towards the top right-hand corner, the better placed it is. Above the top right dotted diagonal, you should be thinking of investing further in that segment. Should the segment approach the bottom left dotted diagonal, however, you should consider exiting.

The strategic position shown in Figure 5.1 is sound. It shows favourable strength in the biggest and reasonably attractive segment C, and an excellent position in the somewhat less attractive segment A. Segment

D is highly promising and demands more attention, given the currently low level of revenues.

Segment B should perhaps be exited – it's a rather unattractive segment, and you're not that well placed. The new segment E seems reasonably promising.

In developing a strategy for this example, you may consider the following worth pursuing:

- Continued development in segments A and C
- Investment in segment D (with the arrow showing the resultant improvement in competitive position)
- Entry to segment E (with competitive position improving over time as market share develops)
- Exit from segment B (crossed out in the figure).

How is your strategic position? Hopefully your *main* segments, from which you derive most revenues, should find themselves positioned above the main diagonal.

Which segments are so important that you would derive greatest benefit from improving your competitive position? Where should you concentrate your efforts?

Do you have any new segments in mind? How attractive are they? How well placed would you be?

Are there any segments you should be thinking of getting out of?

One final word on strategic position. The above example showed the strategic position of a small company involved in five product/market segments.

Exactly the same analysis can and should be undertaken for a larger company involved in, say, five businesses – or strategic business units (SBUs, in management-speak). The bubbles of Figure 5.1 would now represent businesses, as opposed to segments.

Each business can be plotted against both competitive position (itself a weighted average of that business's competitive position in each of its addressed segments) and market attractiveness (again a weighted average).

And the same conclusions could be drawn: invest in one business, hold another for cash, exit a third, and so on.

If you have plans for improving your strategic position, they should be in your business plan. Your backer needs to know.

Essential example

Reggae Reggae's strategy

Reggae Reggae Sauce is a classic example of the success of test marketing. For many years, Jamaica-born reggae musician Levi Roots and his family set up a stall (named 'Rasta'rant'!) at the Notting Hill Carnival and sold jerk chicken to passing revellers. He received so many compliments about the sauce, made to his grandmother's 'secret recipe', that he decided to bottle some in his kitchen and sell it separately. For this he received backing of £1,000 from Greater London Enterprise. At the 2006 carnival, these bottles flew off the stall as fast as the jerk chicken itself.

Encouraged, Roots took his bottles around various trade shows, marketing it innovatively by playing the guitar to a reggae beat and singing a song about the sauce. At one such show he was spotted by a BBC producer and a few months later he reprised the song in front of 3 million viewers on the BBC's *Dragons' Den*. He walked away with an investment of £50,000 for 40% of his company in February 2007, a success attributable partly to his charisma (and song), but mainly, one suspects, to the proven success of the product. It had been test marketed again and again, on the streets, and found to be a winner.

The rest of the story is a phenomenon. The Dragons helped it get onto the shelves at Sainsbury's, where it was expected to shift 50,000 units a year and ended up selling almost that amount a week. Soon the sauce range was extended, most recently with a Red Hot version, followed by the *Reggae Reggae Cookbook,* processed foods flavoured with the sauce, Levi Roots branded sandwiches, a Reggae Reggae pizza at Domino's, a Reggae Reggae box meal at KFC, a Levi Roots Caribbean Crush drink, and so on.

Roots's company is now valued at tens of millions of pounds, giving the Dragons one of their best ever returns and making Roots a very wealthy man. No wonder he has written a book titled *You Can Get It If You Really Want*!

Strategy in a start-up

The process set out in this chapter is not that different for a start-up, whether serving an existing market or creating a new one. You need to assess your likely opening competitive position in the main segments where you intend to compete and develop a strategy to enhance that competitiveness over time.

There are three key differences:

■ Your competitive position is in the future rather than the present tense.

■ It will be affected adversely from the outset by a low rating against all key success factors pertaining to experience.

■ Your backer will want to know whether it is defensible once achieved.

Your competitive position in a new venture is a judgement on the future. For an established business, the debate revolves as much around the present and recent past as it does around the future – around the weighting of KSFs and/or your ratings against specific KSFs, as justified by evidence from customer, supplier and other interviews, each of which will be based as much on fact and performance track record as on judgement.

But for a start-up, the debate will in large part be conjecture, especially if your venture is in a new market. So your arguments must be stronger. And you must find evidence from any possible source.

Best of all for a business-to-business start-up is a letter of intent from a prospective customer – even better, a handful of them. Failing that, and this is the same for a business-to-consumer start-up, your evidence must lie in your rigorous analysis of market demand, competition and your competitive distinctiveness.

Your argument must set out what customer need or want you are filling – and why your offering will serve that need better than current providers, whether direct or indirect competitors.

Your storyline must be simple, focused and clear. It should be deliverable as an elevator speech.

You have no business as yet. You are invisible. Your storyline is a promise to the customer – of delivery sometime in the near future.

And your challenge is to get your backer to buy into that storyline.

The second difference in a start-up, your initial rating against those KSFs that demand experience, you can do little about. Your rating against market share will be near zero at the outset and that against some cost-related factors, especially those pertaining to scale, will also be low.

Likewise your rating against some differentiation factors. Your lack of track record may count against you in areas such as consistency of product quality, delivery, customer service and sales and marketing.

In that case, how will your firm compete? It's not easy being a new entrant to an existing market. You are inevitably facing a low competitive position relative to the leaders at the outset. However, if you are addressing a growing market and/or you can differentiate your product or service sufficiently, things should improve.

Your competitive position in three to five years' time should have improved measurably – your market share rating should be up, your unit costs down and your service performance improved.

But this analysis further highlights what we discussed (in Chapters 2 and 3) about segmentation. If your new venture does not serve an existing market but creates its own new niche, then all changes. The analysis of competition will be undertaken not for the market as a whole but for your addressed product/market segment. And if that is a new segment, created by your new venture, you effectively have no *direct* competition.

But there are two caveats:

∎ You will have indirect competition (as discussed in Chapter 4).
∎ You may in due course face competition from new entrants, who will be after your niche.

This brings us to the third of the main differences between strategy for a start-up and that for an established business: its defensibility.

Remember the definition we used for strategy: 'Strategy is how a company deploys its scarce resources to gain a sustainable advantage over the competition.' The all-important word for a start-up in a new market is 'sustainable'.

If your new venture succeeds, you will be targeted. Competitors will eye your newly carved space with envy. They will come after you. And soon.

How will you protect yourself against that competitive response? Your backers need to know this. If they are venture capitalists, they will be looking for an exit after five years or so. Could this be when your competitors have started taking chunks out of your market share? If so, your backers won't be able to sell out, or only at a discounted price. If there's a chance of that scenario from the outset, they won't back you.

There are a number of ways you can try to sustain your competitive advantage:

- Patent protection of key products
- Sustained innovation, staying one step ahead in product development
- Sustained process improvement, staying ahead in cost competitiveness and efficiency
- Investment in branding, identifying in the mind of the customer the particular benefit brought by your offering with its name
- Investment, for business-to-business ventures, in customer relationships.

However you aim to do so, this must form a key component of your business plan. Set out here not only how you are going to achieve a competitive advantage in this newly created market, but also how you will sustain it.

For further reading on strategy in a start-up, or indeed for further thoughts on market demand (see Chapter 3) and competition (Chapter 4) in start-ups, along with more case studies on what worked, what didn't and why, try John Mullins's terrific book, *The New Business Road Test* (3rd edition, FT Prentice Hall, 2010). This is essential reading on all the preparatory work and research you should undertake before drawing up a business plan for a start-up, especially in a new market.

Strategic risks and opportunities

In Chapters 3 and 4 of your plan, you pulled out the main risks and opportunities relating to market demand and industry competition in your line of business. Now you can add those that relate to your competitive position and strategy over the next few years.

In the pages above, you have assessed your competitive position (or prospective position if your venture is a start-up) in key segments. You have set out your strategy for strengthening your position in each key segment, as well as your overall strategic position.

That is what you believe to be the most likely scenario. What are the risks that your competitive positioning could turn out to be worse than that? Suppose, for example, a competitor were to steal a major customer from you? How likely is that? And what sort of impact would it have? What could happen to make your positioning even worse than that?

Conversely, what could happen to improve your competitive prospects significantly? Could a major competitor exit from the market, for example? How likely is that, and with what impact?

What are the *big* risks – those that are reasonably likely *and* with reasonable impact (as defined in Chapter 3)? How can they be mitigated? What are the big opportunities? How can you exploit them?

We will return to these big risks and opportunities later (see Chapter 8).

Essential case study
The Dart Valley Guest House and Oriental Spa business plan, 2015

Chapter 5: Strategy

Dick Jones has found that competition in the three- and four-star hotel/spa business in Devon is of medium to high intensity (see Chapter 4), with the main risk being that the spa goes the way of a fad. But what of Dart Valley's competitive standing in this market and how might that be improved if they achieve the funding needed for the proposed Phase II development?

Dick is a former management consultant and appreciates that his findings must be rooted in research and analysis, as set out in Appendix A of this book. He rolls up his sleeves. He scans the Web, talks to people he knows in the Spa Business Association, reviews notes and literature from the UK Spa & Wellness Conference he attended the previous year and examines the *Spa Industry Survey Report for Great Britain & Ireland* sponsored by VisitBritain.

He compares this research with his own experience at Dart Valley over the past three years and concludes that the main purchasing criteria for customers of spa services are these: the effectiveness of the treatment (the customer must feel that the treatment has done them good); the standard of the premises (preferably clean, hygienic, spacious and with a relaxing ambience); and, of course, price.

▶

He finds that as customers also consider the range of facilities provided important, from hot tubs to swimming pools, saunas to Jacuzzis, and as they become more savvy, they will place greater emphasis on the range of treatments provided – as shown in Table 5.1.

He then translates these customer purchasing criteria into key success factors (KSFs) – see Table 5.2. He finds that the winning provider of spa services will have highly skilled and experienced therapists, quality premises, a positive, upbeat culture and tight control of cost.

| table 5.1 | Customer purchasing criteria from spa services |

Spa customer purchasing criteria		Importance	Changes
Effectiveness	▪ Therapist capabilities	*High*	→
	▪ Benefit awareness	*Low/med*	→
	▪ Confidence in process	*Med*	→
Efficiency	▪ Effort	*Low/med*	→
	▪ Timeliness	*Low*	→
Relationship	▪ Rapport	*Med*	↑
	▪ Enthusiasm	*Med/high*	→
Range	▪ Facilities	*Med/high*	→
	▪ Treatments	*Low/med*	↑↑
Premises	▪ Cleanliness, hygiene, space, decor	*High*	↑
Price		*Med/high*	↑

Finally, he allows for the two incremental KSFs of market share and management factors and computes the weighting to each. He is now ready to rate the Dart Valley offering against these KSFs. He is mildly surprised but proud to find that Dart Valley's overall competitive position in spa services in the South Devon area comes out as favourable to strong, or 3.5 on a scale of 0 to 5 – see Table 5.3 for the Dart Valley results and Appendix A on the methodology for how ratings are calculated.

The Palace, a grand institution in Torquay, with 250 rooms and a full suite of spa, swimming and aquatic facilities, emerges top, of course, but not that much further ahead. Dick believes that his team of

table 5.2 Key success factors in spa services

Spa customer purchasing criteria		Importance	Change	Associated key success factors
Effectiveness	▪ Therapist capabilities	High	↑	▪ Therapist skills
	▪ Benefit awareness	Low/med	↑	▪ Qualification
	▪ Confidence in process	Med	↑	▪ Track record
Efficiency	▪ Effort	Low/med	↑	▪ Availability
	▪ Timeliness	Low	↑	▪ Work ethic
				▪ Delivery
Relationship	▪ Rapport	Med	←	▪ People skills (communication)
	▪ Enthusiasm	Med/high	↑	▪ Positive, upbeat culture
Range	▪ Facilities	Med/high	↑	▪ Range of facilities
	▪ Treatments	Low/med	↑↑	▪ Range of treatments
Premises	▪ Cleanliness, hygiene, space, decor	High	←	▪ Spa quality premises
Price		Med/high	←	▪ Cost competitiveness

table 5.3	Dart Valley competitive position in spa services

Key success factors	Weighting	Dart Valley	The Palace	Fit4U	Smugglers' Cove	Dart Valley Phase II
Relative market share	15%	2	4	3	2	3
Cost factors:	25%	3	4	4	1	3.5
Overhead control, scale economies						
Management factors:	10%	2	5	4	4	4
Marketing						
Differentiation factors:	10%	5	4	4	5	5
Effectiveness – standard of therapists						
Efficiency – work ethic, delivery	5%	5	3	4	5	5
Relationship – communication, attitude	10%	5	4	4	5	5
Range – facilities, treatment	10%	2	5	4	1	4
Premises – hygiene, decor, space	15%	5	3	4	5	5
Competitive position	100%	3.5	4.0	3.9	3.1	4.1

Key to rating: 1 = weak, 2 = tenable, 3 = favourable, 4 = strong, 5 = very strong

Note on selected competitors: Dart Valley Guest House & Spa, Torbay; The Palace Hotel & Spa, Torquay; Fit4U Fitness Club & Spa, Torquay; Smugglers' Cove Hotel & Spa, South Hams

therapists is more skilled and more enthusiastic than the team at The Palace, thanks to the personal care taken over their recruitment and motivation by Dick's wife, Kay. He also believes that the sense of personal space and relaxation, not to mention the extraordinary views, at Dart Valley is in contrast to the slightly cramped and rather overpopulated feel at The Palace's spa.

Not far behind The Palace is the Torquay branch of the national Fit4U chain, a slick operation focusing primarily on its fitness suites and courses, but with an impressive set of spa facilities added on. Good as they are, Dick doesn't believe they match the standards of excellence and ambience at Dart Valley.

There are a number of other competitors in the Torquay area, but they tend to fall a little behind The Palace and Fit4U, certainly in terms of range of facilities. One other spa offering stands out, how-ever, and that is Smugglers' Cove, a top-of-the-range boutique hotel perched above its own cove in South Hams. It claims to offer 'spa' facilities, but in reality there's a treatment room and a sauna and that's it. But guests are truly pampered there, and one or two of Dart Valley's excellent therapists also work there, so it ranks as a credible competitor, albeit in its luxury market niche.

Dick knows that little of this analysis, and certainly none of these figures, will find their way into his business plan (we will see later on what will go in). But what the exercise has given him is analysis in depth and thinking in depth, findings rooted in research. And balance.

Dick has shown to himself that Dart Valley is a credible player in the spa services business, with its strong points not overexaggerated and its weak points not glossed over. This must shine through in the plan.

Even more importantly, this analysis has provided a construct for framing the project at the heart of his business plan, the proposed Phase II development of 16 more rooms plus a swimming pool. The final column of Table 5.3 shows clearly that the project could render Dart Valley the leading spa operator in South Devon, thanks to:

■ increased market share, hence spread of message

■ greater contribution to overheads, hence lower unit costs

■ broader range of facilities, not far below that offered by The Palace.

▶

Dick now reproduces the analysis above for Dart Valley's other two main business segments – accommodation and catering. For the purposes of this book, we need not go into similar detail, but suffice it to say that Dick's conclusions are similarly encouraging.

Dick can now put into words, wrapped up into just three to four pages of A4, what his analysis of competitive position has concluded, namely as follows:

- Dart Valley has come from nowhere to be a credible competitor in its niche.

- It has done so, on the one hand, by:
  - offering the overnight visitor an experience somewhat out of the ordinary – clean, crisp, comfortable accommodation spiced with a hint of the Orient, with stunning views over the Dart Valley
  - offering the diner the choice of traditional European fare or home-cooked, delicately spiced oriental cuisine, with the same lovely views
  - creating a spacious, relaxing environment, a high quality of therapy and a culture of service and enthusiasm in its spa services – factors that counterbalance the limited range of facilities offered compared to leading local competitors.

- And, on the other, by:
  - keeping a tight control over overheads.

- That Dart Valley has become a serious competitor in this industry is evidenced by its occupancy rates, having achieved room occupancy by year three of operations of 71%, well above the average for guest houses, countryside establishments or Torbay as a whole (see Chapter 4).

- Completion of the two-phase strategy could make Dart Valley the leading provider of spa services in the Torbay and South Hams area, not in terms of scale or market share, but in terms of competitive position, hence profitability.

- Strategic risks are low – Dart Valley will offer in Phase II more of the same successful formula of Phase I and it seems unlikely that this concept, so successful so far, will become dated or of lesser appeal over the next five years.

Dick will proceed to assess the resource implications of this strategy in the next chapter of his plan. Before that, however, he cannot resist comparing what he has written in Chapter 5 with what he would have written four years earlier, when starting up the venture. For Phase I, he had used a mortgage plus the proceeds from the sale of the family home in South-West London as finance – and he had never got round to writing a business plan for himself as the backer (though it might have been a useful exercise).

He finds that much of what he has written in 2015 would have been the same as in 2010. He had researched the spa services market in depth at the time, so his findings on customer purchasing criteria and key success factors would not have changed much in the interim – only perhaps in the weighting attached to, for example, the range of treatments offered.

The main difference would have been in the use of tense. In 2010 his plan for the new venture would have been in the future tense throughout. The first three bullet points above would have been virtually identical four years earlier, except that they would reflect aspirations for the future, not the factual present.

Thus the first two bullets would have read:

- Dart Valley *should be* a credible competitor in its niche *by 2015.*
- It *will do* so, on the one hand by:
  - offering the overnight visitor an experience somewhat out of the ordinary – clean, crisp, accommodation spiced with a hint of the Orient, with stunning views over the Dart Valley – and so on.

Things have worked out pretty much as planned, which gives Dick a feeling of great satisfaction and indeed optimism that Phase II will be worthy of securing a backer.

Essential checklist on strategy

Your chapter on strategy will stand out from 9 out of 10 other business plans due to its underpinning in research and analysis. Your backer will appreciate this thoroughness.

Very little of the research you undertook when following the guidelines in Appendix A of this book will find its way directly into this chapter. But it will be there indirectly. This chapter will be just three to four pages long, but it will radiate latent power. The impression will be conveyed to your backer that each statement is rooted in either fact or rigorously supported judgement.

Derive your firm's competitive position coherently:

- Demonstrate your understanding of customer purchasing criteria in key business segments – make cursory but pertinent reference to research you have done on this, with further detail as appropriate in an appendix to your plan.
- Demonstrate likewise your understanding of key success factors.
- Set out objectively your assessment of your firm's competitive position – lay out the sources of competitive advantage in each key segment.

Explain how your firm's strategy will improve performance over the next few years:

- Which of the generic strategies you will deploy.
- What steps will be taken to strengthen competitive position in key segments, by building on strengths and/or working on weaknesses.
- How your firm will boost its strategic position by optimising its portfolio of business segments.

If your business is a new venture in an existing market, set out why you have a sufficiently distinctive angle to survive in the early stages. If you are creating a new product or service, demonstrate how you will find ready buyers, in the right quantities and at the right price.

Finally, alert your backer to the key strategic risks your firm may face and how you intend to mitigate them. And, conversely, highlight the strategic opportunities that may be there for the taking, which will represent the upside to your plan's forecasts.

6

Resources

❝❝ It's not the size of the dog in the fight, it's the size of the
fight in the dog.

Mark Twain

In this chapter

- Management
  - In an established business
  - In a start-up
- Marketing
  - In an established business
  - In a start-up
- Operations and capital expenditure
  - Supplies
  - Purchasing
  - Manufacture or service provision
  - Research and development
  - Distribution, storage and logistics
  - Sales
  - Customer service and technical support
  - Systems and IT
  - Quality and financial control
  - Regulatory compliance
- Resource risks and opportunities

I n the last chapter you set out your firm's strategy over the next few years. You explained how you plan to strengthen its competitive position in strategically selected product/market segments – whether by building on your strengths against key success factors (KSFs) or by working on weaknesses.

In short, you explained *what* your firm planned to do to achieve the goals set out in Chapter 2 of your plan. In this chapter you will set out *how*.

You will show how you will deploy the firm's scarce resources to implement that strategy.

One caveat: if yours is a medium-sized business or bigger, you may be tempted to delegate each of the sections in this chapter to the respective heads of department – to the marketing director, the operations director, the chief information officer, or whomever. Fine, but make sure you edit the output in the style of the rest of the document. This business plan must flow with one style only. And remember that each departmental head would be capable of writing a 25-page report on their pet function alone. Restrict them to three to four pages, summarise their main findings in half a page or so and put their reports into an appropriate appendix.

All your firm's resources must be competently deployed for your business plan to be successful. But some resources are more critical than others.

In my experience, having reviewed hundreds of business plans on behalf of investors or lenders, the backer's pecking order of priority goes like this:

1 Management
2 Marketing
3 Operations.

Many investors say they back people, not products or services. That's not the whole story (see below) – but it's a hefty chunk of it.

And investors know that it's no good having the best widget on the market if customers are unaware how good it is. So they are always keen to learn in detail about a firm's marketing plans.

They also realise that management and marketing must permeate every link in the value chain in a successful organisation (see Figure 6.1). Managerial capability must be as evident in the inbound logistics as in the service ends of the business. A pervasive culture of marketing should ensure that product development, indeed the full R&D programme, is driven by the needs of the customer.

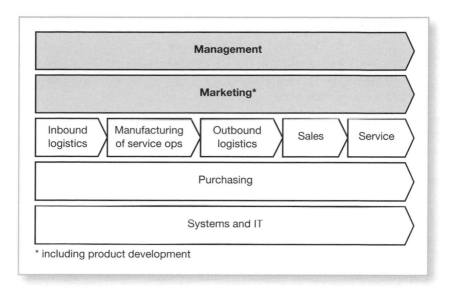

figure 6.1   **The value chain as seen by your backer**

Then there's the rest of the value chain. Each link is important; no link can be broken. But each link can be strengthened relatively painlessly if there is a weakness. Getting the supply chain right, streamlining the manufacturing process, outsourcing the logistics function, installing new enterprise resource or customer relations management software, and so on, can arguably be fixed – whether within the firm's existing resources, through targeted recruitment or with the appropriate guid ance from external consultants.

This is not necessarily the case with management. If a manager is not up to the job, and this is seldom a black and white issue, it can take time for this to be fully appreciated, whereupon finding the right replacement manager available at the right time can be a bit hit and miss.

Nor is this the case with marketing. It can be difficult to change the culture of an organisation which believes that this is the way we have always done it here, or this is the kind of product we have always made here, and hang the customer. Your backer needs to know that your firm is market-led, not production-led.

So you'll start Chapter 6 of your business plan with how your management resources are up to the task of delivering your plan. You will move on to your marketing resources and then address the rest of the value chain.

Management

In this section, you'll set out why you have the right management team to ensure delivery of the plan. But be aware that your backer will be looking for a different balance of capabilities in an established business compared to a start-up.

In an established business

There are two schools of thought on management in an established business. There are some private equity players who say that, as in a start-up, management is the most important of all considerations in deciding whether or not to invest. To back up that belief, they will offer management teams extremely generous, ratcheted equity packages conditional upon delivery of the plan.

At the other extreme are private equity players who regard management effectively as units of production. They should do their job, be rewarded very well if they deliver and be replaced, ruthlessly, if they don't. These players will undertake detailed due diligence on the market, finances, legals, and so on, but little on the management. No need – management is replaceable.

Most private equity players lie somewhere in between. They conduct detailed management due diligence before investing. They would rather not have the hassle of replacing a manager during the plan period – better to weed the team before investing and stick with those they back.

Wherever they lie on the management dispensability spectrum, all private equity players will agree on this. They are looking for managers who can implement the strategy, who can deliver against the plan.

They want managers who can not only identify where the firm needs to strengthen its performance against one or another KSF, but also execute that performance improvement.

This has implications for what should go into your business plan, for each key manager:

- A one-page curriculum vitae, specifying roles held, with which firm and for how long, and highlighting major achievements against specific objectives within those roles – as an appendix to your plan
- A one-paragraph summary, with a sentence or two on relevant experience, including length of service at the firm, and selecting one example of how the manager delivered in a relevant role or against a relevant project – for this section of Chapter 6.

By the time your backers have read through six paragraphs for six key managers, they should be left with an overriding impression of *action*. These guys are doers, your backers will think, they look like they can deliver this plan.

So, who should be these six key managers? It depends on the size and nature of the business, but it should certainly include your firm's heads of strategy (this will probably be the managing director in a small firm), sales and marketing (this may be one person in a small firm), finance and operations. In a larger firm it may well include your heads of technology, human resources and IT, as well as the heads of the most important business units.

Your backer will also want to know about organisation and governance in your firm. Here may be the place to include an organisation chart, kept simple and showing in particular who reports to whom in the top management team.

One paragraph on governance should suffice, unless yours is out of the ordinary. Who is who on the board of directors may be useful, especially if one or two play an important guiding role in the firm's strategic direction, functional performance or networking.

In a start-up

There is no debate that management is a more important factor in a start-up than in an established business. It is crucial. You will not find any venture capitalist dismissing management as dispensable, as you may find in some buyout houses.

The earlier the stage in the investment cycle, the more crucial typically is management. The right managers are more important to the backer in seed capital (for the very early stages of a business, often proof of concept) than venture capital (for the early, high-risk, high growth years of a business), and more in venture capital than development capital (for growth businesses with an established track record).

Many venture capitalists say that they back the person, rather than the product or service, in a start-up. With the right spirit, passion and dedication to the cause, an entrepreneur is well on the way to obtaining backing.

But this is a great oversimplification. As has been pointed out in earlier chapters, first and foremost is the business proposition. The offering must have a sustainable competitive advantage. There must be customers prepared to pay the right price for it. If those boxes are ticked, and the entrepreneur is the right person, then the venture capitalist will get excited.

Note the use of the word 'entrepreneur', not 'manager'. That is because backers are looking for someone quite different in a start-up. They are not looking for a solid, steady, nine-to-fiver, with a proven track record of delivering to plan. They are looking for a visionary, a leader, a person who believes wholly in the product or service, who will inspire and motivate through passion, energy and darned hard work.

Think Branson, Dyson, Roddick. Or, on the other side of the channel, Jobs. Think Levi Roots, whom you read about earlier (Chapter 5). But these are exceptional people – surely your backers can't expect you to be like that?

Yes, they can, and they will. I have worked over the years with managers working in the least glamorous businesses you can imagine – from the makers of sewage pumps to the makers of stairlifts for the elderly and infirm – and have found leaders who genuinely convey passion to their employees, customers and other stakeholders. If they can do it, so can you. So must you.

If you are starting up a new business, you must feel and convey that passion. You may even possess the Celtic *hwyl* – the passion, spirit, fervour that can lift you to extremes of success (for further reading, try this author's *Backing U! A Business-Oriented Guide to Backing Your Passion and Achieving Career Success,* Business & Careers Press, 2009).

But passion won't be everything. As we saw for an established business, you must also be able to deliver. And in this section of your business plan, you must explain succinctly how you have delivered in the past – how you met the objectives set, whether by you or your boss.

As for the passion, don't leave that just for the pitch. You may not get that far. The passion should shine through on every page of the plan. And when you do get to that presentation, let it rip.

Essential tip

Let your backer be infused with your passion.

Marketing

Again, what underpins your section on marketing has different nuances depending on whether yours is an established or start-up business.

In an established business

Your backer needs to know that yours is a market-driven firm. You make products or supply services to customers that fill an identified and researched customer need, and that convey definable benefits to customers.

And your backer needs to know that you will deploy a coherent array of marketing tools to ensure that customers are sufficiently aware of these benefits that they will purchase your products or services in sufficient quantities and at the right prices for you to make your plan.

Don't make the mistake of confusing marketing with advertising. The latter is just one component of a component (promotion) of the former.

Marketing is much bigger than that. It is a mindset. It is about the orientation of a firm towards serving the customer.

In a classic text, *Basic Marketing: A Managerial Approach* (Irwin, 1960), which has been much elaborated since, but not markedly improved, E. Jerome McCarthy set out four components of the marketing mix, the four Ps: product, place, pricing and promotion. This categorisation should more than suffice for this section of your business plan. It should contain a paragraph or three on each, as follows:

- Product – if your firm follows a differentiation as opposed to a low-cost generic strategy (see Chapter 5), show how it is the satisfaction of identified customer needs that has shaped your products (or services). Show too how product development, and also research, is oriented to meeting future customer needs – and does not exist in an ivory tower, presided over by boffins with little knowledge of or interest in the needs of the marketplace.

- Place – show which distribution channels are of greatest importance to your firm, now and over the next few years. Do you focus on direct sales or indirect, via agents, wholesalers or distributors? Why? What channels does the competition use? How have your online sales developed in recent years? To what extent have they cannibalised offline sales or brought in additional business? What are the prospects for the future?

- Price – how is your firm's price positioning relative to the competition? Broadly in line with the average, at a discount, at a premium? Why? How is this pricing aligned with strategy? How elastic are volumes sold in your business to price? What are the prospects for raising prices in line with inflation over the plan period? What are your assumptions?

■ Promotion – what have been the main ways you have been pro-moting your products in recent years? Advertising (through which media – print, screen, radio, internet?), trade promotions, public relations, sponsorship, exhibitions, trade shows, seminars/confer-ences? Why? How will this promotional mix change over the plan period?

Finally, you should include here a word or two on the results of all this marketing. How aware is your addressed market of your presence? How aware is it of the benefits of your offering?

Furthermore, how satisfied are your customers with your product or service and with your performance? If you have undertaken any sat-isfaction surveys, here is the place to include the headline results. You may even include a one-page synopsis as an appendix – along with other marketing data you think might be useful evidence for your backer (for example, a breakdown of your marketing budget over the last three years).

To what extent is this customer satisfaction expressed in repeat busi-ness? This is the lifeblood of every business. The cost of winning a new customer exceeds greatly the cost of winning repeat business. If you have some good statistics on repeat business, set them out here. And emphasise how much better your ratio is than that of your competi-tors (assuming that is the case!).

Essential example

Gocompare's resources

How did a girl who left Croesyceiliog Comprehensive in Cwmbran at the age of 16 with a handful of GCSEs become worth £44 million 25 years later when esure.com bought her company? Use of resources, namely marketing, is one answer.

After school, Hayley Parsons worked her way up at Admiral Insur-ance and, when passed over for the top job when Admiral formed Confused.com, an insurance price comparison website, she quit and started her own rival firm, Gocompare.com. Her point of differentia-tion was to compare not just prices but also product features, although it was not until she embarked on an in-your-face marketing campaign that the firm raced into market leadership.

While Comparethemarket.com was rising up the ranks into fourth place with a campaign featuring a loveable meerkat named Aleksandr Orlov, and Omid Djalili's wit was keeping Moneysupermarket.com highly profitable in third place, Parsons shot above her old, market-leading firm Confused.com with the help of an irritatingly uplifting character – a tubby Welsh/Italian opera singer with a ludicrous moustache called Gio Compario, who pops up in wacky situations and locations to sing the benefits of Gocompare. 'We wanted to get our brand into people's heads – we needed a catchy song,' said Parsons to the *News of the World.* 'To be memorable, it had to be annoying. People love it or they hate it – it really is the Marmite of adverts.' The public swallowed it.

In a start-up

The questions are all the same in a start-up. But the answers differ in two respects. They are in the future tense. And they aren't just important, they're critical.

Marketing is the lifeblood of a start-up. Before you started up, your firm didn't exist. Now you exist, most customers won't know that.

If customers don't soon get to know you exist, you'll have no custom. You'll be one of the thousands of companies that start up and disappear each year without trace.

In Chapter 3 of your plan you identified promising market demand prospects. In Chapter 4, you concluded that the competitive environment was favourable. In Chapter 5, you set out why your offering enjoyed a distinctive competitive edge.

Here, in this section of Chapter 6, you'll set out how customers are going to be put in touch with your offering. It is crucial. It will require you to set out a detailed marketing plan in an appendix and summarise it here, convincingly.

You'll show how each component of the plan will reinforce the other, how the customer will be bombarded with the same message, from different angles, different people, different media, until they are eager to try out your offering.

You'll write this section of the plan with passion, even with some marketing hype thrown in. But your marketing plan must be sensible, rational and doable too. It must convince.

Essential tip

If no one knows you're there, you sure won't get your share.

Operations and capital expenditure

This is the section for your chief operating officer, if you have one. Or for you again, if you don't. Here you need to cover the main issues affecting your firm through the value chain, from the sourcing of supplies through to customer service. Remember that your backers don't need to know the detail. They want the helicopter view in general and the ground-level view only when an issue arises which could have a material impact on your business plan.

In this section, you'll consider the resource implications of your firm's strategy over the next few years on the following aspects of operations:

- Supplies
- Purchasing
- Manufacture or service provision
- Research and development
- Distribution, storage and logistics
- Sales
- Customer service and technical support
- Systems and IT
- Quality and financial control
- Regulatory compliance.

Under each link in the value chain, you'll consider what resources – physical and financial – are required to meet the plan.

And, of particular relevance for the next chapter on financial forecasts, you'll set out, under each link, the key items of capital expenditure needed to support the plan and beyond. State the following – in no more detail than is needed, but convincingly – for the major items of capital expenditure:

- The nature of the capital project
- Why it is needed
- The alternatives considered and rejected

- How much it will cost
- How long it will take to be implemented
- What impact it will have on future revenues or costs
- The risks associated with the investment.

Again, your backer doesn't need to know about every item of capital expenditure, just the main ones – the value impacting ones.

Supplies

Supply of raw materials can be a critical issue. If your company is a metal converter, making, say, aluminium car parts or wear-resistant cobalt cutting tools, your backer needs to know that the metal inputs to the production process are going to be available as and when you need them. And when the metal price goes up, as indeed it will, as for any commodity raw material, to what extent will you be able to preserve your margins through the pricing mechanism?

Metal converters are an extreme case. Few manufacturing companies, and no service companies, are as sensitive to raw material supply and pricing as a metal converter. But think of producers of plastics, glass and folding cartons – all are highly sensitive to availability and price of their key raw materials, respectively polypropylene (itself hugely sensitive to the price of crude oil), silica and cartonboard (itself highly sensitive to supplies of recycled and virgin pulp).

Think of an automotive manufacturer – sensitive to the price of galvanised, low carbon steel for chassis, but with a whole range of other suppliers, of seats, plastic fuel tanks and tyres, for example, serving to spread the risk and limit exposure to the availability or price of steel.

The higher the proportion of cost from a single raw material in your business, the more your backer will need to know the detail. If you run a metal converting business, you should devote a page or two in an appendix to the pricing cycle of that metal over the last few years, highlighting the drivers behind each major upswing or downswing.

How dependent is your firm on the provision of supplies not just of one commodity but from one supplier? If that supplier fails to deliver, or exploits its bargaining power to raise prices dramatically, what options do you have for shifting to another supplier? And with what switching costs?

If yours is a service business, don't think this section doesn't apply to you. It is likely that your main supplies will be people. But how easy is it to find people of the right background, qualifications and experience to replace employees who move on?

And even service businesses can be reliant on goods. A dental practice needs regular supplies of equipment, products and materials, not just hygienists. How reliant has an insurance broker become on its main software supplier? Can your building firm find sufficiently well-qualified, competent and enthusiastic plumbers?

Most businesses will have a range of supplies, a reasonable choice of suppliers and relative predictability in the cost of the supplies. But not all. Your backer needs to know where your business lies.

Purchasing

Supplies and purchasing used to come under the same heading in the old days. A manufacturer would purchase the supplies, convert them into some product, ship them out, sell them and provide service support.

Then along came outsourcing. Now every stage in the value chain can be outsourced. Manufactured modules can be bought in (or even the whole manufacturing process can be outsourced), transport operators contracted, distributors engaged, agents hired and service companies instructed.

And it's not just in manufacturing. It's the same with service companies. Insurance companies now outsource chunks of claims management. Banks outsource software development and payment processing. Prisons outsource prisoner transfer.

Whatever the sector, whether manufacturing or services, cleaning, maintenance, IT services and catering are often outsourced. Likewise customer service and technical support, often to offshore providers.

Today's firm can often be seen as an aggregator of products and services, overlaid with design, management and marketing value added.

At every stage in the value chain, the firm can be a purchaser. Not just in supplies, but also in operations, logistics, sales and service.

How sharp is your purchasing capability? Do you consider purchasing to be a key success factor? If not, why not? How well trained is your team in negotiation?

Do your competitors buy their raw materials cheaper than you do? Even if their quantities purchased are of similar scale to yours?

What about the bought-in products in your manufacturing? Are they competitively priced? And logistics? Technical support? Customer service? Are you getting consistently good deals in your purchasing, relative to your competitors?

This section could be anything from one paragraph to one page, again depending on whether your firm's purchasing capabilities may be an issue to your backer.

Essential example

Dyson's resources

The furore which surrounded the relocation of Dyson vacuum cleaners from Malmesbury to Malaysia in 2002 was extraordinary – understandable, but misplaced. The story of James Dyson's invention is well known – numerous prototypes and 15 years' persistence before getting the product to market and the taking of it by storm, despite much higher prices. This was followed by an aggressive response by Hoover, leading to a prolonged but ultimately victorious court case on patent infringement.

By 2001, Dyson's sales had multiplied tenfold since 1995. But growth had slowed, UK market share had slipped and competitors were pricing at up to 60% below. It was time for radical action. Dyson looked to its resource base. Malaysian labour rates and real estate unit costs were one-third of those in Britain. Elsewhere in Asia, unit costs were even lower, but Malaysia had infrastructural and workforce benefits. Six hundred jobs in Malmesbury had to go, but 1,200 jobs would remain – more than the total number of jobs at Dyson just four years earlier and including 400 engineers and scientists in research and development.

Dyson's strategy of relocating manufacturing offshore has been an unqualified success. The vacuum cleaners became more cost competitive, sales trebled, Dyson continues to be a beacon of engineering innovation in the UK and the firm now employs 2,000 in Malmesbury, including 1,000 in R&D. Meanwhile, Dyson announced plans in 2014 to invest £250 million in the expansion of the Malmesbury site to create jobs for a further 2,000 engineers.

Manufacture or service provision

This is where you explain succinctly how you make your product or deliver your service.

If you are a manufacturer, where are your facilities? What size are they? For how long have you been there? What scope is there for expansion, and what constraints would need to be overcome (for example, in relation to planning permission)? What are the options if you have to move to another site? How do your facilities compare with those of the competition?

What are your main items of capital equipment? How have they changed in recent years? Where do they sit on the value/quality spectrum – are they the Rolls-Royce, the BMW or the Ford Mondeo equivalent in their field? What additional equipment do you need – as replacement or for growth? How does the equipment you deploy compare with that of your competitors?

What are your main manufacturing processes? How have they developed in recent years? Do you ask the 'make or buy' question at each stage of the manufacturing process? Which components or processes have you outsourced in recent years? What plans do you have for future outsourcing? What do your competitors do?

If yours is a service company, the same questions generally apply – except that you may be delivering your service from an office or a depot rather than a factory, the equipment deployed may be more computer-related than manufacturing-related (although many service firms, for example in dentistry, use highly sophisticated equipment) and your processes centre more around the movement of paperwork (or e-information these days) than goods.

Above all, how do the facilities, equipment and processes you deploy in providing your service compare with those of your competitors? What are you planning to do to stay ahead, keep apace or catch up?

Research and development

You will have already discussed product development in your section on marketing resources, earlier in this chapter. But here is the place to tell your backer a bit more about your research and development operations. How many staff members, and what have they been working on in the last few years? How long have products taken to come on stream? How successful have the launches been? What impact have new products had on your manufacturing processes and equipment?

What products are currently in R&D? Are these new products or revamped versions of an existing product range? Are they being developed to meet gaps in the market? Define the gaps, and set out the timeline for launch and the implications for manufacturing and distribution.

Is your product line regarded in the market as being up to date, long in the tooth, somewhere in the middle? Or varied? What plans do you have to improve that positioning?

How extensive is your current product pipeline compared to the recent past?

How do your firm's R&D capabilities compare with the competition? Who is recognised in the industry as the innovator? Are you more of a follower? Are you happy with that positioning?

In short, are there any issues with R&D that your backer needs to know about?

Distribution, storage and logistics

Set out here how your goods get out of the factory and into the hands of the customer. What are the various routes to market? Do they go via a wholesaler or distributor? To an agent? Directly to the customer? A mix of all three? How has this changed in recent years? How will it change in the future? Why? What logistics do your competitors deploy? Does that work better or worse? What do you plan to do about it?

Again, only go into detail here if there is an issue that your backer needs to know about – for good, in that you want to demonstrate a competitive advantage, or for bad, in that you need to highlight a competitive weakness, albeit one that you are in the process of rectifying. That may well have cost implications – your backer needs to know.

Sales

Marketing is fine, but can only create awareness. You need sales people to seal the deal.

How large is your sales team? How well qualified are they? How has your sales force changed over time?

How well do they perform? If you have the data, and you think it helps your cause, you may want to include measures of sales force effectiveness such as lead response time, rate of contact or opportunity-to-win ratio.

How cost effective is your sales team? How have your ratios of sales to number and cost of salespersons changed over time?

How do those ratios compare with those of the market leader? If below, what are you planning to do about it?

Customer service and technical support

These are areas where, again, you must be candid and up front. If you're not, you will be found out. Remember, your backer will probably insist on speaking to a few customers, and if your customer service or technical support is not up to scratch, your customer will seize the opportunity to tell it like it is.

It is not the end of the world if you don't have the best reputation in customer service, in every place, for every customer, for every product line. It's a trade-off. Customer service is expensive, so too is technical support. Often it is the largest player that has the best service and support, because it can afford to with its economies of scale.

I reviewed the business plan of a company recently that had superb technical support in one region, but very limited support in the region into which it wanted to expand – a key growth component of the business plan. The company recognised this constraint and was assessing options for strengthening its capability via partnering with a service company in that region.

This was an issue for the backer, rightly recognised by the company and argued credibly in this section of its business plan. How is your customer service and technical support? Is it outsourced? Does it work well? And in relation to the competition? To the market leader? How can it be improved? What would be the cost implications?

Systems and IT

What are the key systems and IT you use in your manufacturing or service operations? How long have they been in place? What did you use before? How effective have these new systems been? How do they compare with the systems and IT of the competition?

What are the shortcomings of your systems and IT? How can they be improved? What are the cost implications?

I recently helped review the plan of a global player in payment systems. Its systems were an acknowledged weakness and any prospective buyer was made fully aware that a major investment would be needed in updating the systems very soon after taking over the company. The backer needed to know and was told explicitly up front.

Your situation is unlikely to be so drastic, but are there any systems or IT issues that your backer needs to know about? Here is the place to lay them out.

Quality and financial control

Control is important to your backer. Even if things work out as per the assumptions in your business plan on market demand, industry competition, your strategy and plans for improving competitive advantage, can your backer rest assured that you have sufficient control over quality and finances that the whole thing won't crumble?

What controls do you have in place for ensuring quality of output? And this question applies as much or more to a service business as to a manufacturer. How do your controls compare with those of your competitors? What is best practice?

And if something goes wrong in quality of output – think Perrier or Toyota – what contingency plans do you have to put it right? At what cost?

What financial controls do you have? How do you ensure that invoices are paid on time or very soon after? Can your systems prevent stock-building getting out of control if there is a dip in sales? How can you detect fraud at an early stage?

Again, if you feel that all is indeed under control, or as much as anywhere else in the industry, just refer to that here. There may be no need to go into the issue in great detail.

Regulatory compliance

This is similar to the above issue. Your backer needs to know that your firm is on top of all compliance issues – whether in environmental or health and safety areas, which are of particular relevance to manufacturers.

Taking environmental compliance as an example, what is your firm's track record on compliance over the past few years? How has legislation changed in this period, and how have you responded? How does your response compare with that of your competitors? How may legislation change further in the future, and how will you respond? What are the cost implications?

Address similar questions in all major areas of compliance. If your firm is in financial services, how have you responded to tighter capital adequacy controls following the financial crash of 2008?

If all is under control in major areas of compliance, say so here. If there are issues, explain what they are and how you will address them. If there are major issues, for example on the environment, detail them in an appendix and summarise them and their costs here.

Resource risks and opportunities

You have already pulled out the main risks and opportunities relating to market demand (Chapter 3 of your plan), industry competition (Chapter 4) and strategy (Chapter 5). Now it's time to add the major resource risks to your plan, as well as resource opportunities.

These resource risks could relate to management (e.g. a key manager lured away to a competitor), marketing (e.g. an expensive advertising campaign that produces little benefit) or operations (e.g. distribution disruption if a new regional depot's systems fail).

What are the resource risks that are at least reasonably likely to occur and with reasonable impact if they do occur? These are the *big* risks (as defined in Chapter 3). How can they be mitigated? What are the *big* opportunities? How can you exploit them?

We will return to these big resource risks and opportunities later (see Chapter 8).

Essential case study
The Dart Valley Guest House and Oriental Spa business plan, 2015

Chapter 6: Resources

Dick Jones has set out his strategy to make Dart Valley the leading provider of spa services in South Devon through completion of the second phase of the development. Now, in Chapter 6 of his plan, he sets out the resource implications, along with their risks and opportunities. Here are his highlights:

■ Management – unlike for the Phase I development three years earlier, management is now proven. Before Dart Valley, neither he nor his wife, Kay, had had any experience of hotel or spa management and this could have been a problem in obtaining external funding. Now, with three years' proven experience behind them – with ups and downs, yes, but overall success – management is a strength of this plan, not a weakness. But Dick must also set out his plans for how he will recruit a manager for the new spa offering, preferably someone with an oriental heritage to complement the business's positioning.

▪ Marketing – Dart Valley has developed to date through judicious use of local and regional advertising, attendance at regional promotions, competitive pricing off-season and other special packages, such as for weddings. Dick recognises that marketing to fill 33 rooms will be a greater challenge than for 17 rooms, but he sees it largely as more of the same, rather than an entirely new tack; one possibility is to do more partnering with successful spa hotels elsewhere, giving them a cut on business referrals and offering the customer greater variety in where to stay next time.

▪ Operations – Dick doesn't see any likely issues with regard to supplies, purchasing, provision of services, systems (the reservation system has worked very well after the inevitable teething problems), controls or compliance (the major issue there being the planning permission, which, after some toing and froing, Dick's architect has now secured from Devon County Council).

Dick sums up the major resource risks and opportunities as being the slippage and/or cost escalation in construction works and any upsets in the health of the owners. As regards the former, and given his experience in Phase I, Dick has already built an extra two months and 10% contingency into his construction plans. As regards the latter, he and Kay are firm believers that no one is indispensable – if something happens to them, others would come in to take their place.

Essential checklist on resources

Demonstrate how your firm will deploy its scarce resources to implement the strategy of Chapter 5 to achieve the goals and objectives of Chapter 2.

Set out your plans for deploying resources in three main fields – management, marketing and operations:

- **Management** – how you will have the right team of managers, with the right experience, qualifications and skills to implement the strategy.

- **Marketing** – how you will create sufficient awareness of the firm's offering over the plan period, a crucial issue in a start-up.

- **Operations** – how you will deploy your resources to ensure that supplies, purchasing, manufacturing/service provision, R&D, distribution, sales, customer service, systems, control and compliance are sufficiently aligned to deliver the plan.

Finally, describe the big resource risks and opportunities that may impact on the achievability of your business plan.

7

Financials and forecasts

> In the business world, the rearview mirror is always
> clearer than the windshield.
>
> *Warren Buffett*

In this chapter

- Historic financials
- Market-driven sales forecasts
- Competition-driven margin forecasts
- Funding the plan
- Full financial forecasts
  - Profit and loss account
  - Cash flow
  - Balance sheet
- Forecasts in a start-up
- Financial risks and opportunities

n **Chapter 6 of your plan** you set out how you would deploy your firm's scarce resources to achieve the goals of Chapter 2, following the strategy of Chapter 5. In this chapter, you will show how that strategy will translate into results – in terms of both key measurable parameters and money.

And you are going to do it in a way that will convince your backer. A way that you won't find in other guides to business planning.

You will forecast your sales growth in a way that is consistent both with the trends in market demand you identified in Chapter 3 and with your growth plans outlined in Chapter 5.

You will forecast your profit margin development in a way that is consistent with the competitive dynamics assessed in Chapter 4 and your profit improvement plans of Chapter 5.

Then you'll translate these forecasts into full financial statements – the detail that your backer will expect to see in the business plan (though, in reality, they may well have their own financial model to slot your numbers into).

But, first, we will start with the actual numbers, the historic financials.

Historic financials

Start by setting out your last three years' actual financials, as well as those for the current year's budget.

If your firm has only been going for a couple of years, set out as much as you can. If your firm is 5, maybe 10, years old, don't put down the whole history, just the last 3 years – unless circumstances suggest otherwise.

Remember, we are trying to give your backers enough information for them to make their backing decision. We don't want to overload them with data and information. If the last three years have been reasonably indicative of what is likely to come in the future, then three years should be sufficient.

But if your business operates in a highly cyclical industry, or if some extraordinary event occurred in a particular year, like the loss of a major customer or a warehouse fire, you may need to set out four or even five years of historics.

If your business is a start-up, you will have no historics. Your financials will all be forecasts, and these will be addressed in a later section of this chapter.

I won't go into detail here on how to draw up historical accounts. This is a book not on accounting but on planning. If yours is an established business, your accountant has already drawn up the accounts and you hopefully have a reasonable idea of what they mean. But I shall show you how to draw up coherent financial *forecasts* later in this chapter.

For now, you should set out four major financial statements – for each year, the historic actual years and the budget year – namely:

- sales and profit margins by main business segment
- profit and loss (P&L) account (overall, for all segments)
- cash flow statement
- balance sheet.

Then, in one to two pages of narrative, you should describe the highlights that underpin these financials. Start with the basic structure of your firm's current financials. Describe:

- which business segments contribute most to sales (already covered in Chapter 2 of your plan)
- which contribute most to profit (also in Chapter 2)
- the growth (or otherwise) in overall sales over the years and in the budget
- the major constituents of expense in the P&L
- the change in gross and operating profit over the years and in the budget
- the major influences in the cash flow statement and the balance sheet.

Then, while addressing each of those bullets, look for items of interest in the financials. Look for change from year to year. Look in particular for anomalies, for unexpected or untypical change. Look for what your backer will look for – anything that did not perform to trend, that could not easily have been predicted.

And explain why. What was behind that change? Was it a one-off or could it happen again?

Here are some examples of anomalies that you might need to address:

- A dip in sales in one business segment due to the loss of a customer. Was this due to a situation change for the customer – bankruptcy, takeover, change of management – or a plain, old, dastardly switch to a competitor?

- A jump in cost of goods sold. Was this due to costlier raw materials (in which case, to what extent was this passed through to the customer?), a new supplier, a renegotiation of volume discount terms?

- A sharp increase in a particular overhead item, say rent. Was this due to the taking on of more square feet, a lease renewal, relocation of premises?

- Counter-intuitive trends in working capital, with, for example, stocks rising one year despite flat sales. Was this due to inadequate production or inventory controls?

- Ups and downs in annual capital expenditure. What were the big items? Did they come in on time and within budget?

Again, remember, this is not a thesis. Only highlight those items that your backer should know about. But don't overlook any, whether deliberately or accidentally, that they really must know about. Because when (not if) they find out, you may have to look elsewhere for your backing.

Market-driven sales forecasts

Without sales, you have no business. Sales forecasts matter. But they need to be credible and convincing.

The secret is to lay out your sales forecast in a market context. This will give you a market-derived perspective on its achievability. It's a 'top-down', market-driven approach. The 'bottom-up' approach, where you set out the specific initiatives planned for developing business in each of your segments, can then be added to get total revenues in each segment.

Deriving market-driven sales forecasts is best done by assessing average change over a fixed period of time, typically a three-, possibly a five-year, time frame. You'll relate your forecast sales growth to medium-term trends in the market over that time period. Having completed this process, however, you will still have to set out your sales forecasts, at least the totals, for each intervening year. These will be needed for the yearly P&L and other financial forecasts later in this chapter.

The process is straightforward, as long as you take one step at a time. The flow set out below is a process of eight steps, each following logically from the previous step:

1 Business segments. List each main segment, which will be forecast separately.

2 Revenues. What revenues were achieved in this segment in the last financial year? If this year is untypical in some way, you should substitute a 'normal' level of revenues for the year (from Chapter 2 of your plan).

3 Market demand prospects. How do you expect the market to grow (preferably in per cent per year) over the next few years in this segment (from Chapter 3)?

4 Competitive position. How does your firm measure up relative to the competition in this segment, and how may this change over the next few years (from Chapter 5)?

5 Likely revenue growth. Based on future competitive position, is your firm likely to keep pace with, exceed or fall short of market demand growth in this segment? What is your likely revenue growth rate?

6 Top-down revenues. What are the resultant revenues from the market-driven forecast growth rate?

7 Bottom-up revenues. What initiatives are planned to grow sales by above (or below) market growth rates in this segment – for example, through the launch (or removal) of new products within the product group, entry into (or withdrawal from) new markets within the market group or the taking on (or loss) of new customers? Or a significant marketing investment in a segment? What are the likely incremental revenues from such new, bottom-up initiatives in three years' time?

8 Total revenues. Add up the market-driven and bottom-up revenues to get the total forecast revenues for each segment in three years' time.

The beauty of this process is the transparency. Your backer will see to what extent your revenue forecasts are:

- consistent with market demand prospects and your firm's competitive position, within each segment
- dependent on new initiatives in sales and marketing for their achievement.

The process is best captured in a table. There are eight entries in the process flow, so we take eight columns, as shown in Table 7.1.

The first four columns are easy to fill in – you've already done the work, in Chapters 2, 3 and 5 of your plan. Here you just need to add columns 5–8.

Column 5 is the clincher. Your selected likely market-driven revenue growth rate must be consistent with:

- market demand forecasts, as set out in Chapter 3 of your plan
- your firm's competitive position, as set out in Chapter 5
- your firm's track record over the last few years.

table **7.1** Drawing up a market-based sales forecast

Business segments	Revenues (£000)	Market demand growth (%/year)	Company competitive position (0–5)	Likely revenue growth (%/year)	Top-down revenues (£000)	Bottom-up revenues (£000)	Total revenues (£000)
	Latest year	Next three years	Next three years	Next three years	In three years	In three years	In three years
1	2	3	4	5	6	7	8
Source:	*Chapter 2*	*Chapter 3*	*Chapter 5*	←——— Here in Chapter 7 ———→			
A							
B							
C							
Others							
Total							

Here's an example of consistency. If you find that the market in a business segment is set to grow steadily, and you assess your firm as having a favourable competitive position (and you have a track record), then, all else being equal, you should be able to grow your business apace with the market in that segment. If, however, your plan is to grow much faster than that, you will need convincing reasons on how.

Your backer won't necessarily be fazed by a high growth plan, as long as it's consistent. Suppose your competitive position in a business segment has been and should remain strong (around 4 on Appendix A's 0 to 5 scale), and is demonstrated by your having outperformed the market in the past. If you're planning to continue to beat the market in the future, then your backer should find the assumptions *consistent.*

But suppose your competitive position in a segment is just tenable (around 2) and you've underperformed against the market in the past. Suppose too that your position isn't expected to show any significant improvement in the future. If your plans for this segment show you beating the market in the future, your backer's eyebrows will be raised. Your plans are *inconsistent* with both your future position and your previous performance.

Suppose, however, you've underperformed against the market in the past, but you've recently taken steps to improve your competitive position to favourable (around 3). If you're planning to grow with the market in the future, then your story will at least be *consistent.* All your backer will need to do is confirm that you have indeed sharpened up your act.

Take a look at the example of RandomCo in Table 7.2. Whoever prepared these forecasts was all over the place. Some forecasts seem consistent with market prospects and the firm's positioning, but others are way out. Have a go yourself at filling in the boxes in the final column!

table 7.2			A test: how consistent are RandomCo's market-based sales forecasts?			

Business segments	Revenues (£000)	Market demand growth (%/year)	RandomCo competitive position (0–5)	Forecast revenue growth (%/year)	Forecast revenues (£000)	How likely is the forecast?
	Latest year	Next three years	Next three years	Next three years	In three years	
A	10	5%	3.0	17%	16	☐
B	10	5%	3.0	5%	12	☐
C	10	5%	3.0	0%	10	☐
D	10	5%	2.0	9%	13	☐
E	10	5%	3.5 to 4.0	12%	14	☐
F	10	−2.5%	3.0	14%	15	☐

Key

1 = Most likely 2 = Likely
3 = Unlikely 4 = Most unlikely

Answers: A:3, B:2, C:1, D:3, E:1, F:4

Did you get them all correct?!

This is unrealistic, you may think. No one in their right mind would forecast revenue growth as, for example, in segments A or F. Not so. I have come across countless examples over the years of good companies with atrocious forecasts. The worst are the so-called hockey stick forecasts, which show a recent or imminent downturn in sales followed by future explosive growth.

In segment F, market demand is set to decline, thus competition is likely to get tougher. RandomCo is no more than favourably placed in that segment, so, other things being equal, is likely to show sales decline in line with the market. Yet this forecaster is showing strong revenue growth, despite having no new initiatives in the pipeline, beating the market by a wide margin. This wild forecast fully justifies the *most unlikely* answer.

There's one extra flourish you can apply to this chart. Since historical performance is such an important factor in assessing achievability of forecast performance, I often add a couple of extra columns before column 2, setting out revenues for each of the previous two years. I then add a column after column 2 for the average annual revenue growth rate per segment over the last three years. Column 3 is then split into two, showing average annual market demand growth in the *last* three years and that of the *next* three years. I find that this helps set the forecasts in a historic context, enabling forecast future performance against the market to be compared with past performance against the market. But I have encountered some colleagues and clients who find that the extra four columns make the chart a bit unwieldy and harder to comprehend.

A final word on these market-driven sales forecasts. You won't find them in most business plans. If you include them, or something like them – a variant tailored to the circumstances of your business – your plan will be distinctive. It will show you understand and are confident about where you sit in the market and where it and you are going. It will impress your backer.

Essential tip

In these forecasts your backer is looking for three of the Seven Cs: consistency, coherence and credibility. Your coherent sales forecasts will be consistent with market demand forecasts, your firm's competitive position and bottom-up sales initiatives. And your coherent margin forecasts will be consistent with trends in industry competitive intensity and bottom-up profit improvement initiatives. They will have enhanced credibility.

Competition-driven margin forecasts

You have placed your sales forecasts in a market demand context. Now you need to put your profit margin forecasts in a market supply context, or, in other words, a competition context. Again, this will be distinctive. You will impress.

The process has three parts – current profitability, competitive environment and forecast profit – and flows like this:

1 *Business segments.* As above, you look at one segment at a time.

Current profitability

2 Revenues this year. From Table 7.1.

3 Profit margin this year. What percentage profit* margin will you make in this business segment this year?

---

* Gross profit is typically used, which is revenues less costs of materials and other direct costs. Better, where data is available, is contribution to fixed overhead, which also takes into account variable overhead costs. In many small businesses, marketing spend can differ greatly by business segment. If that's so in your business, you might choose to define marketing as a direct cost and the pertinent profit margin as revenues less costs of materials, other direct costs, and marketing costs.

4 Profit this year. Revenue multiplied by profit margin.

Competitive environment

5 Recent competitive intensity. How tough is competition compared to other segments – high, medium or low (from Chapter 4 of your plan)?

6 Future competitive intensity. How tough is competition likely to be over the next few years compared to other segments – high, medium or low (also from Chapter 4)?

Forecast profit

7 Planned profit margin. What percentage profit margin are you planning to make in this business segment in three years' time?

8 Forecast profit. Forecast revenues from Table 7.1 times planned profit margin of step 7.

9 Planned profit improvement measures. What measures are you planning to improve margins to support your planned profit margin (from Chapter 5)?

Again, this forecasting process works well in a table. There are nine entries in the process flow, so here in Table 7.3 we have nine columns.

Most of the work needed to fill out this chart you have already done. Columns 2–4 are your current margins by segment. In columns 5 and 6, you put in indicators of how intense competition is today and how that is likely to change over the next few years – your conclusions from Chapter 4.

The meat of column 9, your profit improvement measures, has already been set out in Chapter 5 on resources. Here you just need to flag references to the specific initiatives underway or planned.

Now you need to add the critical column 7, whereupon column 8 falls into place from column 7 times the revenue forecast of Table 7.1.

There are three main factors that will determine how credible your margin forecasts in column 7 are:

- top-down external pricing pressures from competitive forces in the marketplace (as in columns 5 and 6)
- bottom-up operational initiatives to improve the cost effectiveness of your business (as in column 9)
- bottom-up investment initiatives you may have to invest in strengthening a business or in launching another (also in column 9).

table 7.3 Drawing up a competition-based margin forecast

Business segments	Revenues (£000)	Profit (£000)	Profit margin (%)	Competitive intensity (Low-Med-High)	Planned profit margin (%)	Forecast profit (£000)	Planned profit improvement measures
	Latest year	Latest year	Latest year	Latest year / In three years	In three years	In three years	
1	2	3	4	5 6	7	8	9
Source:	◄── Chapter 2 ──►			Chapter 4	Here in Chapter 7		Chapters 5 and 6
A							
B							
C							
Others							
Total							

As in the first stage, your backer is looking for *consistency* in the profit margin forecasts. If competition is going to get stiffer, pricing is likely to come under pressure, and your backer will expect profit margins to be slimmed. If your plans show profit margins moving the other way – actually improving – you'll need some good bottom-up reasons why.

Conversely, if competition is set to ease up and your profit margins are planned to stay flat, or even shrink, your backer may think you're being rather conservative – unless there are bottom-up reasons why you feel the need to be adding cost.

Whatever your plans for driving down cost and improving profit margin from the bottom up may be, they'll need to be consistent and convincing to your backer.

As with the market-driven sales forecasts, however, your competition-driven margin forecasts will be distinctive. Few business plans will present margin plans within such context. Your backer will find your plan more credible.

Funding the plan

By now, you have a set of market-driven sales forecasts and one of competition-driven margin forecasts. You have identified capital expenditure requirements from your analysis of resources in Chapter 6.

Before you proceed to draw up the full suite of forecast accounts, you should pause to think about how your business plan will be funded. If your forecasts are showing serious growth, and certainly if your firm is a start-up, the business may well need an external cash injection up front to enable and underpin that growth.

The fact that you are writing a business plan suggests that your business is in need of some incremental funding, some backing. If your business was throwing out enough cash each year to fund its growth prospects, you may well not need to be writing a business plan – unless instructed to do so by your divisional manager or your board.

Funding for your plan can come in the form of equity or debt, or various, rather complex hybrids of the two. We'll keep it black and white here – equity and debt.

The huge advantage of *equity finance* is that it does not require servicing, unless you make such a good profit that your board decides to pay dividends. But there is no commitment to pay out anything to shareholders unless the company can afford to do so, unlike with debt finance.

The problem with equity is that it is expensive. An equity backer expects a rate of return commensurate with the risk they are taking on. For an established business, that could be in the region of 30–40% per annum. For a start-up, they may well be looking for double that return.

The return expected will be directly in line with the perceived risk of the venture. The lower the risk, the lower the expected return demanded by the investor. Start-ups are by definition riskier than investments in established businesses. Venture capitalists expect that 3 or 4 in 10 of their start-up investments will go under, the same number will do alright, and hopefully 1 or 2 will be stellar. If your business plan offers just a 10% per annum return to the venture capitalist, they will walk away – they are effectively being offered a 10–20% chance of a 10% return. Not a great deal.

Debt finance, on the other hand, demands a fixed return, one that is not in line with the performance of the business. It demands a fixed rate of interest, or more usually a fixed spread over a specified benchmark rate of interest, which has to be paid irrespective of the performance of the business. Whether in times of plenty or scarcity, the interest payments must be made.

Debt finance is cheaper, but more onerous and less flexible than equity finance.

In general, the more confident you are in your business plan, the more you should try to obtain debt funding in preference to equity. If you can fund all future growth through debt finance, then once the debt is paid down the residual cash flow is all yours.

But by maximising the debt finance, you are raising the risk of financial instability. You raise the risk of having to go cap in hand when times get hard and asking the bank to restructure its loans and covenants. That it may do, but at a punitive cost. Or it may not and elect instead to close your business down.

It is a balance. If you do need a significant equity cushion, you should try to argue your case so well that your backer gives you a preferential class of equity – one that incentivises you to maximise profit growth of the business. Such incentives to owner-managers can include the following:

■ You retaining a larger shareholding than the proportion of cash you will inject into the business. Suppose the business needs £1 million in cash to get going. Your equity provider puts in £900,000 and you put in £100,000, but you manage to negotiate from the start a shareholding not of 10%, but of, say, one-third.

■ An equity ratchet, whereby your level of shareholding reaches a higher level once the company has met certain, pre-specified performance targets. You may be given a 20% shareholding up front, say, which could be ratcheted up to 25%, 30% or 35% should operating profit reach certain levels by, say, year three.

For the time being you can assume that the funds needed to drive your plan forward all come in the form of debt finance. All backers will be interested in seeing how the full financial forecasts develop on the assumption of all debt finance. They will want to stress test the forecasts to see how sensitive the cash flows are to adverse assumptions, whether an all-debt capital structure can weather such fluctuation and, if not, how much of an equity cushion the business needs to survive hard times.

An assumption of all-debt finance presents a worst-case scenario from the perspective of cash flow in the business. It is a good starting point for discussion and negotiation.

Full financial forecasts

You have already forecast the main guts of your business over the next three years. You have set out and *justified in a market context* where sales are going to be heading. And you have set out and *justified in a competitive context* what contribution these sales will make to the overheads of your business.

You have forecast the capital spending needs of your business in the appropriate sections of your Chapter 6 on resources. All that remains to be forecast are the overheads, interest and tax expenses for your income statement and the working capital needs for the cash flow statement.

Much of the rest of the financial forecasts is padding, 'accountantese'. But it does need to be done nonetheless, if only because your backer expects it.

The frustrating thing is that if your backer is a finance house, as opposed, say, to your board of directors, it will have its own financial models to slot your sales and margin numbers into – which means that all the effort you'll put into creating a full set of projected accounts will be in vain!

But that's life – it's part of the price you pay to get the backing. So this section outlines the basic financial forecasts you need to compose.

You should set out the current year's budget numbers plus three-year forecasts for three different, interlinked sets of accounts:

- ▪ Profit and loss account, including overheads
- ▪ Cash flow, including capital expenditure
- ▪ Balance sheet.

We'll take them one at a time.

Profit and loss account

The top line of the profit and loss account has already been done. That's the sales forecast – by far the most difficult and important line in financial forecasting. You have also forecast the gross profit line, or possibly the contribution line, or even a hybrid of the contribution line defined as gross profit less marketing expense.

Now you can fill in the bits in between – the various items of direct cost, such as cost of goods sold – to ensure that the margins emerge as already forecast.

That just leaves overheads to be forecast before you get to operating profit, and overheads are the easiest of the cost items to forecast.

So we are almost there with a P&L before we seem to have started!

Let's remind ourselves exactly what items need to be forecast in a P&L, using Table 7.4.

table 7.4   Forecasting the profit and loss account

P&L item	Notes
Sales	Already done!
less direct costs	To be consistent with gross profit forecast – see Note 1
Gross profit	Already done!
Gross margin (%)	= *Gross profit divided by sales*
less depreciation	The main non cash provision in the P&L – see Note 2
less other overheads	Forecast each main item separately – see Note 3
Operating profit	= Gross profit less depreciation and overheads
Operating margin (%)	= *Operating profit divided by sales*
plus other income	Typically investment income – see Note 4
EBIT	= Earnings before interest and tax – see Note 5
less interest	That's net interest – see Note 6
PBT	= Profit (or earnings) before tax
less tax	Easier said than done – see Note 7
PAT	= Profit after tax, aka Net Profit, the 'bottom line'
Net margin (%)	= *PAT divided by sales*

▶

Notes

1 You have already determined that gross margins are going to be a certain percentage in three years' time. Now you need to project the various items of direct cost, like raw materials and direct labour, to ensure that the gross margin emerging in year three is as you have forecast.

2 Depreciation is not a cash expense – it is a provision for future capital expense. Capital expenditure is by definition a lumpy, one-off investment designed to spread benefits over more than 1 year, sometimes 5 (like some IT investment), 7 (a vehicle), 10 (equipment) or 20 (a building). You won't need to spend on that item again the following year, but you will at some stage in the future. You need to provide for that, and the tax authorities will allow you to offset that provision against tax. Your annual depreciation provision on an asset equals the capital expenditure divided by its anticipated length of useful life. Amortisation is usually added in here too, and represents capital expenditure on an acquired intangible asset (like brand value), again divided by the anticipated useful length of life of the asset.

3 Overheads are easy to forecast, but do not make the mistake of leaving them as is – 'Oh, we have plenty of office space and staff to handle a trebling of sales!' Your backer won't believe you. But, yes, overheads tend not to rise as fast as sales. Indeed, that is where the source of future profit typically resides. But they do rise – some overheads (like the sales function) at around (very roughly) one-half of the rate of growth of sales, others (like the admin function) a bit slower. Don't forecast them to remain at the same percentage of sales as they are today – that is far too conservative and negates the purpose of growth. But, on the other hand, don't forecast costs to grow so unrealistically slowly that your operating margin by year three becomes insupportably high.

4 Investment income is the item that differentiates between operating profit and EBIT and relates mainly to the dividend income from minority shareholding positions in other companies (not subsidiary companies, whose results would be consolidated into the accounts of your firm). But this item is typically not a factor in an SME's accounts. For an SME, operating profit and EBIT can often be taken as one and the same.

5 EBIT is the parameter based on which one often hears a company valued, as in 'company ABC is worth X times EBIT'. An alternative parameter, nowadays more commonly used, is EBITDA, which is EBIT plus depreciation and amortisation. It is the closest indicator in the P&L to the pre-tax cash (as opposed to profit) generated by the business. Whether you use EBIT or EBITDA as the basis for valuation, you are assuming an all-equity capital structure, and when the appropriate multiple is applied you derive a value for the enterprise, against which the value of the debt can be deducted to give the value of the equity.

6 Remember that you need to include here not only the interest your firm pays on its short- and long-term debt, but also the interest it has earned over the same period from its bank deposits. It is your net interest paid that should represent the difference between EBIT and EBT (or PBT).

7 Tax calculations are an esoteric art, with their intricate patchwork of allowances and rates seemingly known only to highly paid tax advisers. But for purposes of forecasting, keep it simple. Apply the standard rate of corporation tax to PBT less any accumulated tax losses in your business.

And that's it! Simple enough. To check you have picked up all the main points, take a look at how Dick Jones forecasts the P&L of the Dart Valley Guest House and Oriental Spa later in this chapter.

Now do a sense check. What's your net margin today? What have you projected it to be in three years' time? Does that make sense?

If it has grown significantly, what are the main factors driving that growth – revenue growth, expense items growing less quickly, cost taken out? Can those assumptions be justified? Robustly?

The Dart Valley's forecasts show net margin leaping from 15% to 24%. How? In a high fixed cost business like the hotel trade, profits are highly sensitive to volumes. By adding more rooms and more visitors, Dart Valley will have higher gross profits to spread across the overhead expenses of facilities such as the spa and swimming pool. Logically it makes sense.

Do your net margin forecasts make sense?

Cash flow

These are the forecasts your equity backer is most interested in. Investors want to know how much cash they have to put into the business and how much cash the business will throw off each year to generate a return on that investment.

We start with the end result of the P&L, the net profit, or profit after tax, and make a few adjustments to derive the cash implications of the business activity, as summarised in Table 7.5.

The end result of all this cash flow, including all inflows and outflows of cash over the 12-month period, will be an accretion or diminution of the accumulated cash reserves of the company. In cash flow forecasts these are best assumed to be retained within the company and, for the sake of clarity, not distributed to shareholders as dividends in the forecast period. In reality, of course, dividends may well be paid and unnecessarily high cash reserves taken out of the company. But for purposes of financial forecasting it helps to see how the cash surplus accumulates on the cash flow statement and how the cash reserves build up on the balance sheet.

This leads us on to the final financial statement you need to prepare, the balance sheet.

table 7.5   Forecasting the cash flow statement

Cash flow item	Notes
Profit after tax	The bottom line of the P&L account
plus depreciation	Add back depreciation (and amortisation) – see Note 1
Operating cash flow	= Operating cash flow before working capital
less change in stocks	See Note 2
less change in debtors	See Note 3
plus change in creditors	See Note 4
Cash flow from operations	= Operating cash flow after working capital
less capital expenditure	See Note 5
Cash flow pre-financing	
plus finance provided	See Note 6
Cash surplus (year)	The end result, the cash added to or subtracted from cash reserves after 12 months' trading
Cash surplus (cumulative)	The cash retained in the business at the end of the period

▶

Notes

1 Depreciation is a non-cash item in the P&L, so needs to be added back for the cash flow statement. In other words, the cash generated by one year's trading is larger than what is recorded as 'profit' due to the often hefty provision for future capital expenditure called depreciation.

2 The three working capital adjustments are effectively items relating to timing. Stocks (known in the US as inventories) bought (or finished goods manufactured) today may not be sold for many weeks. An increase in stocks should be subtracted from operating cash flow, a decrease added. Excel makes working capital forecasts easy. If your stock levels today are, say, the equivalent of 45 days' worth of revenues, you take the change in revenues in one year and multiply by 45/365 to get the increase in stock holding. You then replicate the formula across the years.

3 A sale may be made today, but payment as registered by cash in your hand or bank account may not be received until 10, 30, even 60 days hence. An increase in trade debtors (what your customers owe you, known in the US as accounts receivable) should be subtracted from operating cash flow, a decrease added – as for stocks.

4 Supplies received today may not be the same as payment made to that supplier, which may be 10, 30, even 60 days later. An increase in trade creditors (what you owe your suppliers, known in the US as accounts payable) should be added to operating cash flow, a decrease subtracted – the opposite to stocks and debtors. It can represent, in effect, an extra source of funding for your business.

5 Capital expenditure is defined as that designed to produce a benefit to the business that should last beyond the 12 months of the accounting period. It is allowable against tax only in the form of a depreciation charge spread over the useful life of the asset. In your Chapter 6 on resources, you set out your plans for capital expenditure for each of the next three years on buildings and works, equipment and vehicles. Here you should enter the total capital spending for the year.

6 Net long-term finance provided to the firm over the previous 12 months should include loans raised and/or equity injected, less loans repaid in part or full. In many years, this item will be a blank, since the cash required to grow the business will be raised from cash generated from within the business and there will be no need for the addition of funds from external sources.

Balance sheet

While the previous two statements represent a flow over a 12-month period – profit in the case of the P&L account and cash in the case of the cash flow statement – the balance sheet represents a snapshot in time. If your firm's financial year ends on 31 March, the balance sheet represents a statement of your firm's financial situation as of midnight on 31 March.

It shows the assets your firm holds and the liabilities it owes at that moment of time.

It is the financial statement most beloved of your banker. While your equity investor loves the cash flow statement, the banker, while also admiring the other two statements, loves the balance sheet best. It shows how indebted your firm is. It shows them how much security their loan has, how much of an equity cushion there is if things go wrong. It shows them whether they have cause for concern.

It is fairly straightforward to draw up a balance sheet in Excel from your P&L and cash flow statement worksheets. They are all interlinked. The changes in the balance sheet from the previous date to the current date will be exactly the same as what you have already computed for the relevant items of the P&L and cash flow statements.

If you find this DIY prospect a tad daunting, there are plenty of off-the-shelf software packages you can acquire to guide you through it. Take a look at them on the Web – like the curiously named **www. upyourcashflow.com**, which ranks high on Google – and check out some review sites before acquiring one. They all have similar functions – this is not rocket science. Go for whichever is rated the simplest to understand for the end user.

Essential tip

If stuck, take a break. When numbers go wonky, walk away. Better, sleep on them. Return afresh and, hey presto, you'll spot the wrong link or formula in your spreadsheet in an instant!

I have a confession. I had never before drawn up a set of balance sheet forecasts from P&L and cash flow forecasts. By the time Lotus 123 and Excel came on the scene, I was already a fairly senior consultant, so all such modelling was done by my more junior colleagues. I just had to examine their output to make sure it made sense.

But for the purposes of this book, I thought I should try it myself. Like you, probably, I am not an accountant. So I tried it out on behalf of you, a fellow layperson, on the Dart Valley case study. It wasn't that hard, but I did make mistakes. And it took me longer than envisaged – a whole morning just on the balance sheet forecast and reconciliation. Some readers may well be smarter and faster. Others may struggle even more than me – in which case you may choose to invest in the software. The exercise has meant, however, that I am able to give you at first hand some tips on what can go wrong – see Note 3 to Table 7.6.

table 7.6	Forecasting the balance sheet
Balance sheet item	*Notes*
Current assets	= Cash and other assets that can be expected to be converted into cash over the next 12 months
Stocks	= Stocks held at start-year plus the change in stock levels during the year *in the cash flow forecast*

Debtors	= Debtors at start-year plus the change in debtor levels during the year *in the cash flow forecast*
Other	= Deposits, prepayments, etc. made by customers at start-year plus the change in such levels during the year *in the cash flow forecast*
Cash	= The figure for cumulative cash surplus *in the cash flow forecast* – see Note 1
Total	= Total current assets
Capital assets	= Assets which are not easily converted into cash and are usually held for a period in excess of one year
Net fixed assets at start-year	= Net fixed assets at start-year, namely the net fixed assets shown in the previous balance sheet
plus capital expenditure	= Capital expenditure during the year *in the cash flow forecast*
less depreciation	= Depreciation during the year *in the P&L forecast*
Net fixed assets at end-year	This will be the same as fixed assets at cost less cumulative depreciation from the date of asset acquisition to end-year
Other	= The value of investments or intangibles (if any) held at start-year plus the change in such levels during the year *in the cash flow forecast*
Total	= Total capital assets
TOTAL ASSETS	= Total current assets plus total capital assets
Current liabilities	= Liabilities which can be expected to be paid in cash to creditors over the following 12 months
Creditors	= Creditors at start-year plus the change in creditor levels during the year *in the cash flow forecast*
Provision for taxation	= Provision for taxation at start-year plus the change in such levels during the year *in the P&L forecast*
Short-term loans	= Short-term loans (i.e. those due within the next 12 months) at start-year plus the change in such loans during the year *in the cash flow forecast*
Total	= Total current liabilities
Long-term liabilities	= Liabilities which are not expected to be paid out in cash over the next 12 months
Long-term debt	= Long-term debt, including mortgages on business property, at start-year plus any change (new loans taken out, less debt paid back) during the year *in the cash flow forecast*

Pension obligations	= Pension obligations (if any) at start-year plus any change during the year *in the cash flow forecast*
Total	= Total long-term liabilities
Owner equity	= Total assets less current and long-term liabilities = residual claim of owners on the assets = 'net worth'
Share capital paid up	= Equity investment paid in cash, cumulative to date, at start-year plus any further injection during the year *in the cash flow forecast*
P&L account	= Cumulative net profit at start-year (i.e. the total of all net profits (or losses) in all previous P&L accounts) plus the net profit (or loss) during the year in the P&L account less any dividends paid out during the year *in the cash flow forecast* – see Note 2
Total	= Total owner equity
TOTAL LIABILITIES	= Current liabilities plus long-term liabilities plus owner equity = current liabilities plus 'capital employed' – see Note 3

Notes

1   This 'cash' figure may of course be spread over a number of places – in the till, a current account, a deposit account – but for purposes of forecasting it is best to have just the one total number. Then it can be compared directly with the cumulative cash surplus number in the cash flow statement each year. They are one and the same.

2   It is best to assume that no dividends are paid out in the forecast. Then your backer can see clearly how the P&L (which, together with paid-up share capital, comprises owner equity) builds up over time in the balance sheet and how this build-up is reflected in the cash item in current assets.

3   Total liabilities are, by definition, equal to total assets. It is best to insert in your spreadsheet a check item – a row showing one minus the other. This should at all times and in all cells be zero. But of course it may not be. Mistakes may have crept in while trying to reconcile the balance sheet with the P&L and cash flow. If the check cells don't all show zeros, here are some areas that may have gone wrong. You need to ensure that:

   ▪ you have given the right signs to the changes in working capital in your cash flow forecast – an increase in stocks is a cash outflow, as for debtors, but an increase in creditors is a cash inflow

   ▪ your cash row in the balance sheet is identical to the cumulative cash surplus row in the cash flow forecast

   ▪ your net fixed asset number at end-year picks up both the capital expenditure during the year from the cash flow forecast as well as the depreciation provision from the P&L forecast

   ▪ any increase in long-term liabilities, whether in debt or equity, is reflected in a corresponding increase in net fixed assets in that year (assuming the finance raised is for such purposes)

   ▪ what goes into the P&L account item in the balance sheet is the cumulative, historical P&L, not just the P&L result for that year.

You now have all the financial forecasts you need for your business plan. You have a market-driven sales forecast, a competition-driven profit margin forecast and a full set of financials.

One final word of advice: make sure you specify clearly and throughout the bases for each of your forecast assumptions. By their very nature, forecasts are dependent on judgement. One person's reasoning will not be the same as the next person's. Set out your assumptions and justify them. Draw on evidence where possible.

These forecasts should represent your base case, defined as the most probable outcome. They should not be what you hope will happen, but rather what is most likely to happen.

In the next chapter you will re-examine these forecasts from different perspectives. What would happen if all goes right? This is the so-called upside case, one that an equity investor will enjoy hearing about.

And what if all goes wrong? This is the downside case, one that your banker will want to know all about.

Forecasts in a start-up

Drawing up market-driven forecasts for a start-up is different from that for an established business. There is no track record on which to base one's judgement. There is no past, nor present, only future.

Nevertheless, it has to be done. In Chapter 3, you identified the market you will be addressing – whether an existing market, a new one or a variant of the two. In Chapter 5, you assessed what your competitive position will be upon entering this market and how that may improve over the next three years.

Now you need to try to place some numbers around this. Let's assume for now that yours is an existing market, which you are entering with a business proposition with a difference. What is the size of this market? What share of this market are you likely to capture after three years? What revenues does that translate into?

Of course, this is easier said than done. If you are starting up the fourth mobile phone network in a country that already has three, you can readily find data on the size of the market (say $1 billion) and its growth rate (10%/year), and you can make various assumptions on your market share development over time. It is most unlikely you will reach a one in four share (25%) within three years, unless you are launching something sensationally different or at much lower cost. But, based on the prior experience of fourth operators in other countries, you might hope for 8–10% following an intensive marketing campaign, and that will translate into $1,000 × 1.33 × 0.09 = $120 million sales in three years' time.

Small to medium-sized companies may not have that sort of data available. But, depending on your market and your circumstances, you should consider giving it a go. Do you have the kind of data that could fill in Table 7.7?

Your backer would love to see your revenue forecasts framed in something like Table 7.7. It will give them a concept of the scale of the gamble they will be making. Are you forecasting to gain a 25% share of market, from a standing start? Or 5%? That's a big difference in the nature of the bet.

And are you forecasting to gain 25% of the market with a competitive position of 3.5 (favourable to strong) or 2.5 (tenable to favourable)? Again, a different sort of bet.

Don't worry if your business proposition doesn't lend itself to this form of analysis. In the example of the Dart Valley Guest House and Oriental Spa, we don't use this framework. The data is difficult to come by and market share so small as to be misleading. Instead we use benchmark data on room occupancy and rates.

But the important thing is to frame your sales forecasts in a market context. However you choose to do it, you should attempt to provide points of *market reference* for your backer. You will greatly strengthen your case if you can do that.

Likewise with your margin forecasts. If you can set them in a competitive context, that would be most useful to your backer. Try to find out whatever you can about the profitability of competing players, whether competing directly or indirectly. If you know that competitor X is highly profitable, with an operating margin of 20%, say, then your forecast of achieving an operating margin of 15% by year three will seem more achievable to your backer than if most competitors are registering margins of just 5–10%.

Even more so than with the sales forecasts, however, a small to medium-sized company is likely to be constrained here in its margin forecasts by the availability of data. You probably won't be able to find such data on your competitors-to-be. But you can look for clues. What evidence of prosperity do your competitors display? Are the owners or managers leading new-Mercedes or aged-Mondeo lifestyles?

Once you have put your sales and margin forecasts in a market framework, you need to build up the full financial statements, as set out

table 7.7   Drawing up a market-based sales forecast for a start-up

Business segments	Market size (£000)	Market demand growth (%/year)	Forecast market size (£000)	Company competitive position (0–5)	Likely market share (%)	Likely revenues (£000)
	Latest year	Next three years	In three years	Next three years	In three years	In three years
1	2	3		4	5	6
Source:		Chapter 3		Chapter 5	Here in Chapter 7	
A						
B						
C						
Others						
Total						

above. The process for drawing up P&L and cash flow forecasts will be the same as for an established business, and the only difference in the first balance sheet forecast will be that your start-year assets and liabilities are zero.

Thus the cash surplus entry in your first year balance sheet will be the same as the cash surplus for the year in your cash flow statement. And the P&L equity entry in your balance sheet will be the same as your net profit for the year in your P&L account. For subsequent years, all financial forecasts will be as for an established business.

Financial risks and opportunities

So far, you have identified the main risks and opportunities relating to market demand (Chapter 3 of your plan), industry competition (Chapter 4), strategy (Chapter 5) and resources (Chapter 6). Now you need to add the final set – those relating to specific financial issues.

The most obvious financial issues that could impact your business plan will be interest rates, exchange rates and tax rates. Ask yourself to what extent your business plans would be affected if there were a significant change in any of these rates, whether in a favourable or an unfavourable direction.

What are the financial risks that are reasonably likely to occur *and* with reasonable impact if they do occur? These are the *big* risks (as defined in Chapter 3). How can they be mitigated? What are the *big* opportunities? How can you exploit them?

All big risks and opportunities, whether financial or related to market, competition, strategy or resources, will be examined together in the next chapter.

Essential case study
The Dart Valley Guest House and Oriental Spa business plan, 2015

Chapter 7: Financials and forecasts

Dick Jones starts by setting out the financial history of Dart Valley since it started trading in late 2011. He lays out the main business parameters and the three major financial statements, shown later alongside the forecasts in Tables 7.9–7.11, and makes explanatory comments only when helpful to the prospective backer, including the following:

- Occupancy may seem low in retrospect in 2012, but the 39% seemed like a major achievement at the time, and a hugely welcome outperformance on his expected 25–30%.

- They have been able to push up the AARR (average achieved room rate) by 7.5% per annum since the first year, with the budget for 2015 showing a further 3% increase.

- Breakeven at the operating profit level was achieved in early 2013 and at the bottom line towards the end of the year, both ahead of plan.

- Marketing expenditure peaked in the first year at over £25,000 and can be expected to return to that level or beyond with the opening of the Phase II development.

- Following the financing at the outset of a mortgage of £500,000 and owner equity of £550,000, the venture has needed no further cash injection and has been operationally cash positive since 2013.

- By the end of 2014, the book value of owner equity had reached £431,000 and seemed set to exceed the £550,000 invested by 2016. This takes no account of the enhancement in the value of the property since purchase and renovation.

Dick then moves on to the forecasts. He has read carefully the section in this Chapter 7 on preparing market-based sales forecasts, but suspects they are not directly appropriate to his plan. After all, he is planning a doubling in bed capacity over the plan period, so his revenues should grow much faster than the market.

Nevertheless, he has a go, if only because the book says that it will impress a backer – see Table 7.8. Lo and behold, the exercise is quite useful. It shows the backer the following:

- How Dart Valley seems well placed to beat the market even in the absence of the Phase II building programme.

- That it can do so in two main ways:
  - Growing accommodation revenues faster than the market, due to its strong competitive position – this would be done more by nudging up room rates than through higher occupancy, since Dart Valley already enjoys high occupancy.

| table 7.8 | How achievable are Dart Valley's sales forecasts? | | | | | | |

Business segments	Revenues (£000)	Market demand growth (%/year)	Company competitive position (0–5)	Likely revenue growth (%/year)	Top-down revenues (£000)	Phase II-derived revenues (£000)	Total revenues (£000)
	2014	2014–19	2014–19	2014–19	2019	2019	2019
1	2	3	4	5	6	7	8
Source:	Chapter 2	Chapter 3	Chapter 5		Here in Chapter 7		
Accommodation	326	3–4%	3.6 to 3.9	5%	416	217	633
Catering	82	2–3%	3.3 to 3.5	3%	95	64	159
Spa	105	4–5%	3.5 to 4.1	7.5%	151	133	284
Total	**513**			**5.2%**	**662**	**414**	**1,076**

  - Deriving a higher share of revenues from spa services, for both
    overnight and outside guests, even in the absence of the Phase II
    facilities, as Dart Valley's range of services continues to develop and
    becomes better known.

- That over three-fifths of revenues by 2019 would be derived from the
  existing business, with the balance from the Phase II development.

Dick thinks carefully about drawing up competition-based margin
forecasts, but decides there is no benefit in doing this – he envisages
no significant competitive intensification over the forecast period. The
risk identified in Chapter 4 of a new, directly competitive entrant will
be treated separately in Chapter 8.

Dick moves on to the financial forecasts and sets out the three main
financial statements forecast to 2019 – see Tables 7.9–7.11. He sets
them against the historics for 2012–14 and the budget for 2015 to
show continuity and consistency to the backer. His explanatory comments include the following for the P&L (see Table 7.9):

- An assumed 10% drop in average achieved room rate and a 20% drop
  in occupancy rate once the new accommodation capacity comes on
  stream in 2017. Given how full the guest house has been in recent
  months and the healthy forward booking for this year and next, Dick
  believes these assumptions are reasonable.

- An assumed doubling in staff costs, spread across room cleaning, waiting, cooking and spa services, with no increase in the bar, reception,
  accounts or gardens.

- A major marketing campaign planned for both 2016 and 2017.

- Debt finance of 100% assumed for the time being for the £1 million to
  be raised.

- The forecasts show operating margin rising from around 20% today to
  around 33% by 2019, a reflection of an almost doubled revenue stream
  spread across an overhead base increasing much more slowly – indeed
  just 50% higher at the end of the period than budgeted for 2015.

From the cash flow forecast (see Table 7.10), Dick observes that Dart Valley should be throwing off an average of over £300,000 a year cash from operations in the three years following the Phase II investment.

And from the balance sheet forecast (see Table 7.11), Dick notes with some satisfaction that the book value of owner equity should exceed £1 million by the end of the period.

Since he has assumed all debt financing, Dick addresses the risk of a rising interest rate. A 3% rise would mean an extra £30,000 per year in interest charges, which Dick believes would be adequately covered by the cash generated from operations. But the bankers will want to take into account market and strategic risks too, which will be addressed in the next chapter.

▶

table 7.9 Dart Valley's profit and loss account forecast, 2016–19

	Actual			Budget		Forecast		
	2012	2013	2014	2015	2016	2017	2018	2019
Average number of rooms available	17	17	17	17	17	33	33	33
Average achieved room rate (£/night)	64.1	69.5	73.9	75.5	79	70	72	74
Average room occupancy	39.2%	55.9%	71.4%	75.0%	75%	60%	65%	71%
Revenues	**£000**	**£000**	**£000**	**£000**	**£000**	**£000**	**£000**	**£000**
Rooms	155	240	326	354	368	506	564	633
Restaurant and bar	45	65	82	87	87	135	145	159
Spa	76	92	105	109	109	263	273	284
Total revenue	**276**	**397**	**513**	**550**	**564**	**904**	**982**	**1,076**
Cost of goods sold	–14	–15	–20	–22	–22	–34	–36	–40
Gross profit	**262**	**382**	**493**	**528**	**542**	**870**	**946**	**1,036**
Gross margin	94.9%	96.2%	96.1%	96.0%	96.1%	96.2%	96.3%	93.3%
Expenses								
Directors' salaries	–100	–100	–100	–100	–100	–100	–100	–100
Wages	–64	–71	–77	–80	–84	–173	–178	–184
Maintenance	–16	–15	–22	–20	–20	–35	–37	–40
Gas, electricity and water	–15	–17	–19	–20	–22	–35	–37	–40
Telecoms and IT	–7	–7	–9	–10	–11	–11	–12	–12

Insurance	−10	−11	−11	−12	−13	−20	−20	−20
Vehicle running	−5	−5	−6	−6	−6	−7	−7	−7
Admin	−7	−7	−8	−8	−9	−12	−12	−12
Marketing (incl. travel)	−25	−18	−22	−20	−30	−30	−25	−20
Property taxes	−10	−11	−11	−12	−13	−20	−22	−25
Miscellaneous	−19	−9	−14	−20	−20	−30	−30	−30
Total expense	**−278**	**−271**	**−299**	**−308**	**−328**	**−478**	**−480**	**−490**
EBITDA	**−16**	**111**	**194**	**220**	**214**	**397**	**466**	**546**
Depreciation	−101	−101	−101	−101	−101	−185	−185	−185
EBIT	**−117**	**10**	**93**	**119**	**113**	**212**	**281**	**361**
Investment income	0	0	0	0	0	0	0	0
Operating profit	**−117**	**10**	**93**	**119**	**113**	**212**	**281**	**361**
Operating margin (%)	−42.4%	2.5%	18.1%	21.6%	20.0%	23.5%	28.7%	33.6%
Interest	−35	−35	−35	−35	−35	−105	−105	−105
Profit before tax	**−152**	**−25**	**58**	**84**	**78**	**107**	**176**	**256**
PBT margin (%)	−55.1%	−6.3%	11.3%	15.3%	13.8%	11.9%	18.0%	23.8%
Cumulative PBT	−152	−177	−119	−35	43	151	327	584
Tax	0	0	0	0	−16	−23	−37	−54
Profit after tax	**−152**	**−25**	**58**	**84**	**62**	**85**	**139**	**203**
PAT margin (%)	−55.1%	−6.36%	11.3%	15.3%	10.9%	9.4%	14.2%	18.8%
Cumulative PAT	−152	−177	−119	−35	27	112	251	454

table 7.10 Dart Valley's cash flow forecast, 2016–19

£000	Actual			Budget		Forecast		
	2012	2013	2014	2015	2016	2017	2018	2019
Profit after tax	**-152**	**-25**	**58**	**84**	**62**	**85**	**139**	**203**
Depreciation	101	101	101	101	101	185	185	185
Operating cash flow	**-51**	**76**	**159**	**185**	**163**	**269**	**324**	**387**
Change in working capital								
Change in stocks (increase = −)	−1	0	0	0	0	−1	0	0
Change in debtors (increase = −)	−23	−10	−10	−3	−1	−28	−6	−8
Change in creditors (increase = +)	11	0	1	0	1	6	0	0
Net change (increase = −)	**−12**	**−10**	**−9**	**−3**	**0**	**−23**	**−6**	**−8**
Cash flow from operations	**−63**	**66**	**150**	**182**	**162**	**246**	**318**	**380**
(= Sales receipts less expense payments)								
Capital expenditure								
Buildings and works	−996	0	0	0	−1,030	0	0	0
Equipment	−15	0	−4	−9	−15	−2	0	−5
Vehicles	−30	0	0	0	0	0	−10	−5
Total	−1,041	0	−4	−9	−1,045	−2	−10	−5

Cash flow pre-financing	-1,104	66	146	173	-883	244	308	375
Financing								
Mortgage taken on property	500	0	0	0	1,000	0	0	0
Share capital paid in	550	0	0	0	0	0	0	0
Cash surplus for year	**-54**	**66**	**146**	**173**	**117**	**244**	**308**	**375**
Cash surplus (Cum)	**-54**	**11**	**157**	**331**	**448**	**692**	**1,000**	**1,375**
Net cash inflow to shareholders	-604	66	146	173	117	244	308	375
Net cash inflow to shareholders (cum)	-604	-539	-393	-219	-102	142	450	825

table 7.11   Dart Valley's balance sheet forecast, 2016–19

£000		Actual			Budget		Forecast		
	31.12.12	31.12.13	31.12.14	31.12.15	31.12.16	31.12.17	31.12.18	31.12.19
Current assets								
Stocks	1	1	2	2	2	3	3	3
Debtors (= accounts receivable)	23	33	42	45	46	74	81	88
Other (deposits, prepaid, etc.)	0	0	0	0	0	0	0	0
Cash	-54	11	157	331	448	692	1,000	1,375
Total	-31	45	201	378	496	769	1,084	1,466
Capital assets								
Net fixed assets at start year	1,041	940	843	751	1,695	1,596	1,422	1,242
less depreciation during year	-101	-101	-101	-101	-101	-185	-185	-185
Net fixed assets at end year	940	839	742	650	1,594	1,412	1,237	1,058
Other (e.g. investments, intangibles)	0	0	0	0	0	0	0	0
Total	940	839	742	650	1,594	1,412	1,237	1,058
TOTAL ASSETS	909	884	943	1,028	2,090	2,181	2,321	2,524

Current liabilities								
Creditors (= accounts payable)	11	11	12	13	13	19	20	20
Provision for taxation	0	0	0	0	0	0	0	0
Short-term loans due in 12 months	0	0	0	0	0	0	0	0
Total	11	11	12	13	13	19	20	20
Long-term liabilities								
Long-term debt	500	500	500	500	1,500	1,500	1,500	1,500
Pension obligations	0	0	0	0	0	0	0	0
Total	500	500	500	500	1,500	1,500	1,500	1,500
Owner equity								
Share capital paid up	550	550	550	550	550	550	550	550
P&L A/C b/f	0	-152	-177	-119	-35	27	112	251
P&L this year	-152	-25	58	84	62	85	139	203
less dividends paid	0	0	0	0	0	0	0	0
P&L A/C	-152	-177	-119	-35	27	112	251	454
Total	398	373	431	515	577	662	801	1,004
TOTAL LIABILITIES	**909**	**884**	**943**	**1,028**	**2,090**	**2,181**	**2,321**	**2,524**
Check: Total assets less liabilities	0	0	0	0	0	0	0	0
	Yes!	*Yes!*	*Yes!*	*Yes!*	*Yes!*	*Yes!*	*Yes!*	*Yes!*

Essential checklist on financials and forecasts

Draw up a set of financial forecasts rooted in a strategic context. Let your backer see that your analysis of market demand and supply (Chapters 3 and 4 of your plan) and your firm's strategy and resource deployment (Chapters 5 and 6) translate rationally into the numbers of this Chapter 7.

You should produce the following:

- **A forecast P&L account** – where the sales will be framed in a market demand context and profit margins in an industry competition context.

- **A forecast cash flow statement** – where the capital expenditure needed to drive the profit growth in the P&L account will be evident and framed in the analysis of resource development of Chapter 6.

- **A forecast balance sheet** – which will show how your forecasts can be achieved with the assumed capital structure (the balance of debt and equity).

Finally, set out the big financial risks and opportunities that may impact on your business plan.

Note: Here's a plea to you, the reader. Please do not load your business plan with irrelevant financial detail! In particular:

- Do not lay out monthly financial forecasts unless your business is in trouble or is a start-up. If your business has serious cash difficulties, monthly data will be needed. If not, annual is fine. If yours is a start-up, showing monthly data for the first three months, quarterly to the end of the year and by year thenceforth should be fine.

- Do not burden your backer with spurious accuracy in your forecasts. Sales in three years' time will emphatically not be £1,654,729.43, so don't say that; they will not even be £1,654,729 and they almost certainly will not be £1,655,000; they may perhaps be of the order of £1.66 million. Three, or a maximum four, significant figures are all that are needed to convey the sense of whether or not your plan is backable.

Less is more. Less detail yields more clarity.

8

Risk, opportunity and sensitivity

❝ When written in Chinese the word crisis is composed of two characters. One represents danger, and the other represents opportunity.

John F. Kennedy

In this chapter

- Meet the Suns and Clouds chart
- What the suns and clouds tell you
  - Extraordinary risk
  - The balance
  - Bankers and investors see different skies
- Sensitivity testing

Y ou're almost there. You have set out the market context in which your firm exists, how it is positioned in that market and how your strategy will deploy the firm's resources over the next few years. You have developed a set of financial forecasts that are consistent with that context.

All you need do now is set out what could go wrong with these forecasts – and also what could go even more right with them.

In other words, what are the risks and opportunities behind those forecasts? And how likely are those risks and opportunities to occur? And, if they did, what impact would they have?

The good news is that you've already done the work. Not some of it, not even much of it, but all of it. At the end of each chapter of your business plan you have pulled out the risks and opportunities you have encountered. And not just any old risks and opportunities, but the *big* ones.

We defined in Chapter 3 a *big* risk (or opportunity) as one where:

- the likelihood of occurrence is medium (or high) *and* impact is high
- the likelihood of occurrence is high *and* impact is medium (or high).

You have gathered all these big risks and opportunities along the way, relating to market demand (Chapter 3 of your plan), industry competition (Chapter 4), your firm's competitive position and strategy (Chapter 5), your firm's resources (Chapter 6) and your financial forecasts (Chapter 7). All you need to do now is assemble them, weigh them up and address the key question: do the opportunities surpass the risks?

And I have just the tool to help you with that.

Meet the Suns and Clouds chart

I first created the Suns and Clouds chart in the early 1990s. Since then I've seen it reproduced in various forms in reports by my consulting competitors. They say imitation is the sincerest form of flattery, but I still kick myself that I didn't copyright it back then!

The reason it keeps getting copied is that it works. It manages to encapsulate in one chart conclusions on the relative importance of all the main issues in the plan. It shows, diagrammatically, whether the opportunities (the suns) outshine the risks (the clouds). Or vice versa, when the clouds overshadow the suns. In short, in one chart, it tells you whether your plan is backable. Or not.

The chart (see Figure 8.1) forces you to view each risk (and opportunity) from two perspectives: how likely it is to happen; and how big an impact it would have if it did. You don't need to quantify the impact, but instead have some idea of the notional, relative impact of each issue on the value of the firm.

In the chart, risks are represented as clouds, opportunities as suns. The more likely a risk (or opportunity) is to happen the further to the right you should place it along the horizontal axis. In Figure 8.1, risk D is the most likely to happen, and risk B the least likely.

The bigger the impact a risk (or opportunity) would have if it were to happen, the higher you should place it up the vertical axis. In the same chart, opportunity B would have the largest impact and opportunity C the smallest.

For each risk (and opportunity), you need to place it in the appropriate position on the chart, taking into account *both* factors – its likelihood *and* its impact.

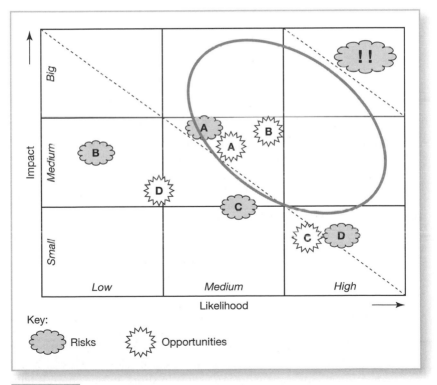

figure 8.1   **The Suns and Clouds chart**

Don't worry if things don't make that much sense initially. This chart changes with further thought and discussion. *Always.* Arguably its greatest virtue is that it serves as a stimulus to discussion. I have often given PowerPoint presentations of 100 slides or so, with no more than a couple of questions for clarification every now and then. Then when the Suns and Clouds chart comes up, towards the end of the presentation, it can remain on the screen for half an hour or more. It stimulates discussion and provokes amendment. A client may choose to debate for 10, maybe 15 minutes the precise positioning of one risk, or opportunity, *and what can be done to shift its position favourably.*

Remember, you cannot be exact in this chart. Nor do you need to be. It is a pictorial representation of risk and opportunity, designed to give you a *feel* for the balance of risk and opportunity in your business.

It is up to you whether you include a Suns and Clouds chart in your business plan – 99% of plans won't have anything like it. If you include it, your plan will be distinctive, special, backer-sensitive. But if you're grilled on it, will you be able to respond vigorously?

Whether or not you include the chart doesn't matter. The critical thing is the thought process. You *must* try to visualise the balance of risk and opportunity inherent in your plan. You must separate out those risks and opportunities of little significance from those of great significance. You must screen out the background chatter and let the metaphorical voices of the main proponents of risk and opportunity be heard – and may the most convincing win.

Because this is what your backers will do. They, or their advisers, may well use a tool like the Suns and Clouds chart, but, whether they do or don't, for sure they will be assessing risk and opportunity. That's their job. It's what they do, day in, day out. Whether analytically or instinctively, that's how your backer thinks.

And you must be prepared to answer from the same perspective.

Essential tip

The last of the Seven Cs that make for a good business plan is to be convincing. It is in your analysis of risk and opportunity that you need to be just that. If you can convince your reader that the opportunities facing your business outshine the risks, you may have a backer.

What the suns and clouds tell you

The Suns and Clouds chart tells you two main things about how backable your plan is: whether there are any *extraordinary* risks (or opportunities); and whether the overall *balance* of risk and opportunity is favourable.

Extraordinary risk

Take a look at the top right-hand corner of Figure 8.1. There's a heavy thundercloud there, with two exclamation marks. That's a risk that is both very likely *and* very big. It's a showstopper risk. If your backer finds one of them in your plan, that's it. It's unbackable.

The closer a cloud gets to that thundercloud, the worse news it is. Risks that hover around the diagonal (from the top left to the bottom right corners) can be handled, as long as they are balanced by opportunities. But as soon as a cloud starts creeping towards that thundercloud – for example, to around where opportunity B is placed – that's when your backer starts to get itchy feet.

But imagine a bright shining sun in that spot where the thundercloud is. That's terrific news, and your backers will be falling over themselves to invest.

It's not unusual for a backer to find a showstopper risk. Think of the excellent BBC TV programme, *Dragons' Den*. Most aspirant entrepreneurs leave with no investment. Often it's just one risk that turns off the Dragons. It may be incredulity that anyone would buy such a product or service. Or that the entrepreneur has been trying for so long, or has invested so much, for such little result. Or the product is too costly to yield a profit. Each is a risk that the Dragons see as highly likely and with big impact. Each is a top right-hand corner thundercloud, a showstopper.

Some risks are huge but most unlikely to happen. That's not to say that they won't happen. The unlikely can happen. But these are not showstopper risks. They are top *left*-hand corner risks. If we worried about the unlikely happening we would never cross the road. Certainly no backer would ever invest a penny!

In the autumn of 2001, my colleagues and I were advising a client on whether to back a company involved in airport operations. After the first week of work, we produced an interim report and a first-cut Suns and Clouds chart. In the top left-hand corner box, we placed a risk entitled 'major air incident'. We were thinking of a serious air crash that might lead to the prolonged grounding of a common class of aircraft. It seemed unlikely but would have a very large impact if it happened. Then 9/11 came just a few days later. We never envisaged anything so catastrophic, so inconceivably evil, but at least we had alerted our client to the extreme risks involved in the air industry. The deal was renegotiated and completed successfully.

The balance

In general, for most investment decisions, there's no showstopper risk. The main purpose of the Suns and Clouds chart will then be to present the *balance* of risk and opportunity. Do the opportunities surpass the risks? Given the overall picture, are the suns more favourably placed than the clouds? Or do the clouds overshadow the suns?

The way to assess a Suns and Clouds chart is to look first at the general area above the diagonal and in the direction of the thundercloud. This is the area covered in Figure 8.1 by the parabola. Any risk (or opportunity) there is worthy of note: it's at least reasonably likely to occur *and* would have at least a reasonable impact.

Those risks and opportunities below the diagonal are less important. Either they are of low to medium likelihood *and* of low to medium impact, or they're not big enough, or not likely enough, to be of major concern.

A backer will look at the pattern of suns in this area of the parabola and compare it with the pattern of clouds. The closer each sun and cloud to the thundercloud, the more important it is. If the pattern of suns seems better placed than the pattern of clouds, your backer will be comforted. If the clouds overshadow the suns, they will be concerned.

In Figure 8.1, there are two clouds and two suns above the diagonal. But risk D lies outside the parabola. The best placed is opportunity B. Risk A and opportunity A more or less balance each other out, likewise other risks and opportunities. Opportunity B seems distinctly clear of the pack. The opportunities seem to surpass the risks. The business looks backable.

One of the best features of the Suns and Clouds chart is that it can be made dynamic. If the balance of risk and opportunity shown on the chart is unfavourable, you may be able to do something about it – and the chart will show this clearly.

For every risk, there are mitigating factors. Many, including those relating to market demand and competition, will be beyond your control

– though some you may be able to insure against. Those relating to your firm's competitive position, however, you may well be able to influence. There may be initiatives that can be undertaken to improve competitiveness and lower the risk. Some risks, indeed, may be wholly within your firm's control. You may even be able to eliminate them from the chart.

Likewise, there may be opportunities where your firm's chances of realising them can be enhanced through some initiative.

Risk mitigation or opportunity enhancement in the Suns and Clouds chart can be illuminated with arrows and target signs. They'll show where your firm should aim for and remind you that it's a target. It will improve the overall balance of risk in your plan.

Essential example

The Beatles' risks and opportunities

If you were a music producer at Parlophone in the first few months of 1962, would you have backed the Beatles? Remember that this was a distinguished record company that had never previously backed any rock 'n' roll artists. At the time, there were dozens of young rock 'n' roll groups with persistent promoters doing the rounds of the studios. One such group, the Beatles, had done a couple of tours in Hamburg and had developed a bit of a following at a nightclub in their home town of Liverpool.

You knew that one other record company, Decca, had shown some interest but had turned them down in favour of a similar group, Brian Poole and the Tremeloes. Some Decca executives also believed – in a now classic quote – that 'guitar groups are on the way out'. For your studio's first venture into rock 'n' roll, would you have chosen these four mop-topped lads from Liverpool? Let's look at their suns and clouds in Figure 8.2.

It couldn't have been an easy decision. On the one hand, there were so many wannabe groups around (risk 3) and the Beatles seemed unexceptional musically (risk 5). On the other hand, they seemed to have charisma and humour (opportunity 2). And, on the back of their Hamburg experience, they had built a loyal following among

▶

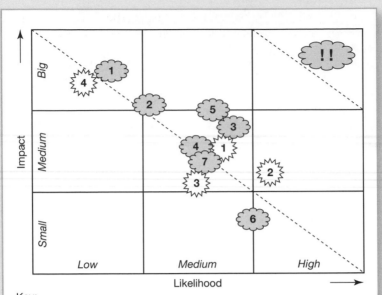

Key:

 Risks   Opportunities

1 Stuck in the 1950s   1 May be popular, as in Liverpool?
2 Risk to Parlophone's image   2 They have humour and charisma
3 Many similar in Liverpool alone 3 A catchy name
4 Members chopping and   4 Writers and composers?
  changing
5 Unexceptional musicians
6 Silly mop-top hairstyles
7 Drinking and swearing on stage

figure 8.2 **Risks and opportunities facing the Beatles, early 1962**

club-goers in Liverpool (opportunity 1). These may have been the
four issues that stood out, two risks and two opportunities, above
the diagonal, within the parabola (as shown in Figure 8.1).

No one would blame you, you would have thought, if you turned
these guys down. Yet you had a hunch. They seemed to have
something. Maybe they could improve their musical abilities.
Maybe they could be marketed. Maybe some of the risks could be

mitigated – perhaps they could develop their singing and songwriting capabilities, and bin (contractually) their drinking and swearing on stage. You backed them.

As a postscript to this tale, let's envisage how the backing decision would have changed one year later, in spring 1963. After the release of their first album, would you have backed the Beatles? You know the answer, but it's fun to think what the Suns and Clouds chart would now look like.

One year on, the Beatles' first single *Love Me Do* had reached the UK Top 20. Their second single, *Please Please Me,* and their first album, of the same name, were riding high as number ones in both the single and album charts. Was this a flash in the pan? Would these guys come and go with little trace like many before them?

You weren't to know then that their album would stay at number 1 for 30 weeks, before being replaced by, yes, their second album! That their fourth single, *She Loves You,* would become the biggest seller of all time, topping hits by their role model, Elvis Presley, and would remain so for more than a decade.

What you did know was that you'd sure made the right decision the year before. You had also greatly underestimated them as musicians. They could write and compose catchy songs. The Suns and Clouds chart was transformed – see Figure 8.3.

All the risks in the earlier Suns and Clouds chart had retreated left-wards into insignificance. Even the risk of the four members splitting up was greatly reduced. Meanwhile the opportunities were dazzling. Their popularity as performers had soared. Their potential as song-writers was astonishing. And to cap it all, a new, huge opportunity had arisen (opportunity 5). Could they conceivably become the first British group to wow a US audience?

Would you have backed the Beatles in the spring of 1963? The suns and clouds say it all. Would you play the lottery if you knew what numbers were coming up?

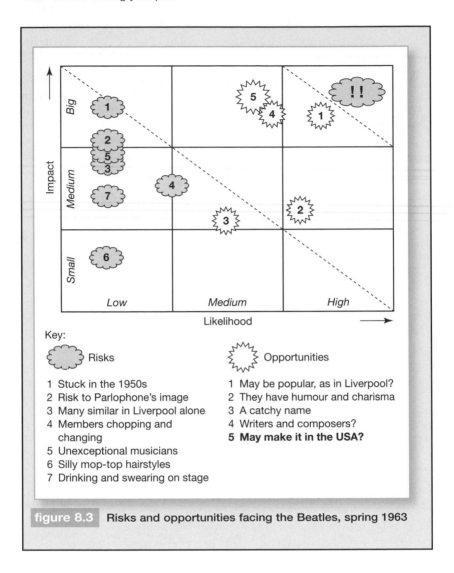

figure 8.3 Risks and opportunities facing the Beatles, spring 1963

Bankers and investors see different skies

The Suns and Clouds chart can be shown to any backer, whether your board, an investor or a lender. But they will view it from different perspectives.

Bankers will focus on the clouds. They will want to know what can go wrong. Then they'll want to know what can go seriously wrong. They may even want to know what happens when everything goes wrong.

Investors will also be interested in the clouds, but will focus on the suns. They'll want to know what you can do to shift these suns up and to the right.

Same chart, different perspectives. The risks and opportunities faced by the entrepreneur translate into the risks and returns analysed by the financiers. Bankers like low risk for which they are prepared to accept a relatively low return. Investors seek a higher return, for which they are prepared to accept higher risk.

It's all there on the Suns and Clouds chart.

Essential example

Woolworths' risks and opportunities

It still seems inconceivable that Woolworths is no more. Even though Frank Woolworth started the group in Pennsylvania in 1879, opening in Liverpool in 1909, it came to feel like a very British company. We grew up with Woolies – we shopped there for Pick 'n' Mix sweets and toys as children, for records/cassettes/CDs as youngsters, for cheap crockery as students, for Ladybird and school clothes as parents and, of course, for sweets and toys for the kids, the grandkids, and so on. The New Cross branch was the site of one of the most tragic incidents on British soil during the Second World War, when a direct hit from a German V-2 rocket killed 168. Yet Woolies is gone, in the very year it was to celebrate its one hundredth anniversary.

It was the financial crash in the autumn of 2008 that drove the final nail into Woolworth's coffin. There had been plenty of nails before then, yet Woolies remained a major force on the high street. It was the market leader in sweets, number two in entertainment and toys, number four in homewares and number five in children's clothes. Overall, it turned over £2 billion and was the UK's eighth biggest retailer. How could it have been put up for sale for just £1?

Imagine you were advising a turnaround specialist on buying it as a going concern. What was the balance of risk and opportunity? A Suns and Clouds chart (indicative, drawn up with no inside information) may help – see Figure 8.4.

It is not a pretty sight, the clouds are omnipresent. No investor would back a risk profile like that, even with a clean balance sheet. The main item of value would have been the online business – and that

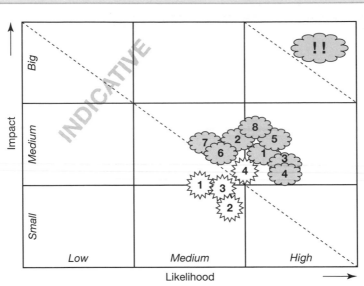

figure 8.4 **Risks and opportunities facing Woolworths, late 2008**

was bought separately by Shop Direct (formerly Littlewoods), who also took the Ladybird brand.

Woolworths had failed to adapt to meet changing consumer tastes. For the fast-moving entertainment items it stocked, it struggled to compete on price with the supermarkets. It could not provide a broader range like the specialist entertainment retailers, because the likes of Virgin, Our Price, Tower, Zavvi and HMV were themselves being usurped, first by e-commerce and then by downloading. Finally Woolworths' positioning constrained it from competing purely on price like Poundland and its successors. Sadly, Woolies had become a relic of yesteryear.

Sensitivity testing

The y-axis in the Suns and Clouds chart specifies impact on cash flow, or impact on value. But the chart is looking only for *relative* impact, in the sense that one risk will have a greater impact than another.

But your backer may be interested in *specific* impact. They may want you to quantify one or more risks or opportunities, to put actual figures on them.

Indeed, you would be wise to pre-empt your backer's question and prepare some quantified impacts in advance. This is sensitivity testing. You test the financial statements to see how they change in response to a specific risk or opportunity or a general adjustment.

This is easy to do, assuming you have built up your financial forecasts on Excel or with specialist software. You should be able simply to plug in an amended value for the parameter to your spreadsheet and see the impact ripple down to the bottom line on your financial statements.

Pull out three or four big risks, assign specific, quantitative impacts to them and observe the effects on your P&L and cash flow forecasts. Also stick in a couple of general risks beloved by bankers, such as operating costs up by 5% or expenditure on a key capital project up by 20%. Then take a look at the output and see how sensitive the financial forecasts are to these scenarios.

For an example of sensitivity analysis, see that for our Dart Valley case study below.

Finally, you may choose to prepare a 'downside case' for your banker – one where you combine two, three or more risks and examine their cumulative impact. But beware. No matter how conservative and unlikely your downside case may emerge, the guys on the bank's credit committee will go further. They will assume bigger impacts on more risks, until your P&L resembles a battleground.

So go gently in your downside case. And balance it with an upside case, where the opportunities in your Suns and Clouds chart materialise and/or have a bigger impact than in your base case financial forecasts.

At the end of the day, your base case forecasts are what you believe are most likely to happen. They have been drawn up coherently in a market and competitive context. Stand by them, defend them resolutely against undue pessimism and counter the latter by highlighting similarly irrational optimism.

Essential tip

Stay realistic in your sensitivity testing. In the old days, that was taken for granted. Each test took many minutes of laborious manual calculation, so only meaningful tests were contemplated. Nowadays, with electronic spreadsheets, any test can be done in a millisecond. Don't do tests on improbable values or scenarios – they will aggravate your backer. Stick to the reasonably likely.

Essential case study
The Dart Valley Guest House and Oriental Spa business plan, 2015

Chapter 8: Risk, opportunity and sensitivity

Dick and Kay Jones are quite surprised when they set out their Suns and Clouds chart. All the way through drawing up the business plan, Kay has been diligent in teasing out of Dick the main risks, whether arising from market demand and industry competition or from Dart Valley's strategy, resources and financials.

They have tried to envisage how a banker would view things and feel they have been conservative, much more so than when they started the venture four years before.

Yet when they draw up their Suns and Clouds chart (see Figure 8.5), it looks so sunny, so favourable. Have they over-egged it, they wonder?

Perhaps not. Most of the risks they have identified have been of low probability and/or of low impact. They have not been *big* risks, as defined above. Only one seems to merit placing to the right of the diagonal – a slower build-up of occupancy than in the plan (risk 6 in Figure 8.5).

On the other hand, there is one opportunity, one sun (opportunity 2) that shines all on its own – the Dart Valley concept, proven in Phase I, due to be rolled out and made more financially viable in Phase II.

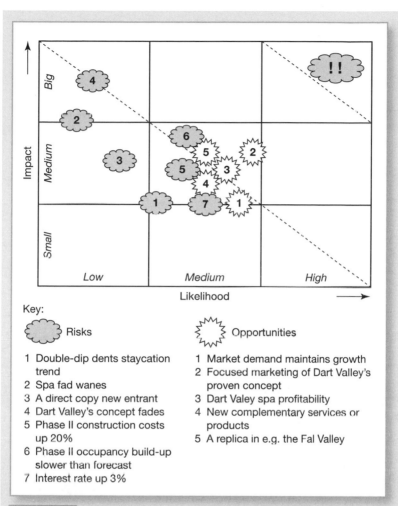

figure 8.5 **Risks and opportunities facing Dart Valley**

Other opportunities that offset risk 6 are the transformation of Dart Valley's spa services to a profitable segment in its own right (opportunity 3), rather than a loss leader for the accommodation segment, and the introduction of complementary services and products (opportunity 4), such as day trips, sporting trips and aromatherapy products.

Finally, there is the opportunity to replicate Dart Valley's success (opportunity 5). Dick and Kay have already identified a rambling, characterful B&B business nestled into the Fal Valley in Cornwall that would be ideal and whose owners are planning to retire in a couple of years. Even if the timing of that particular deal doesn't work out, there will be other properties on the market when the time is right for Dick and Kay.

Dart Valley is a lovely business. It has a healthy P&L, assets that the most conservative of bankers will lend against and forecast cash flows that more adventurous bankers and equity investors would find attractive.

Whether or not this is a business that can attract 100% debt finance for this Phase II investment is an altogether different issue. While opportunities seem to outshine risks, it is also a business that is highly geared operationally – in other words, it has a high proportion of fixed cost. That's good news when things go well, but not so good when things go poorly.

Dick figures that bankers will need to see some stress testing of certain key parameters, especially those flagged in the Suns and Clouds chart. He does some sensitivity testing, as shown in Table 8.1.

The impact on profit before tax (PBT) from inflated Phase II construction costs of 20% seems limited and containable, Dick thinks – and, of course, there is only a minor cash flow impact in later years resulting from higher depreciation/lower tax. The impact is mainly felt in the year of occurrence, 2016, when financing for an incremental cash outflow of £200,000 would need to be found.

table 8.1   Dart Valley sensitivity testing

	Profit before tax (£000)		Cash flow (£000)	
	2017	2019	2017	2019
Business plan	107	256	244	375
Sensitivity tests				
Phase II construction costs up 20%	94	243	247	377
Occupancy rates down 15%	–6	113	164	273
Both of the above	–19	100	167	276

If occupancy rates turn out to be 15% below plan – for example, 51% in 2017 instead of the forecast 60% – the impact on P&L is much greater. The P&L in 2017 drops into the red and the profit forecast for 2019 is halved. Cash flow, however, remains positive, though shrunken.

Dick can show that such a drop is unlikely. A 51% overall occupancy rate in 2017 would imply a level of just 23% in the new rooms of Phase II (compared to a forecast 44% in the business plan), yet Dart Valley managed to achieve 39% occupancy in its first year of operations in 2012.

However, Dick understands that bankers tend to look at things rather more gloomily. They may view risk 6 in the Suns and Clouds chart as of higher probability. It will be quite a challenge to get 100% debt financing, he figures, but he'll give it a go.

Essential checklist on risk, opportunity and sensitivity

Set out and weigh up the big risks and opportunities facing the achievement of your business plan, by considering the following:

- Their likelihood of occurrence
- Their impact on cash flow if they do occur.

Use the Suns and Clouds tool to do this, at least for yourself. You do not have to include it in the plan.

Assure your backer of two fundamentals on the nature of their risk

- There is no showstopper risk in your plan.
- On balance, opportunities to beat your plan surpass the risks faced.

Finally, quantify certain key risks and opportunities and assess their impact on the financial forecasts in a sensitivity analysis. Show that your cash flow forecasts are able to withstand the impact of reasonable adverse assumptions derived from specified risks.

Show that your plan is robust and backable.

9

Conclusion

❝❝ Drive thy business or it will drive thee.

Benjamin Franklin

In this chapter

- Conclusion
- Executive summary
- Investment highlights

Y ou are all but there! All that is left now are a conclusion and an executive summary. And possibly an investment highlights section. Hopefully you have saved your best until last. These sections must be punchy. They should knock out your backer!

Conclusion

This is the fun bit. All, yes, *all* the hard work has already been done. In each chapter you've had to do some serious research and thinking – about market demand, competition, strategy, resources, financials and risk.

All you need do now is take your headline conclusions from each of those chapters and weave them into a coherent storyline. One that puts the case for obtaining backing in full context. In half a page.

You should set the storyline out as follows:

The overall conclusion on why your business is worthy of backing (in which you summarise, preferably in bold, the main findings from the headlines below):

- *Market demand prospects.* State your conclusions on what's going to happen to market demand, by key business segment (Chapter 3 of your plan).

- *Competition.* Your conclusions on whether competition is intense and set to get tougher (Chapter 4).

- *Strategy.* Your conclusions on your firm's competitive position and its strategy for further developing competitive advantage (Chapter 5).

- *Resources.* Your conclusions on the resources your firm will deploy to implement that strategy and meet its goals (Chapter 6).

- *Financials and forecasts.* Your conclusions on how your firm will grow revenues and operating margin over the next few years (Chapter 7).

- *Risk, opportunity and sensitivity.* Your conclusions on why opportunities before your firm outshine risks in your plan (Chapter 8).

You can either develop these conclusions into half a page's worth of normal text or just set out your conclusion in the above format, with one overall conclusion supported by six bulleted sentences.

If you choose the latter format, make it super-concise. Force yourself to get right to the point. *Each bullet point should be no more than one sentence.* It can have a couple of commas, with some back-up qualifying phrases, if necessary – maybe even a dash or a colon. But just the one sentence.

The more long-winded you make this storyline, the more difficult it will be for the backer to see how you have derived your overall conclusion. The conclusion itself should also be just the one sentence. It should answer the question: *why is this plan worthy of backing?*

Essential tip

Save the best until last. Make your conclusion punchy. And remember the Seven Cs – make it clear, crisp, concise, consistent, coherent, credible and convincing.

Essential case study
The Dart Valley Guest House and Oriental Spa business plan, 2015

Chapter 9: Conclusion

Dick has come to the end of his business plan for Phase II of his Dart Valley business. He has thoroughly enjoyed working on it – every page he has relished and imbued with a passion for the business he genuinely feels. He's going to miss it.

Here is his crisp, concise, six-bulleted conclusion.

Dart Valley is distinctive, well placed in a growing market and poised to become a leading, highly profitable provider of spa services in South Devon, with opportunities to exploit a proven concept outshining risks of construction cost overrun or slower build-up of occupancy:

- *Market demand prospects.* The market for West Country tourism was boosted temporarily by the staycation effect during the economic downturn and should hold firm over the next few years, faring better in the three- and four-star category.
- *Competition.* The industry is competitive, with low barriers to entry, but with the most highly differentiated businesses thriving, with above average occupancy levels.

- *Strategy.* The Dart Valley is distinctive in its stunning location and oriental offering, has achieved a favourable to strong competitive position in three years, with room occupancy budgeted at 75% in 2015, and is poised to become the leading provider of spa services in South Devon with the planned Phase II investment.

- *Resources.* The £1.05 million Phase II investment will add 16 rooms to Dart Valley's current 17-room capacity, plus a swimming pool, and involve a doubling of staff and a return to the marketing levels of the early days of Phase I.

- *Financials and forecasts.* Dart Valley's sales are forecast almost to double by 2019, greatly surpassing the planned 50% increase in overhead and boosting profitability from 2015's budgeted 21.6% operating margin to 34%.

- *Risk, opportunity and sensitivity.* The opportunity to exploit Dart Valley's proven concept outshines the main risks of construction cost overrun or a slower than anticipated occupancy build-up.

That should do the trick, thinks Dick. Time to collar the bank manager.

Executive summary

The executive summary, to become Chapter 1 of your business plan, is an extended version of the conclusion, no more, no less.

It should have the same overall conclusion, perhaps even the same one sentence, but instead of one sentence per bullet it should have a couple of paragraphs for each.

The executive summary should be two pages of A4 text, perhaps three or four including tables and/or charts. At six paragraphs per page, that gives you an average of two paragraphs per bullet. One or two bullets might merit more than two paragraphs, others fewer.

Again, as for the conclusion in your Chapter 9, remember that you must be clear, concise and convincing in your executive summary.

Don't fall into the trap of dismissing the executive summary as a drag. You are presenting a case for why your firm is worthy of gaining backing. Your case will be well researched and analysed, but it must also be well presented. Nowhere is presentation more important than in the executive summary. For all readers it will be the first few pages they read. Some senior decision-makers in your board or bank will read nothing else.

Spend time on it, nurture it, hone it and edit it remorselessly, even give it to a professional to edit. It may be the best investment you make.

Once perfected, it becomes Chapter 1 of your business plan.

Let's take another look at the executive summary of the Dart Valley case study, shown at the outset of this book in Chapter 1. Hopefully it will give you an idea of how to make your plan crisp, coherent, convincing – and backable!

Essential case study
The Dart Valley Guest House and Oriental Spa business plan, 2015

Chapter 1: Executive summary

The Dart Valley Guest House and Oriental Spa ('Dart Valley') is a destination with a difference. It is set overlooking a spectacularly beautiful valley in South Devon and yet offers visitors a touch of the Orient in its rooms, cuisine and spa. It has 17 rooms for hire, with spa and restaurant facilities also open to day visitors. It turned over £513,000 in 2014, having grown by 36% per year since 2012, and operating margin is expected to top 20% in 2015. Further investment of £1.05 million in a 16-room extension and a swimming pool is forecast to double sales by 2019 and boost operating margin to 34%. Opportunities to exploit a proven concept outshine risks of cost overrun or slower build-up of occupancy.

Dart Valley has three main business segments – rooms, catering and the spa. Room revenues have been growing fastest, at 45% per year, with spa revenues (20% of total) slower (at 18% per year) due to buoyant custom from non-resident visitors from the start and subsequent capacity limitations, to be eased with the planned Phase II development.

The market for West Country tourism was worth £225 million in 2014 (Source: VisitBritain). Key long-term drivers are the growth in UK population and per capita incomes and the propensity for people to take multiple holidays each year. The main short-term driver since 2008 was the boost to domestic tourism caused by the financial crisis – the so-called staycation effect. This reversed in 2013–14 with the recovery in the economy and overseas holidays, and the market can be expected to remain flat over the next few years.

There are many excellent hotels, guest houses and B&Bs throughout Devon and the West Country. The industry is competitive, with low barriers to entry, with occupancy rates, depending on size and location, improving over time and with the most highly differentiated businesses thriving and enjoying repeat custom. Spa facilities are less widespread in rural Devon than in a big city like Plymouth, but there are good spas to be found in neighbouring Torquay and Totnes. Restaurants offering oriental cuisine, namely Chinese, Thai, Japanese and Vietnamese, can also be found in either one or both towns.

The Dart Valley Guest House is distinctive in two main ways: it enjoys a spectacular location atop one of the most beautiful valleys in England; and it has an oriental theme. The theme is understated, with a hint of the Orient applied to the bedroom decor and oriental treatments available, in addition to standard ones, at the spa. Oriental cuisine is offered in the restaurant, but so too is European fare. The customer is given the choice. In the three years since opening in December 2011, occupancy rates at the Dart Valley have grown from 39% to 56% to 71% and are budgeted conservatively for 75% this year. Restaurant take-up by overnight visitors has risen to 35% of visitor nights and spa occupancy to 26%, both above budget.

Dick and Kay Jones bought the freehold to the premises in 2010 for £715,000, against which they took on a mortgage of £500,000, and spent a further £280,000 of their own funds on renovation. The owners work full-time in the business and employ a staff of three full-time equivalents, with part-time help added as appropriate. Spa professionals are contracted as required.

The business broke even at the operating profit level during 2013, the second year of operations, and achieved a profit before tax of 11% in 2014, budgeted to rise to 15% this year. The owners believe that profitability will be greatly boosted with the planned Phase II expansion, costing £1.05 million for a new building with 16 rooms and an outdoor, heated swimming pool. Overheads, other than financing costs, will rise by 50%, but revenues, once occupancy rates return to today's levels by (conservatively) 2019, will have almost doubled. Operating margin, assuming no change in directors' remuneration, is forecast to reach 34% by 2019 and profit before tax 24%. The speed of growth will continue to yield challenges of cash flow, and the owners will look to their backer to provide the necessary flexibility of finance.

The key risks to this plan are a slower build-up of occupancy, whether caused by a further drop in staycation tourism as economic recovery gathers pace, the opening of direct competition, a peaking of interest in the offering or insufficient awareness, slippage in construction works and the health of the owners – all of which are examined in depth in the plan and found to be containable.

Upside opportunities lie in raising occupancy rates higher than in the plan through marketing focused on exploiting a proven concept, the introduction of new, complementary services or products, lift-off in the spa segment profitability and the acquisition of another site (Phase III), like one identified in the Fal Valley, to replicate the oriental spa concept in Cornwall.

In conclusion, the Dart Valley has established itself as a serious player in the West Country tourism industry, offering visitors something very special. It is now poised, through this expansion, to become the leading player in spa services in South Devon and make healthy profits. Its owners seek a financial partner who shares this vision.

Investment highlights

There is one final element that may need to be added. If the purpose of your business plan is to raise equity finance, and especially if you are seeking to sell your company, you might consider including a section on investment highlights.

I don't take to investment highlights sections. As an adviser to financiers I treat them with suspicion. They can reek of sales spiel. I tend to skim through them and move on to the plan proper.

But they are common. They are often found in a Confidential Information Memorandum (CIM), a document typically put together in an auction situation by the corporate finance adviser to the vendor of part or all of a company's equity.

The CIM itself is a sale document. Good ones will transpose what is in management's business plan into a CIM format, while retaining the balance found in the business plan. Risks will be addressed and measures to mitigate them set out. They will not be swept under the carpet.

A bad CIM is a miserable affair. It reads like the sale particulars of a dodgy estate agent. Everything that is good about a company will be in there, and exaggerated. Anything not so good will be absent. It will resemble the classic sale particular which waxes lyrical about the spacious rooms of this semi-detached Edwardian house, but omits to mention that it is sited alongside a dual carriageway. The house 'might benefit from some updating', meaning the roof needs replacing and the interior should be gutted, with the electrics, heating, plumbing and plastering all best redone before you even think of redecorating.

If a CIM is bad, imagine what its investment highlights section is like! It is the rock hard sell section of a hard sell document! I have seen some horrors over the years. How about these (suitably disguised):

■ 'ABC addresses a booming market, one that has doubled in the last three years' – yes, and it was on the verge of falling off a cliff (due to huge imminent overcapacity in undersea transatlantic cables)!

■ 'DEF is the only UK based producer' yes, all others had withdrawn from the market due to a structural inability to compete with low-cost, well-engineered product from the Far East!

■ 'GHI is the leading player in the dental segment of this market' – yes, but demand for this product in the dental segment was limited and accounted for all of 3% of the company's sales!

If you are going to insert an investment highlights section, here are some tips:

■ *Don't reproduce the executive summary* – keep it short and sharp; restrict yourself to half a dozen bullets, maximum 10. These bullets should highlight the key reasons why a backer would choose to inject scarce resources into your company rather than in a host of other companies.

■ *Don't have a separate chapter* – just drop a text box into the middle of the executive summary chapter; the investment highlights section will of course duplicate some of what is in the executive summary, but both must be stand-alone texts – one summarising the business plan and one pulling out the main attractions for an investor.

■ *Don't mislead* – if you're found out, you'll have no deal, no matter how good your company is, how sound your business plan or how attractive the return on investment.

Let your investment highlights section be a brief venture into sales blurb, albeit in a soft, understated tone, in an otherwise rational, factual and balanced business plan.

Essential case study
The Dart Valley Guest House and Oriental Spa business plan, 2015

Investment highlights

Dick Jones is hoping to raise the funds needed for the Dart Valley Phase II project from his bank. He recognises, however, that his bank manager may well demand more of an equity cushion in case things veer from plan.

Dick is prepared therefore to insert the text below in a box into the executive summary chapter of his business plan. Reluctant as they would be to part with 15–20% of the family equity in Dart Valley, he and Kay would pay that price to see Phase II get underway. These investment highlights seem about right, he thinks, not too hard a sell, but nevertheless compelling.

Investment highlights

The Dart Valley Guest House and Oriental Spa business exhibits these value drivers:

■ A distinctive tourism offering in an area of outstanding natural beauty

■ Recession-proof market

■ 75% room occupancy rate after four years of operation

■ Proven management

■ Phase II investment of £1.05m in extra room capacity and a swimming pool to make it the leading spa provider in the region

- Sales forecast to almost double by 2019
- Operating profit forecast to rise by 2019 to £360,000, a margin of 34%, up from 15% in 2015
- Potential to replicate concept elsewhere in the West Country

The owners are seeking to raise £350,000 in equity finance in exchange for a minority shareholding. This represents an exceptional investment opportunity.

3

Using your plan

10

Pitching your plan

> There are worse things in life than death. Have you ever spent an evening with an insurance salesman?
>
> *Woody Allen*

In this chapter

- Focusing the content
- Using PowerPoint
- Delivering the message

You have a plan. It is clear, crisp, concise, consistent, coherent, credible and convincing. It sails the Seven Cs. Job done?

Not quite. Now you need to sell it.

This should be the easy part. After all, the plan has been written from the perspective of the backer. So all you need to do is stick it in the backer's lap and, hey presto, it's a yes?

In theory, perhaps. In practice, the process can be greatly facilitated if you do some modest selling.

The place to do that is in the pitch. And the first thing to remember about a pitch is that it is but one form of public speaking.

Public speaking at its most extreme is standing on a soapbox at Speakers' Corner in Hyde Park, London, and spouting interminably about whatever you want. Or picture David Lloyd George addressing the multitude, in his frock coat, winged collar and flowing white locks, mesmerising his flock with Celtic passion and oratory.

At its other extreme public speaking is communicating one on one, namely conversing. Somewhere in the middle is standing on your feet and addressing an audience of three, four or even a dozen on the merits of your business plan.

That means that you need to follow some basic guidelines of public speaking for your pitch. I have written a whole book on this, *Stand, Speak, Deliver! 37 Short Speeches on How to Survive – and Thrive – in Public Speaking and Presenting* (Little Brown, 2015). This is a book designed as much to entertain as inform, but let me summarise below its key points as they relate to the pitch.

Focusing the content

The first golden rule in public speaking is to know your audience.

If you are delivering a speech to the Women's Institute, bin the raunchy jokes. Or maybe stick one or two in? Do some research – find out how much titillation is just right for the blue-rinse brigade!

If you are presenting to an audience of a hundred plus at a conference, think about what you as a member of the audience would want to see and hear. Would it be 55 minutes of analytical content, followed by 5 minutes of Q&A? Or would it be 40 minutes of mixed content, interspersing analysis with examples and preferably anecdotes, followed by 20 minutes of Q&A? What will the audience wish to hear from you? Find out.

In this case, in pitching your plan to potential backers, the same applies. You must know your audience, know who you are pitching to. Do some research on your backers. Who have they invested in or lent to before, who have they turned down? Why? What are they looking for? What tickles their fancy?

If you can, find out about the specific individuals you'll be pitching to. Know whether to keep your pitch dead serious or sprinkle it with anecdote, even humour. If in doubt, keep it straight at first and respond to their cues.

Know their expectations of time – most will want to be out of the room once an hour is up. Know what they wear – will they be in City suits or post-dot com boom smart casuals? Remember the old public speaking adage: be as well dressed as the best dressed person in the room.

Above all, know whether you are addressing investors or bankers – or both.

If the former, tailor your pitch throughout with references to the upside – the super results and returns that will emerge when you exploit the opportunities you'll reveal in the plan.

If you are pitching to bankers, go very easy on the upside – they really aren't interested. Be candid about the downsides, don't try to sweep them under the carpet, but take care to specify how you will mitigate the risks or avoid them altogether.

Depending on whom you are addressing, you may choose to amend the actual wording of your PowerPoint to accentuate the nuances for your audience. But take care – a presentation tailored for an investor may find its way to the inbox of a banker, who may have already received a banker-orientated version and will relish playing 'spot the difference'.

It is safer to stick to more neutral wording in the PowerPoint and voice over the appropriate nuances during the pitch itself.

As for the structure of the pitch, that should be the same for whomever you are pitching to. It should open with the answer to the key question, which is: 'Why should we back ABC Ltd?' The answer doesn't have to be as blatant as 'You should back ABC because . . . ' Rather that should be implicit in an answer such as 'ABC's competitive advantage in [one or two key success factors] should enable it to gain share in the [whatever] market, which is growing at X%/year, and to achieve a Y%/year growth in operating profit over the next three years'.

The structure should then broadly follow that of the PowerPoint example of the Dart Valley Guest House in Appendix D, which itself adheres to a golden rule of business presentation:

- Tell them what you are going to tell them – see the one-page executive summary, where the headline conclusions from each chapter are gathered together beneath an overall conclusion to the report in the headline of the executive summary.
- Tell them.
- Tell them what you have told them – the one-page executive summary again, used as a divider page between chapters.

It may all seem a bit repetitive, especially for those not used to this format, and indeed it is. But I suggest you learn to live with it. It hammers your message home. It is a powerful communication tool, especially in business. It works.

Using PowerPoint

You will use PowerPoint for your pitch. Don't for a second think you will win backing by delivering a five-minute spiel on your business like an aspiring entrepreneur on *Dragons' Den*.

That's TV, that's entertainment. In the real world, your backers will expect PowerPoint. And they will want hard copies in front of them that they can scribble on as you go through. (By the way, print out the presentation two or four slides to a sheet, depending on how dense your text, to make the document less weighty for your backers to carry home!)

I like PowerPoint. I like the discipline it forces on you to be succinct.

But it gets a bad press. It gets lampooned not because of what it is and can do but what people do with it. Business folk misuse PowerPoint to a criminal degree.

It all stems from a misunderstanding of what it is for. Are you using PowerPoint as a visual *aide memoire* to your oral presentation – or as a document of record? Or both?

If the former, remember the adage that 'a picture is worth a thousand words'. Use images or graphs to a maximum, words to a minimum.

If you must use words in a pure *aide memoire* PowerPoint presentation, follow these simple rules: no more than a title plus three, maximum four, bullets per slide, and no more than three, maximum four, words per bullet. On average, 15 to 20 words per slide.

It is when PowerPoint gets used as a document of record that the trouble starts. The worst culprits are the big accounting houses that use PowerPoint in their financial due diligence reports, blanketing slides with multiple charts and miniscule text in an endeavour to cram as much info as possible into one slide. This is sacrilege – it is just writing a report in landscape form, but less intelligibly.

You have a choice: have two separate documents, one a pure *aide memoire* in PowerPoint and the other the plan, in either Word or PowerPoint. Or one PowerPoint document which combines the two.

My personal preference is to combine the two, so there is only ever one business plan document doing the rounds. Here are three techniques to assist in both presentation and readability:

▪ Use charts, tables and images wherever possible, and animation sparingly.

▪ Shove as much data and wordy stuff into the appendices as you can, which are not to be presented but can be fast-forwarded to if necessary to reinforce a point or address a specific question from your backer.

▪ Tell a story, summarising all that is on each slide in a one- or two-line headline at the top of the page, with supporting main points in the body of the slide and supplementary material indented in smaller font size; thus the slide can be talked over by just picking up on the headline, or along with a bullet or two – but not the sub bullets, which are there just for the record; see how the story of the Dart Valley Guest House evolves in Appendix D.

In summary, use, don't abuse PowerPoint. Use it creatively as an *aide memoire,* if you wish, or as presentation-cum-document-of-record, but with a definitive concise storyline and weighty appendices.

One final point: note the flaw in this presenter's chutzpah: 'As you will recall from slide 289 . . . '!

Delivering the message

You have a PowerPoint presentation, punchy, powerfully structured and tailored for your audience. All you need do now is deliver it.

I could write another 100 pages on how you should best deliver your presentation, but my publisher would protest. Let me limit myself here to the top five tips in delivering a business presentation.

But before we get started, please remember this. The PowerPoint document is not a presentation. You are the presenter and what comes out of your mouth is the presentation. The PowerPoint is an aid to your presentation, and can be a document of record for others to read at a later date.

But the presentation itself is all about you. It is up to you to deliver your message clearly and convincingly.

And this is all too often where things go wrong – to the extent where I sometimes suspect that there is a subculture in the world of business where it is considered unbusinesslike to speak clearly and anyone who does so is regarded as being a bit flashy!

You will set out to combat that absurdity.

The first thing you need to get right is the voice. For whatever reason, too many business presenters get the voice wrong. Some feel they should be as casual or laid-back as possible, so their delivery becomes almost soporific. Others think that because everyone is seated around the same table they don't have to speak up. The rule of thumb is the same as in public speaking: you should imagine yourself conversing with the person farthest from you. And animatedly. Imagine that person is your best mate.

Second, there are the hands. This is my personal bugbear. Someone round the table is saying something important while resting his forehead in his hand (it is usually a he!). This immediately robs all vitality from the voice. Worse, he is speaking with his chin resting on his hand. This cuts off the main mode of communication entirely. What is with these guys? Why bother to speak at all if you are going to block your sound waves reaching the ears of the audience? If you do nothing else in presenting, please keep your hands well away from your face!

Where should I put them, you may well ask! Well, anywhere other than on your face is the answer. If you want to be a good public speaker, you'll learn to have a default hand position with your hands hanging loosely by your sides, and with one or both rising now and again to make specific gestures for effect and emphasis.

But for a business pitch you won't need that. Your backers are going to remember your delivery, your message and your PowerPoint, not your hands. Just keep them clear of your face!

Third, as important as the voice and the hands are the eyes. You will almost certainly be speaking to PowerPoint slides. That means you will be referring to PowerPoint slides as you speak to your audience. It does not mean speaking AT PowerPoint slides! This again is an all too common failing. The presenter is speaking while looking down at the laptop screen or at a print-out. Worse, he or she is looking at a projected image, with their back to the audience!

How often have you seen that? It is scarcely credible that presenters do that in business, but it is almost more common to see that happen than otherwise.

Every word that comes out of your mouth should be delivered with your eyes on the audience. Nothing else will do. Anything else gives the impression of being uncertain, unconfident, even shifty – let alone being difficult to hear.

To do that, remember the 3Rs: Read, Reset and Release! Read the note, reset your eyes on the audience, then, and only then, release the information. Do not look at your laptop, print-out or screen while you are actually speaking.

The penultimate of my top five tips on pitch delivery combines eyes and voice. Just because you have with you a beautifully structured and well-argued PowerPoint presentation does not mean that you should read it out to your audience, word by word. Do that and you will bore them so stiffly they'll flee the room – they can read it quicker in the cab on the way back to the office.

Use the PowerPoint as a prompt to your pitch, not as a script. If you can't talk without a script about your business, your baby, for an hour without having to read from a script, you don't deserve a backer. The PowerPoint is there as a document of reference for your backer and as a prompt and guide for you in making your case with conviction. Again, use, don't abuse it.

The fifth and final tip on pitching is simple: enjoy it! Convey your enthusiasm for your business to your backers. Make them as excited about your business as you are. Make them want to join in, get in on the adventure, be a part of your venture.

In summary, don't let your pitch let down your plan. Focus your content, exploit PowerPoint and deliver your message purposefully - with a vibrant voice, meaningful gestures, confident eye contact, plenty of ad lib and, above all, with passion. Wow 'em!

11

Setting targets

❝ In preparing for war I have always found that plans are
useless but planning is essential.

Dwight Eisenhower

In this chapter

■ Choosing key performance indicators

■ Setting milestones

You wrote the plan, you pitched it, you won the backing. Great, but is that it? Can you now archive the files? Nope!

Now you should use the plan for a different purpose – not for obtaining backing, but as a tool for implementation. The plan can be used to assess the performance of both the business as a whole and of individual managers.

If you have managed to get a backer on board, whether an angel, a seed capitalist, a venture capitalist or a private equity house, they are going to be most insistent on you getting this and the next chapter right.

They know that if you deliver to plan, they will achieve their hoped for return. So they will be keen to check how your company progresses against that plan at every stage along the way.

And they will want to incentivise managers to deliver against that plan. Or else . . .

To make such monitoring of progress relevant and easy, your backer will ask you to specify your key performance indicators and draw up appropriate milestones.

Choosing key performance indicators

Your backer doesn't want to be swamped every month, or at every board meeting, with reams of data, destined for the shredder or recycling bin beyond the boardroom.

The data collected and presented should be the minimum required to show clearly the company's overall state of performance.

Progress should be measured against the key parameters which drive value in your business.

In recent years, these have come to be known as key performance indicators (KPIs). KPIs are best regarded as navigation instruments, showing whether the vessel, or company, is on track towards its destination port. Without such instruments, the captain is steering blind – and may be unaware of the rocks or icebergs in her path.

There are two main types of KPI – those that pertain to all companies and those that are particular to your company.

Those that are common to all companies may include the following measures,* relating to:

---

* Note the use of the word 'measures'. A KPI must be measurable. It must be a fact, not an opinion – objective, not subjective. A KPI is an item of data.

- financial performance – e.g. revenues, revenue growth, gross margin, operating profit and margin, net profit and margin, return on capital employed, cash conversion cycle (days of stocks plus days of receivables less days of payables)

- customer satisfaction – e.g. customer satisfaction index, customer retention rate, customer profitability score, 'net promoter score' (the proportion of promoters less that of detractors)

- marketing effectiveness – e.g. market share, opportunity conversion rate, cost per lead, cost per conversion, search engine rankings, click-through rates, social media footprint (but take care, very difficult to measure meaningfully)

- operational effectiveness – e.g. capacity utilisation, order fulfilment time, project cost variance, innovation pipeline strength, rework level, process or machine downtime level, 'six sigma' level (proportion of defective product)

- employee effectiveness – e.g. revenue per employee, employee satisfaction index, employee engagement level, employee churn rate, average employee tenure, time to hire, salary competitiveness ratio

- environmental and sustainability compliance – e.g. carbon footprint, water footprint, energy consumption, supply chain miles, waste recycling rate, product recycling rate.

Already, just from that abbreviated list of examples above, you can see there are far, far too many KPIs for you to monitor regularly on behalf of your backers. They will not be able to see the wood for the trees.

And that is before the KPIs particular to your business are added!

Arguably NONE of the above general KPIs may be the most relevant to your business. You may run an upmarket hair salon on the High Street, for which your most important KPIs may well be the number of heads served and the average revenue received per head – closely followed perhaps by rent, electricity and business rate costs per head served.

Likewise with our central case study of the Dart Valley Guest House: far and away the three most important KPIs for this business are absent from the general list above. They are:

- average number of rooms available
- average achieved room rate (£/night)
- average room occupancy (%).

And that is before we consider the spa side of the business . . .!

Think carefully about the parameters that drive value in your business. Some of them may lie in the general list above, but many, perhaps most, will not. Select the most important. These are the KPIs you should be monitoring.

Setting milestones

Milestones are target values of KPIs over the course of the plan. They represent progress points along the critical path to success.

They should be set at levels that are realistic and achievable. After all, that is the philosophy behind your plan.

Your backer may hold you and your chief managers accountable for the achievement of these milestones. They may be the starting point for reviews of managerial performance during the course of the year.

One caveat: do not fall into the trap of setting too few milestones so that one key milestone can be met by shifting resources from one area to the next. This could be to the detriment of the business. On the other hand, do not set too many – or monitoring may become unmanageable.

Returning to the example of the Dart Valley again, Dick Jones's backer will expect him to meet the milestone of 71% occupancy by year three of his plan, along with an achieved room rate of £74 per night, averaged over the increased capacity of 33 rooms available.

Those are his three most important milestones – and Dick has no qualms about hitting them.

12

Performing to plan

" Strategy without execution is hallucination.

Mike Roach

In this chapter

- Monitoring your plan
- Appraising managerial performance
- Evaluating your plan

Y ou have selected your **key performance indicators** (KPIs) and set your milestones. Now you need to perform to plan.

The progress you make needs to be monitored on a regular basis, at least for each board meeting.

And that monitoring process will assist in the semi-annual performance review of your key managers.

Later on, having monitored progress against the plan for a couple of years, you may choose to set aside time to evaluate it properly. There will for sure be lessons to be learnt for the next time you have to write a business plan.

Monitoring your plan

In Chapter 1, I counselled against the use of business planning as a managerial tool for SMEs. This is fine in large organisations – ones that are prepared to devote the required resources to researching and analysing markets, customers, competitors, resources, financial model assumptions, risk and sensitivity, and so on for a month or so each year. It is not so fine when resources are limited, as in the typical SME.

Nevertheless, if you have invested in writing an SME business plan for a specific purpose, typically to obtain backing, whether from your board, a bank or an investor, it will then be worth your while monitoring it. You will have spent many hours drawing up the plan – the least you can then do is see to what extent things turn out as envisaged.

And your backer will almost certainly demand that of you.

As described in Chapter 11, you have chosen KPIs and have set milestones to make the monitoring of the plan relevant and useful.

After a year or so, however, this monitoring will to some extent be usurped by the budget process. Once the new budget is in place, results over the following year will tend to be assessed in relation to the budget, not to the old business plan, which will come over time to be regarded as a document past its sell-by date.

By the third year, the business plan may have become something of a historical curiosity. Monitoring against it runs the risk of becoming a superfluous exercise. To guard against this, milestones will need to be updated carefully in line with market developments and business out-turn. This may entail you having to redo some aspects of the market and competitive research you undertook for the business plan.

Appraising managerial performance

Clearly the performance of your business against plan and the achievement, or not, of specified milestones will be major factors in the semi-annual performance appraisals of key managers.

Whole books have been written on management appraisal, so I dip my toe in the water hesitantly. Suffice it to say that your CEO and/or backer should take due care when using KPIs to assess individual managerial performance, taking into account these factors:

- By tying the performance of one manager to one or more specific KPIs, you run the risk of that manager skewing allocation of time towards achieving those milestones, which might be to the detriment of other aspects of the business.
- It is the overall performance of the business that counts for most, and the more collaborative and less internally competitive the management team, the more likely the business will perform well overall.
- KPI data may be fudged, legitimately, but unhelpfully.

Nevertheless, KPIs are an important starting point in managerial appraisal.

Evaluating your plan

If you needed to draw up a business plan for a specific purpose – probably, as stated above, to obtain internal or external backing – the chances are that you will need to do so again one day.

That may be in a couple of years' time, if things go either badly, and there's a need for restructuring, or extremely well, and you need further growth capital. Or perhaps you will be looking to expand through acquisition or alliance.

Or it may be in 5, possibly 10 years' time that you need to dust off your business plan and write another.

Whichever, you may well have to do this exercise again. So it would be good to find out what you did right and what went wrong this time.

The way to do that is through a structured evaluation process. This is best done after at least three years, but can be done sooner if a new business plan is needed within that period.

The evaluation should be carried out by someone independent of the initial business planning exercise. No vested interests should be at stake. It should focus on examining the outturn against the KPIs forecast in the plan.

table 12.1   Evaluation of a business plan after three years: an example

Key parameter	Forecast	Outturn	Reasons	Lessons
Market growth, 2015–18	3.0%/yr	2.2%/yr		
No. of competitors	4	5		
Average unit pricing growth	2.5%/yr	1.9%/yr		
Customer return ratio	36%	41%		
Sales volume growth	3.7%/yr	5.8%/yr		
Sales value growth	6.3%/yr	7.8%/yr		
Operating margin, 2018	16.4%	14.2%		
Capex, 2015–18	£1.6m	£1.8m		
etc.				

A summary of the evaluation process might look like that in Table 12.1.

The important points in the evaluation process are as follows:

- KPIs – you might choose to compare the actual costs of rental of premises compared with forecast, but you won't compare the costs of paper clips. Select here only those parameters that have a significant bearing on the outcome of your financial forecasts.

- Reasons – if things turned out significantly differently, why? Was this the result of external forces, or were they in areas within your control?

- Lessons – next time round, what should you do differently in the plan process? How can your forecast be made more accurate? What extra research or analysis would be beneficial?

The main point of the exercise is, of course, the final column. What lessons can be learnt for next time?

Monitoring your business plan can be regarded as an option. Evaluation should not be. It is not a time-consuming process. It can be carried out in just a few days. And the lessons may be illuminating and extremely useful for the next time you're asked by the boss to write a business plan – by the end of the week!

Essential tip

'If only I had done this, thought of that . . . !' Evaluations work. Lessons are better learnt late than never. Try to get it right next time.

Epilogue: Beware these characters!

To end on a lighter note, how would you like your backer to talk about your merits as a business plan writer?

An entrepreneur or a chancer? A realist or a smoker? A persuader or a prat?

You should try to leave the right impression with your backer. All too many don't – and we've met some of these characters along the way in this book. Here are a few as a reminder of what NOT to do when writing your business plan.

They are the dreamer, the loner, the magician, the macho, the delusionist and the shot-gunner. Don't do as they do ...!

The dreamer

This is the person who lays out a set of sales forecasts that bear no relation to what market demand is forecast to do and/or how the firm is positioned in the market. We met him earlier (in Chapter 7) when looking at RandomCo's sales forecasts and assessed his forecasts as wild. He's the kind of guy who forecasts 14% per year sales growth in a business segment even though market demand is shrinking, his firm is at best tenably positioned and he has no plans to launch new products or services or enter new markets.

He's a dreamer. His forecasts bear no relation to the market environment in which his firm operates or to his firm's competitive standing. He's unbackable.

The loner

This is the person whose business plan has a sentence, not even a paragraph, let alone a chapter, on competition. Competition doesn't matter. She identifies a market and her firm will serve it. No one else matters, no competitor exists, no new entrant will arrive. Hers will be the sole provider to this market. If others do arrive, customers will be disdainful, since the newcomers won't have what it takes to compete. Only her firm counts.

She's a loner. Her firm alone can serve the addressed market. Others are irrelevant. She's unbackable.

The magician

This person is the clever guy who has forecast sales reasonably, consistent with both market demand and his firm's competitive position, but he has forecast his cost base to grow at a fraction of his sales growth rate. He believes he can use his purchasing skills to drive down direct costs and, as far as he is concerned, overhead expenses are too high at present and by forecasting them to remain flat while sales grow he is being conservative. As for capital expenditure, who needs it? The company should do fine with its ageing capital equipment for a good few years yet and, if space gets a bit tight in the plant, they can always improve the production process flow. Operating margin is thus forecast to grow dramatically year on year.

He's a magician. He can grow sales without deploying the resources, and costs, needed to drive and serve them. Even if he has a sound market development case, he risks rejection by backers due to his unrealistic cost and margin forecasts. He may be unbackable.

The macho

This person is the turnaround guy extraordinaire. No matter that profits took a bit of a dive last year. This year profits are going to bounce back and rise exponentially thenceforth. His are the fabled 'hockey stick' forecasts. Everything that could go wrong went wrong last year. Everything that can go right will go right in years to come.

And why? Because he has taken charge, he's the new MD. He'll sort everything out – he'll get the sales staff re-motivated, the production staff more efficient and the R&D staff more market-focused. The firm will have world-class leadership for the first time ever. That is he.

He is the macho. He may be right. Some hockey sticks do turn out as forecast. But the odds are not on his side and his backers will be wary indeed of his manifold claims. They will examine his track record with a toothcomb. And they will cross-examine him on every sentence and number in his business plan. If they can bear sitting alongside him that long.

The delusionist

This person has completed a rigorous, thoroughly researched and analysed assessment of the market opportunity. She has explained convincingly why it would be unlikely that more than four companies will enter the field. And she has set out in minute detail why her firm will remain at least as competitive as any other player on the assumption that others copy and follow her company's consistently innovative policies. Her sales forecasts assume conservatively no more than a one in four market share by year five. Her expense forecasts are individually well argued and seem reasonable. And yet her forecasts show an operating margin of 40% from year five.

She is deluded. The sales volume forecasts may well prove correct, so too the cost forecasts. But what about pricing? Can she assume that competitors won't price more competitively than her firm in order to gain share faster? Ultra high operating margins tend to get shaved back through competitive pricing either by the incumbents or a new entrant, or through escalating marketing costs, or a mixture of both. She may well win her backing, but not on the terms suggested by her business plan.

The shot-gunner

This guy is good. He started a business from scratch, survived the early ups and downs, and now has a healthy, tidy, little business. But he is not enamoured of that final adjective. He wants to grow, and grow fast. There is little scope for expanding his current business as is. But it could be replicated in another location. Or he could try introducing a new product line, aimed at a different customer group. Or he could try doing something similar with a different product group entirely. Given his track record, he could well succeed in any one of these strategic directions.

The problem is that his business plan shows investment in all three directions. Forecast profit by the end of year three shows a trebling with each new direction contributing its share. It won't happen.

He is going to be stretched in so many directions he will have to be the Fantastic Four's Mister Fantastic to catch all the balls. His plan is unbackable, but he might not be. If he can be persuaded to select one strategy, to focus, he may be backable. He must become a rifleman, not a shot-gunner.

When you write your business plan, don't be a dreaming, lonesome, macho, deluded, shotgun-toting magician. Be a realist. Earn the respect of your backer. Win that backing.

Good luck!

Appendix A: Deriving competitive position

> **❝** All that is human must retrograde if it does not advance.
>
> *Edward Gibbon*

In this appendix

- Identifying customer purchasing criteria
- Appraising key success factors
- Rating performance for competitive position

n this appendix, you will assess how your firm measures up to the competition. You will conclude what your competitive position is, both now and over the next few years. And you will do this for each of your main business segments.

This appendix sets out a systematic way of deriving competitive position, as opposed to the shortcut listing of your firm's strengths and weaknesses discussed earlier (Chapter 5).

You will go through three stages, for each of your firm's main business segments:

1 Identify and weight customer purchasing criteria – what customers need from their suppliers – that is, your company and your competitors.

2 Appraise and weight key success factors – what you and your competitors need to do to satisfy these customer purchasing criteria and run a successful business.

3 Rate your competitive position – how you perform against those key success factors relative to your competitors.

We'll start, as ever, with the customer.

Identifying customer purchasing criteria

What do customers in your business's main segments need from you and your competitors? Are they looking for the lowest possible price for a given level of product or service? Or the highest quality product or service irrespective of price? Or something in between?

Do customers have the same needs in your other business segments? Do some customer groups place greater importance on certain needs?

What exactly do they want in terms of product or service? The highest specifications? Fastest delivery? The most reliable? The best technical back-up? The most sympathetic customer service?

Customer foremost needs from their suppliers are called customer purchasing criteria (CPCs). For business-to-business (B2B) companies, CPCs typically include product quality (including features, performance and reliability), product range, delivery capabilities, technical support, customer service, relationship, reputation and financial stability. And, of course, price.

For business-to-consumer (B2C) companies, CPCs tend to be similar, although typically with less emphasis on product range and financial stability. Depending on the product or service being offered, the consumer will place varying importance on quality, service and price.

CPCs can usefully be grouped into six categories. They are customer needs relating to the:

- *effectiveness* of the product or service
- *efficiency* of the service
- *range* of products or services provided
- *relationship* with the producer or service provider
- *premises* (only applicable if the customer needs to visit the producer or service provider's premises)
- *price* of the product or service.

They can be conveniently remembered, with perhaps a faint redolence of a cult science fiction film, as the *E2–R2–P2* of customer purchasing criteria.

Let's look briefly at each in turn.

E1: effectiveness

The first need of any customer from any product or service is that the job gets done. You, the customer, have specific requirements on the features, performance and reliability of the product or service you need. You want the job done. Not half-done, not overdone, just done.

You want a crew cut. You go to the service provider, the barber. He gives you a crew cut. You pay and go home. Job done.

You may have other requirements, like how long the haircut took, the interaction with the barber, whether he also offers a wet shave, how clean the barbershop is or how reasonable his price. But the most basic requirement is that he is effective at giving you a crew cut. At getting the job done.

Suppose, however, that it's not a crew cut you want, but the cool cut sported by some film star. Now you get a bit more demanding. You'll want your barber, or hair stylist, to be competent technically at delivering such a haircut, to know about the pros and cons of living with such a haircut and to have done a few of these cuts before – you don't want to be a guinea pig, not with your hair!

You'll place more importance on job effectiveness.

What constitutes product or service effectiveness for the customers of your business? How important is it to your customers, relative to other purchasing criteria? Is it of high, low or medium importance?

E2: efficiency

The second main customer purchasing criterion is efficiency. The customer wants the job done on time.

All customers place *some* level of importance on efficiency for all types of service. You may not care whether your crew cut takes 10, 15 or even 30 minutes, but you would care if it took all Saturday afternoon and you missed the big football game.

Different customer groups may place different levels of importance on efficiency for the same service.

How much emphasis do your customers place on the efficiency of your service? How important is it relative to other criteria? High, low, medium?

R1: range

Then there is the range of products or services provided. This is an area that customers may find important for some products or services, even most important, and of no importance at all for others.

Let's return to the example of a hair salon. No self-respecting hair stylist would offer anything less than haircuts, perms and colourings. But is that enough? Would customers prefer a salon that can also offer techniques such as hair relaxing, straightening, plaiting and braiding? How important to the salon's target customer group is the range of services provided?

At the other extreme lies the functional barbershop. If most customers only want a crew cut, they're going to look for a barbershop that is effective and efficient, and where the barber is a good guy. If the barber were also to offer head massage, big deal! Yet to some customers, the head massage may be the unique offering that draws them through the door.

How important a criterion is product range to your customers? High, low, medium?

R2: relationship

Your barber gives a good crew cut and he does it quickly. But do you like the guy? Is he the sort of person you feel comfortable with having his hands on your head? Do you want your barber to chat or stay quiet? How do you want to interrelate? Does it matter to you if he seems bored and uninterested? Or would you prefer him to be interested and enthusiastic?

Never underestimate the relationship component in providing a service. A successful builder knows how to keep the homeowner as content as possible during the extension works. He'll try to ensure minimum disruption to everyday living – no wheelbarrows crossing the living room carpet – and he'll be of good cheer at all times. He knows that his business depends on personal referrals. If the stay-at-home spouse tells a neighbour that he's not only a good builder but also okay to have around the house under trying circumstances, his chances of converting the next sale are greatly improved.

How much emphasis do your customers place on personal relationships? High, low, medium?

P1: premises

This criterion applies only to those businesses, typically services, where the buying decision may be influenced by the environment.

Think about hair salons again. If you're aiming for the rich and famous, then you'll need a presence in Mayfair. And it had better be spectacular. If you're going for the middle-class, suburban housewife, you should be on the local high street, and the premises should be clean, aspirational and tasteful. Premises should be appropriate for the pocket of the customer.

Do you need a storefront for your business? What do customers expect of your premises? How important a criterion is it relative to others? High, low, medium?

P2: price

This is the big one. Set your prices sky high and you won't have many customers.

Think about the buying decisions you make regularly and the influence of price. For non-essential services, we tend to be more price sensitive. When your eight-year-old son's hair is flopping over his eyes, you look for a barber. He has little interest in his appearance (for the time being!), so you look around for the cheapest. But how cheap are you prepared to go? Would you take him to a barber that is (literally) dirt cheap, where the combs are greasy, the floor is covered with hair and the barber is a miserable so-and-so? Probably not. You set minimum standards of service and then go for a reasonable price.

For essential services, we tend to be less fixated on price. When your central heating system breaks down in the middle of winter, will you go for the cheapest service engineer? Or will you phone around your friends and acquaintances to find someone who is reliable, arrives when they say they will, fixes it with no fuss and charges a price that is not exactly cheap but at least is no rip-off?

What are your customers' pricing needs? How important is pricing relative to other purchasing criteria? High, low, medium? Very high?

Finding out CPCs

All this is very well in theory, you may think, but how do you know what customers want? Simple. Ask them!

It doesn't take long. You'd be surprised how after just a few discussions with any one customer group a predictable pattern begins to emerge. Some may consider one need 'very important', others just 'important'. But it's unlikely that another will say that it's 'unimportant'. Customers tend to have the same needs.

The comprehensive way to find out customer needs is through a 'structured interviewing' process, where you ask a selected sample of customers a carefully prepared list of questions.

In developing a strategy for your business, a customer survey is an essential input. If you haven't done one recently, you would be well advised to conduct one as preparation for your business plan. Appendix B shows how this is done.

Finally, you must also find out how your customers' needs are likely to change in the future. If they believe one purchasing criterion is highly important now, will it be as important in a few years' time? You need to know.

Appraising key success factors

We define key success factors (KSFs) as what producers or service providers like you need to do to succeed in a marketplace. They are what your firm needs to get right to satisfy the customer purchasing criteria of the last section *and* run a sound business.

Typical KSFs are product (or service) quality, consistency, availability, range and product development (R&D). On the service side, KSFs can include distribution capability, sales and marketing effectiveness, customer service and post-sale technical support. Other KSFs relate to the cost side of things, such as location of premises, scale of operations, state-of-the-art, cost-effective equipment and operational process efficiency.

To identify which are the most important KSFs for each of your main business segments, you need to undertake the following steps:

- Convert CPCs into KSFs
  - Differentiation-related
  - Cost-related
- Assess two more KSFs
  - Management
  - Market share
- Apply weights to the KSFs
- Identify any must-have KSFs.

Let's look briefly at each of these steps.

Convert CPCs into KSFs

Here we convert the customer purchasing criteria we researched in the last section into key success factors. In other words, we need to work out *what your business has to do to meet those CPCs.*

This is fairly straightforward for those CPCs that are related to how competitors differentiate their product or service from others – so-called differentiation-related KSFs. A KSF can often seem similar to, even the same as, a CPC. Suppose, for example, that you as a customer want your hair salon to be good at colouring. That's one of your needs. So the stylists need to be skilled at colouring. That's a KSF.

But KSFs generally tend to take a different perspective from CPCs. Here's an example. When you call up your internet service provider's technical help desk, you want the technician to fix the problem. You as a customer need someone who can understand and fix your problem. The associated KSFs for the technician are an appropriate technical qualification, subsequent completion of relevant training and experience of handling this and similar problems.

Here's another example. When you jump on the city tour bus in Athens, Barcelona or Copenhagen, you expect to be able to understand clearly what the tour guide is saying. The customer need is clarity of communication. The associated KSFs are 1) proficiency in the language of delivery and 2) clear communication skills.

When converting a CPC, you may find that the associated KSF can sometimes be the same as you've already associated with another CPC. In other words, one KSF can sometimes be sufficient to meet two or more CPCs. Returning to the tour guide, for example, another customer need may well be rapport with the guide. Rapport will be greatly eased through fluency in the language of delivery. In this example one KSF, language proficiency, serves two CPCs, namely clarity of communication and rapport.

What are the main differentiation-related KSFs in your business? How important are they? Of high, low, medium, medium/high, low/medium importance?

There's one CPC that needs special attention, and that's price. Customers of most services expect a keen *price*. Producers need to keep their *costs* down. Price is a CPC, cost competitiveness is a KSF.

In a competitive service business like car repair, middle-income customers tend to be sensitive to price, among other needs such as quality of work and integrity. A small car repair proprietor will therefore try to keep rental costs for premises down by locating the workshop well off the high street, maybe off the side streets too, and on to some commercially zoned land alongside the railway line.

Other determinants of cost competitiveness in your business could include cost of materials, use of subcontractors, outsourcing of business processes, overhead control, including not just premises but also numbers of support staff, remuneration levels and IT systems.

And size may matter. Other things being equal, the larger the business, the lower costs should be *for each unit* of business sold. These are 'economies of scale' and apply not just to the unit cost of materials or other variable costs, where a larger business will benefit from negotiated volume discounts, but also to overheads.

Think of two hair salons competing against each other on the high street. One has double the amount of space of the other and serves on average 80 customers a day, compared to the smaller salon's 40. They are thus similarly efficient and they charge similar prices. But the larger salon has lower rental costs *per customer* because of a discount negotiated with the landlord on the second commercial unit rented. The larger salon also pays lower marketing costs *per customer,* since advertising space in the *Yellow Pages* or in local glossy magazines costs the same per column inch for both salons, irrespective of how many customers the advertiser serves.

What are the main cost-related KSFs in your business? Cost of materials? Use of subcontractors? Premises? Overhead control? Economies of scale? How important are they? Of high, low, medium, medium/high, low/medium importance?

Assess two more KSFs

So far, we've derived two sets of KSFs from the set of CPCs set out in the previous section: differentiation-related and cost-related. There are two more sets to be considered: management and market share.

How important is management in your business? We discussed your firm's managerial capabilities in greater depth in the chapter on resources (Chapter 6), but here you need to identify how important management is in general in your industry. Think about whether a well-managed company, with a superb sales and marketing team reinforced by an efficient operations team, but with an average product, would outperform a poorly managed company with a superb product in your industry.

Management needs to be added as a differentiation-related KSF. And that will include sales and marketing, the lifeblood of any small or medium-sized business. How important is management as a KSF in your business?

There's one final KSF – an important one – that we need to take into account that isn't directly derived from a CPC. This is your firm's market share. The larger the relative market share, the stronger should be the provider.

A high market share can manifest itself in a number of competitive advantages. One such area is in lower unit costs, but we've already covered this under economies of scale in cost-related KSFs, so we must be careful not to double count.

Market share is an indicator of the breadth and depth of your customer relationships and your business reputation. Since it is more difficult to gain a new customer than to do repeat business with an existing customer, the provider with the larger market share typically has a competitive advantage – *the power of the incumbent.*

For example, if your hair stylist fulfils all your customer needs – excellent hair styling, relaxing premises, rapport and a reasonable price, the fact that one or two of your friends are chatting about the superb new stylist who has just set up shop further down the street will not necessarily tempt you away from your usual provider. Why switch? Your stylist would be most upset, especially when there has been no cause for such disloyalty. This is the power of the incumbent. Customers don't like switching, unless they are sorely tempted (the pull factor) or forced to move through deficient quality of product or service (the push factor). Keep the quality levels high and customers will tend to stick with who they know.

It can even be costly to switch – for example, if your current service provider offers you loyalty discounts. Sometimes it's costly in terms of time to switch. If you change internet service provider, you may face the hassle of having to notify all your contacts of your new email address. Sometimes it's costly in emotional terms to switch, as we saw with the hair stylist. The higher the switching costs, the greater the power of the incumbent.

Incumbency tends to rise in importance as a KSF where customers rely on their service provider for historical continuity. It's less of a wrench to change your shoe repairer, even your hair stylist, than to change your psychiatrist or your accountant. The latter two have built up useful knowledge about you, whether it's your mind or your double-entry books. Switching to another provider may mean them taking a long time to build up the relevant understanding of you as an individual or business.

How great is the power of the incumbent in your business? How important is market share as a KSF?

Apply weights to the KSFs

You've worked out which are the most important KSFs in your business. Each one has been ranked in order of importance. Now you need to weight them.

A simple quantitative approach works best. Don't worry, you won't have to compute a weighting of, say, 14.526%. That would be horribly spurious accuracy. But it's helpful to derive a percentage for the weighting, whether to the nearest 5% or even 10%, so that in the next section you can easily tot up and rate your *overall* competitiveness relative to your peers.

So that 14.526% would become simply 15%. No more accuracy than that is needed. How do you do it? There are two ways: methodically or eyeballing.

If you want a systematic approach, take a look at one such in the box below. If you would prefer to eyeball it, to get a rough and ready answer, start from this guideline: market share 20%; cost factors 30%; and management and differentiation factors 50%. Then adjust them to what you have found to be critical to success in your business. And make sure that however you jiggle them they still add up to 100%.

A systematic approach for deriving KSF weightings

Here's a step-by-step systematic approach to weighting KSFs:

- Use judgement on the relative power of the incumbent to derive a weighting for *market share* of i per cent, typically in the range of 15–25%.

- Revisit the importance of price to the customer. If you judged the customer need of medium importance, give *cost competitiveness* a weighting of 20–25%. If low, 15–20%. If high, 35% plus. If yours is a commodity business, it could be 40–45%, with a correspondingly low weighting for relative market share. Settle on c per cent.

- Think about the importance of *management* factors to the success of your business, especially marketing. Settle on m per cent, typically within a 0–10% range.

- You've now used up a total of $(i + c + m)$ per cent of your available weighting.

- The balance, namely $100 - (i + c + m) = D$ per cent, will be the total weighting for *differentiation* factors.

- Revisit the list of KSFs relating to *differentiation issues,* excluding price, which has already been covered. Where you've judged a factor to be of low importance, give it a KSF score of 1. Where high, 5. Rate pro rata for in between (for example, medium/high would be a 4).

- Add up the total score (T) for these differentiation-related KSFs (excluding price).

- Assign weightings to each differentiation KSF as follows: weighting (per cent) = KSF score × D/T.

- Round each of them up or down to the nearest 5%.

- Adjust further if necessary so that the sum of all KSF weights is 100%.

- Eyeball them for sense and make final adjustments.

- Check that the sum is still 100%.

Once you've eyeballed the weightings in general, you need to assess to what extent these weightings differ for each of your business segments. In particular, different customer groups can often place a different emphasis on price, so cost competitiveness may be more of an issue in one segment than in others. Other customers in other business segments may be more concerned about product quality or customer service. You need to know.

Identify any must-have KSFs

There is one final wrinkle. But it may be crucial.

Is any one of the KSFs so important in your business that if you don't rank highly against it you shouldn't even be in business? You simply won't begin to compete, let alone succeed. You won't win any business, or you won't be able to deliver on the business you win. In other words, it is a *must-have* KSF, rather than a mere *should-have*.

Must a business in your marketplace have, for example, the right ISO classification to win future orders in a competitively intensifying environment? Must it deploy the new cost-revolutionary range of capital equipment? Must your product incorporate a particular new feature?

Are any of the KSFs in your business must-haves? Bear this in mind when we assess your competitive position in the next section.

Rating performance for competitive position

Now you are ready to rate how your business performs against each of the KSFs identified previously. You'll then compute a weighted average rating and see how your overall position compares against competitors.

You should do this for each of your main business segments, since your position in one may be very different from in others. Then you should consider how your position is likely to change in each segment over the next few years and what you can do to improve it over time.

Finally, you need to do a reality check. Do you by any chance rate poorly against one of the must-have KSFs we highlighted above? If so, that may mean you don't get past first base. You shouldn't be in this business.

Who are your peers?

The first thing to decide is who to compare yourself with. Sometimes that seems a no-brainer. Often it requires a little more thought.

Take a simple example. For the owners of three hair salons on a suburban high street, the comparison may seem obvious. They judge themselves against the other two. But some of their potential customers may have their hair done in the city during lunch breaks or after work. Others may get it done when they do their weekly grocery shopping at the out-of-town supermarket. They are competitors too.

Don't be stingy. If you think another provider is serving clients who could potentially be yours, rate them too. Remember, this section is the easy bit. It takes just a few minutes to have a first shot at rating each competitor.

Deriving competitive position

How do you compare with your peers? Are you more or less competitive than them? What's your competitive position? And theirs?

To draw up your competitive position, all you need to do is rate yourself against each of the KSFs drawn up in the previous section. If you use a numerical rating system, alongside the percentage weighting system you've already drawn up above, your competitive position will emerge clearly. I suggest a rating system of 0–5.

If you perform about the same as your peers against a KSF, give yourself a score in the middle, a 3 (*good/favourable*). If you perform very strongly, a 5 (*very strong*). Poorly, a 1 (*weak*). If you perform not quite as well as most others, give yourself a 2 (*tenable*). Better than most, a 4 (*strong*).

Now do the same for each of your competitors against that KSF. Who's the best performer against this KSF? Do they merit a 5, or are they better but not *that* much better than others and deserve a 4?

Continue this process for each KSF.

If you've used Excel, your competitive position literally falls out at the bottom of the spreadsheet (see the example for the Dart Valley Guest House in Chapter 5). For the first 25 years of my career, I had to do it by hand – either by totting up in my head or using a calculator if I was feeling lazy. For youngsters today, that must be hard to imagine.

Excel makes things so much easier. But beware. The old manual approach encouraged you to think very carefully about each rating, because you didn't want the hassle of having to do the calculation all over again. With Excel you do no calculating, so sloppy thinking incurs no time penalty. It's a trap, well known in financial planning these days. Think carefully.

Algebraically, your overall rating is the sum of each rating (r) against each KSF multiplied by the percentage weighting (w) of the KSF. If there are n KSFs, your overall rating will be $(r1 \times w1) + (r2 \times w2) + (r3 \times w3) + \ldots + (rn \times wn)$. As long as the percentage weightings add up to 100%, you should get the right answer.

Implications for future market share

The main use of competitive position is to give you and your backer some idea of how your business is likely to fare over the next few years *in relation to the market as a whole.*

If your firm's competitive position turns out to be around 3, or good/favourable, your backer will expect you, other things being equal, to be able to grow your business *in line with the market* over the next few years. In other words, to hold market share.

If your competitive position is around 4 or above, they will expect you to be able to *beat the market,* to gain market share, again other things being equal. Suppose they have already concluded that your Chapter 3 forecast of market demand growth of 10% a year seems reasonable. With a competitive position of 4, they'll feel more comfortable if your plan is to grow business at, say, 12–15% a year.

If your competitive position is around 2, however, your backers will be less confident about your business prospects. It's more likely you'll *underperform the market* and they'll be especially worried if your plans show you outperforming the market! They will wonder if they are backing the right horse.

Finding out performance ratings

The first step is to do it yourself. Over the years, or months if you've only just started in business, you'll already have had occasional feedback from your customers. 'Great piece of work' generally means you've done something right. 'No way am I paying you for that!' suggests the opposite.

Have a go at rating the business yourself. Then stick a question mark against those ratings where you're a little unsure on performance. Investigate those ratings one or two at a time. Next time you're with a customer, throw in the line: 'By the way, you know that job we did for you a couple of months ago – were you happy with the

▶

turnaround time? Did you expect it to be quicker?' Gradually you'll be able to start removing the question marks and firm up your rating.

While rating your own company's performance, you should also be comparing with your competitors. All performance is relative, so if you give yourself a 3 against one KSF, it will be relative to a competitor that you rate as a 4, or another you rate as a 2. Do a first draft of rating your competitors at the same time as your own. Again, stick in question marks against the numbers where you're unsure. Then start throwing in the odd question with your customers, such as: 'What about Company B? Do they turn things around as fast as we do?' Gradually the question marks on your competitors' ratings should also disappear.

The methodical way to derive ratings is through *structured interviewing.* This is what management consultants do on behalf of their clients to derive primary information on business strategy, marketing or due diligence assignments.

A structured interviewing programme differs from the more casual approach in two respects: you select a representative sample of interviewees; and you draw on a prepared questionnaire.

The advantage of a structured interviewing process is that it will in time give you all you need to know. There are two disadvantages. First, it takes up the time of your customers. There's a risk that you'll leave your customers thinking that you've just wasted a quarter- or half-hour of their precious time. Second, you may be a bit sensitive about your customers knowing that you're doing a strategy review. You don't want them to think that you may be moving on to bigger and better things, leaving them in your wake. You also may not want your customers to think too hard about your service compared to others, in case they suddenly realise that they would be better off shifting to another supplier!

These risks should, however, be containable as long as you prepare your story well in advance and try to make the experience as beneficial for the customer as for you.

For a detailed description on how to conduct a sensitive structured interview programme with your customers, see Appendix B.

Competing by segment

We've talked thus far as if your firm has only one business segment. How does your competitive position compare in each of your main product/market segments?

You need to apply the same process for each segment: identifying how customer purchasing criteria differ by segment; assessing key success factors for each; and deriving competitive position for each. You'll find that some ratings are the same, some are different. Take product quality, for example. Your rating against that KSF will be the same in each segment relating to a product group. But the weighting of that KSF may well differ by customer group segment, thereby impacting your overall competitive position in each.

Ratings for the same KSF may differ by segment. For instance, your company may have an enviable track record in one segment, whereas you may have only just started in another segment – rating a 5 in the first, but only a 1 or 2 in the other.

Competing over time

So far your analysis of competitive position has been static. You've rated your current competitiveness and that of others. But that's only the first part of the story. What your backer also wants to know is how your competitive position is likely to change over the next few years. They will want to understand the dynamics. Is it set to improve or worsen?

The simplest way to do this is to add an extra column to your chart, representing your business in, say, three years' time. Then you can build in any improvements in your ratings against each KSF. These prospective improvements need, for the time being, to be both in the pipeline *and* likely for your backer to be convinced. You will look in Chapter 5 at how you can *proactively and systematically* improve your competitive position. How you can develop a strategy to bridge the gap with the ideal provider. But for now we'll just look at how your competitive position seems set to change naturally over the next few years.

Remember, however, that improved competitive position is a two-edged sword. Your competitors too will have plans. This is where analysis of KSF dynamics gets challenging and intriguing. It's easy enough to know what you're planning, but what are your competitors up to?

Try adding a couple of further columns representing your two most fearsome competitors as they may be in three years' time. Do you have any idea what they're planning to do to improve their competitiveness in the near future? What are they likely to do? What could they do? *What are you afraid they'll do?*

How is your competitive position likely to change over time? And for your competitors?

Getting past first base

Previously in this appendix, we introduced the concept of the must-have KSF – without a good rating in which your business cannot even begin to compete.

Did you find a must-have KSF in any of your business segments? If so, how do you rate against it? Favourable, strong? Fine. Okay-ish? Questionable. Weak? Troublesome. A straight zero, not even a 1? You're out. You don't get past first base.

And what about in a few years' time? Could any KSF develop into a must-have? How will you rate then? Will you get past first base?

And even though you rate as tenable against a must-have KSF today, might it slip over time? Could it slide below 2, into tricky territory?

This may be a case of being cruel to be kind. It's better to know. The sooner you realise that you're in a wrong business segment, the sooner you can withdraw and focus resources on the right segments.

Appendix B: Structured interviewing of customers

> ❝ Your most unhappy customers are your greatest source of learning.
>
> *Bill Gates*

In this appendix

- The interviewees
- The storyline
- The questionnaire
- The interview
- The thanks and feedback

n **Chapter 5,** and in more detail in Appendix A, a structured interviewing programme of customers was recommended as the most methodical way to obtain the information needed to derive your firm's competitive position.

Here's how to do it:

1 Select a representative range of customer interviewees.

2 Prepare your storyline.

3 Prepare a concise questionnaire.

4 Interview them, through email, telephone or face-to-face.

5 Thank them and give them some feedback.

The interviewees

The interviewees should represent a broad cross-section of your business. You should select three to six customers from each of your main product/market segments, as well as, or including, the following:

- Your top six customers in terms of revenue
- Long-standing customers as well as recent acquisitions
- Customers who also use, or used to use, your competitors, so they can compare your performance from direct experience rather than conjecture
- Customers with whom you've had problems
- Would-be customers, currently using a competitor, but on your target list
- Former customers who switched to a competitor.

That sounds like a lot, but you'll be selective. Aim for two, perhaps three dozen in all.

The storyline

Here's your opportunity to put a positive light on your business. Compare these two storylines:

1 'Sorry to waste your time but can I ask for your help in figuring out how well our firm performs?'

2 'As you know, our firm has been rather busy over the last couple of years. But we thought we should take some time out to ask some of our most important customers how their needs may be changing over time and to what extent we can serve those needs better.'

Guess which line will get the better response *and* put your business in a favourable light? The first storyline conveys a negative, defeatist impression and is all about your firm and its possible deficiencies. The second leaves a positive impression and is all about your customer's needs. Stick to the second!

The questionnaire

The questionnaire needs care. It must be taken as a guideline, not as a box-ticking exercise. It stays with you, and it doesn't get handed or emailed to the interviewee. It's a prompter to discussion, no more. It needs to be simple. And concise.

It should be in four parts:

1 The storyline

2 Customer needs – which, how important, now and in the future?

3 Performance – how your firm and your competitors rate against those needs

4 The future – how you can better serve your customer's needs.

The storyline

The storyline should be written out at the top of the questionnaire and memorised. It must be delivered naturally and seemingly spontaneously. Stick in the odd pause, 'um' or 'er' to make it seem less rehearsed.

Customer needs

These are the main questions to put on your questionnaire:

- What are your main needs and your main criteria in buying this service? What do you expect from your providers?
- How important are each of these needs? Which are more important than others? How would you rank them?
- Will these needs become more or less important over time?
- Are any other needs likely to become important in the future?

You should allow the customer to draw up their own set of needs, but it's best to prepare your own list to use as prompts, in case your customer dries up, or they miss an obvious one.

Performance

Here are some performance-related questions:

- How do you think our firm meets those needs? How do we perform?

- How do other providers perform? Do they better meet those needs?
- Who performs best against those most important needs?

Again you should allow the customer to select who they think are the alternative providers of your service, but you should include a prompt list of your main competitors – which you may or may not choose to use. No need to alert your customer to a troublesome competitor that they're not yet fully aware of!

The future

What should we be doing to better meet your needs and those of other customers?

The interview

Interviews are best done face-to-face. Then you can see the nuances behind the replies – the shifting glance, the fidgeting, the emphatic hand gestures. But they are the most time consuming, unless you happen to be seeing your customer as part of your service delivery anyway.

If the interviews are done over the phone, they are best scheduled in advance. You can do this by email or with a preliminary phone call. After you've delivered the storyline, then add: 'I wonder if you could spare 5 to 10 minutes to discuss this with me. I know you're very busy, but perhaps we could set up a time later in the week for me to give you a call.'

The call itself must be carefully managed. Don't launch into the questionnaire without a warm-up. Ask the customer how they are doing, how their work is, how their family is, whatever. Then gently shift to the storyline: 'Well, as I was saying the other day . . . '

After you've finished the structured interview, don't forget the warm-down at the closing. Return to one of the topics you discussed at the outset and gently wind down the discussion, not forgetting to thank them sincerely for giving so freely of their valuable time.

The thanks and feedback

A few hours, a day, a couple of days or a week later – whenever you feel it's appropriate – thank your customer again, officially. By letter is best, but that may feel overly formal for you in this electronic world. Email is probably fine, but use your judgement.

The email should be cheerful and full of sincere gratitude. If possible, it should contain a snippet of information that could be of interest or use to your customer. One or two sentences should suffice. It could pick up on one aspect of the discussion and compare what another customer had to say on the same thing. You could give them an indication of the results of your survey: 'Interestingly, most customers seemed to think that track record was their most important need' or 'Encouragingly, most customers seemed to think we were the most innovative service provider!'

That's structured interviewing. Now all you have to do is compile the results, whether on a piece of paper, on an Excel worksheet, or simply in your head, and feed them into your ratings against each key success factor – for your firm and for each of your main competitors.

The intriguing thing then is to compare these customer-derived ratings with your first-draft, do-it-yourself ratings. You may be in for a surprise!

Appendix C: Alternative sources of funding

In this appendix

- Standard sources of funding
- Alternative sources

The digital revolution has changed just about everything – from how we shop to how we pay, from how we communicate to how we learn, from how we go on holiday to how we find a partner.

Now how we get funded is also changing. Crowdfunding and peer-to-peer loans are becoming serious alternatives.

But first let's put them in perspective.

Standard sources of funding

Thus far, this book has kept things simple. You have a business plan and you need funding: that can come either in the form of debt, whereby you are lent the cash and you need to pay the money back over time with interest, or in the form of equity, whereby you exchange paper for cash and your backer shares in the risk and return of your business.

Thus your backer is interested primarily in the downside of your business (the lender) or in its upside (the investor). This is an important distinction and runs throughout this book.

You need to ensure that your plan addresses the needs of one or the other, depending on to whom you are pitching. Or you can make the plan suitably non-committal and voice over the nuances during the pitch.

But the nuances may have to be yet more subtle, depending on the type of debt or the type of equity you are seeking.

Here are the main standard sources and some nuances for debt finance:

- Bank loan, overdraft facility, credit card facility (though with high interest rates), mortgage – for which you will need to offer some collateral, as well as a robust, downside-protected business plan.

- British Business Bank-backed Enterprise Finance Guarantee, enabling unsecured loans to businesses with inadequate levels of security to satisfy commercial lenders – again, you need to focus on downside protection.

- Asset-backed loans such as leasing (e.g. of vehicles or capital equipment), factoring/invoice discounting (cash in advance of standard debtor payment timing), trade finance (cash in advance of paying creditors), pension-led funding (in effect using your pension fund as security) – here your plan will highlight the quality of the relevant assets.

For equity finance, you'll talk to specialists depending on the stage of evolution of your business:

- Seed capitalists, for business concepts at the proof-of-concept phase
- Venture capitalists, for a business where the concept appears viable but needs funding to get going
- Development capitalists, for businesses up and running and needing extra funding to enable further growth
- Business angels, who are high net worth individuals, as epitomised by the dragons on BBC TV's *Dragons' Den*, and who may be interested in any of the above stages, especially when encouraged by the tax-advantageous Enterprise Investment Scheme.

Or you may choose to grow your business in partnership with a complementary business which may contribute capital in exchange for either stock or your business resources or capabilities. Such an alliance can be as loose as a licensing or distribution agreement or as tight as a formal joint venture.

One such alliance could be with a major customer, with whom you might arrange preferential terms or even exclusivity in return for a contribution to development costs.

Before you part with any stock or sign up for any debt, however, don't forget to look for grants and advice that can come for free. Business Link summarises what is available in one document: https://www.gov.uk/government/uploads/system/uploads/attachment_data/file/32258/11-776-solutions-for-business-government-funded-business-support.pdf

And finally of course, remember that your very first port of call in sourcing finance, if yours is a start-up, could well be with friends and family – or foraging around in the attic for whatever you can flog on eBay!

Alternative sources

The digital revolution has enabled two innovative means of raising funds:

- In debt finance – peer-to-peer loans
- In equity finance – crowdfunding.

These are fast moving and exciting areas of finance. Companies like Zopa and Funding Circle have led the way in the former, Crowdcube and Seedr in the latter.

If you wish to pursue these alternative sources, you would be wise to stay abreast with who is doing what, how and why by reading the trade press.

Your best bet is with www.ft.com, the online version of *The Financial Times*. Here is a selection of what the FT has been reporting in recent weeks on the subject at the time of writing (June 2015).

First a word on the business angel scene, which has also been buoyant in recent years.

Easy money helps angels of the north fly into start-ups

By Andrew Bounds, Enterprise Editor

For the past six years, the Bank of England's quantitative easing programme has been credited with, and blamed for, many of today's unusual economic conditions: historically low interest rates, negative bond yields and record share prices. But an even more unforeseen consequence is an increase in the number of entrepreneurs in the north of England.

With central bank asset purchasing increasing the price of both bonds and equities, investors have been hunting for alternatives as they search for higher returns.

Throw in the generous tax breaks for backing riskier ventures, such as the Enterprise Investment Scheme, and it seems more Britons have decided to become angel investors instead: putting their money into entrepreneurial start-ups that they hope will pay them back with high returns.

. . . Individual angels are making more investments than ever before. The average number today is five compared with 2.5 in 2009, according to the UK Business Angels Association.

. . . As more and more wealthy individuals turn to company financing, it has become a bigger source of funds for start-ups than traditional venture capital funds. Private equity provided an estimated £450m in venture capital in 2014. There was at least £1.2bn from angels, though many transactions are unrecorded.

"The angel market is much bigger than the venture capital market," said Jenny Tooth, chief executive of the UK Business Angels Association.

▶

She points out that there are 18,000 active angels in the UK, yet there still remains a significant north/south divide, with more than six out of 10 angels residing in London and the southeast.

With bank lending to small businesses still falling, the government has looked to encourage angel investors with a range of incentives and set up a £100m fund to invest alongside them. Ms Tooth said that future governments must continue the tax reliefs.

EIS was used for a record £1.4bn of investment in 2013–14. It offers 30 per cent income tax relief on the first £1m of investment annually, exemption from capital gains tax on disposal of shares after three years, allowing losses on share sales to be set off against either income or capital gains.

The even more generous Seed EIS offers 50 per cent tax relief up to £100,000 annually but is only available when investing in companies with fewer than 25 employees.

"Some things go pear-shaped," said Ms Tooth. "Tax breaks are incredibly important. They are used in nine out of 10 deals. Some 90 per cent said it influenced them to take the risk of investing in a small business. Tax breaks are a safety net. Angels are not looking for tax avoidance."

. . . [Mr Ajaz Ahmed, founder of Freeserve] said angels such as himself were vital to help exciting businesses grow. "Venture capitalists do not have any venture. They just want safe bets."

Source: Bounds, A. 'Low rates and QE push angels of the north to invest into start-ups', *Financial Times*, 7 May 2015.
© The Financial Times Limited 2015. All Rights Reserved.

This clipping gives a taste of the buzz around crowdfunding.

The search for seed capital

By Jeremy Hazlehurst

In a trendy building in King's Cross, London, a 200-strong crowd of professional-looking middle-aged types and youngsters with fashionable beards and piercings are watching entrepreneurs make 60-second presentations about their businesses.

The start-ups include an online menswear retailer, a website founded by a former Spitting Image puppeteer, a luxury milkshake business run by an ex-Marks and Spencer employee and a company that streams live gigs. Afterwards, everyone mills about eating canapés, sipping beer and discussing potential deals.

This is an investment roadshow run by Crowdcube, one of the UK's biggest and, at the age of four, oldest crowdfunding websites. Along with others, including Seedrs and Crowdfunder, it is revolutionising investing into early-stage businesses.

If you thought crowdfunding was for small fry, think again. Crowdcube has raised £78m for 229 businesses since 2011, and Seedrs raised £10m in the first quarter of 2015. The Chapel Down Winery, a Kent vineyard, raised £3.9m, and in March, JustPark, a peer-to-peer parking business, raised £3.7m (see below). High-profile entrepreneurs such as Steve Smith, founder of retailer Poundland, celebrity chef Hugh Fearnley-Whittingstall and EasyJet airline founder Sir Stelios Haji-Ioannou crowdfunded their latest ventures.

Advocates of crowdfunding like to talk about "democratising investment". The bigger sites have a minimum stake of £10, but six figures are becoming more common. Two people invested £500,000 each in Chapel Down.

A fund manager at the King's Cross event, who wished to remain anonymous, has invested £250,000 across 10 businesses over the past two years via crowdfunding sites. "It is becoming a very interesting space," she says. "It is bringing opportunities to the market that weren't there before — things that are a bit more niche. It's rewarding to be able to invest in something that has literally been started in a basement. It's fun, and there is an altruistic side to it as well."

She has invested in sectors she would not have considered before, such as biotechnology, and in Zero Carbon Food, a company that grows food in tunnels under Clapham Common in south London.

. . .

But crowdfunding isn't a universal panacea, as pointed out in the article below.

New sources of funding bring difficult choices

By Emma Dunkley

The digital revolution is in full swing, spearheaded by entrepreneurs employing technology that is disrupting sectors from finance to food shopping.

Digitally focused companies such as Uber, the taxi application, and Zopa, the peer-to-peer lender, have emerged in the past decade alongside large numbers of others who are shaking up traditional industries.

A benefit that many current start-ups enjoy, compared with immediately after the financial crisis, is that it has become easier to access financing.

. . . Crowdfunding is a way of raising outside finance that has emerged in the past decade, pooling small sums from many individuals who in return, receive a stake in the start-up or rewards, such as a product sold by the company.

[Nick Hungerford, founder of online wealth manager Nutmeg] says crowdfunding has significant advantages. "You can create a brand as you fundraise, you're not subject to the type of restrictions that venture capitalists add, plus your shareholders become your advocates.

"But crowdfunding as a source of business funding is tiny compared with venture capital, where billions of dollars are invested each year."

Indeed, in spite of the hype surrounding crowdfunding, experts doubt it will replace venture capital as the main source of start-up funding.

[Stephen Newton, founder of Elixirr,] says: "Crowdfunding has yet to mature, but it will never replace venture capital. Generating a large number of passive investors can be great for evangelising your product, but it's no substitute for a hands-on investor who will guide you and plug you into their network."

Similarly, [Tim Levene, founder of Augmentum Capital] says crowdfunding will "absolutely not" replace venture capital.

"Crowdfunding is becoming an increasingly viable option for early-stage businesses, but it is still in its infancy and riddled with challenges. Some platforms are adopting more rigorous screening processes, and I have no doubt that there will be several companies crowdfunded on the leading platforms that will fall by the wayside."

So, while it is easier to raise funds now, those in the industry stress that entrepreneurs should not underestimate the challenges involved and the importance of selecting the right source of funding.

"In the end, every company should be grateful for cash if the terms are right," Mr Hungerford says. "Personally, I'd love to see more British companies raising billion-dollar investment rounds. We have the ideas, talent and energy to overtake Silicon Valley in the race to be the world's hottest technology venue."

Meanwhile peer-to-peer lending, which has been around for longer, has also been growing fast and is to be boosted further by new tax incentives to savers – as highlighted in the article below (though the final sentence might serve as a warning!).

Peer-to-peer investors to get savings tax break

By Judith Evans

A new tax-free personal savings allowance will apply to income from peer-to-peer lending as well as from cash savings, in the latest boost to a sector that has lured both investors and borrowers with competitive rates.

From April 2015, savers will be eligible for a £200 annual windfall thanks to a new tax exemption on savings income, announced in the Budget.

The tax break will not apply to income from investments in shares or funds, but will apply to peer-to-peer, the Treasury confirmed on Thursday.

Some £1.7bn was lent in 2014 through fast-growing peer-to-peer platforms, which allow individuals to make loans to others or to businesses online.

"This is great news for the industry and consumers," said Christine Farnish, who chairs the Peer-to-Peer Finance Association. Funding Circle, a platform for loans to small businesses, said that "there will be big gains for a large number of investors".

Under the new tax break, basic rate taxpayers – who are taxed on savings income at 20 per cent – will be entitled to a £1,000 tax-free allowance, and higher-rate taxpayers, taxed at 40 per cent, will receive an allowance of £500. Additional rate taxpayers, who earn more than £150,000 a year, are not included.

The extension of the tax break to peer-to-peer is the latest in a series of measures aimed at fostering the sector and acknowledging its rapid expansion. These have also included a promise to make peer-to-peer loans eligible for inclusion in individual savings accounts (Isas).

The industry has just celebrated its tenth birthday: the oldest peer-to-peer platform, Zopa, was set up in 2005. But its growth has accelerated in the past two years and new platforms have multiplied.

Lenders have been lured in by rates higher than those available on cash, which are currently at record lows. In a low interest-rate environment, yields can also exceed those from other forms of investment.

Platforms such as Zopa, RateSetter and Funding Circle currently offer annualised rates of between 5 and 7 per cent to investors on five-year loans, with the income generally higher from riskier business lending.

However the Financial Conduct Authority, the City regulator, emphasises that peer-to-peer investments are risk-based and not equivalent to cash savings; they are not covered by the Financial Services Compensation Scheme. Most of the sector has yet to weather a major downturn.

. . .

Source: Evans, J 'Peer-to-peer investors to get savings tax break', *Financial Times*, 19 March 2015.
© The Financial Times Limited 2015. All Rights Reserved.

But alternative sources of funding have some way to go before making a serious dent in the overall market for business finance.

State lender says banks need further help

By Andrew Bounds

High street banks need more government help to lend to small businesses, the head of the British Business Bank has said.

Keith Morgan, chief executive of the state-owned bank set up to improve the lending market, said sources of finance such as peer-to-peer lending and equity crowdfunding had not yet filled the gap left after banks retreated because of the 2008 financial crisis.

"Bank lending is still very important to small businesses. We have seen encouraging signs of growth from alternative lenders [but] they still represent something very small," Mr Morgan told the Financial Times.

Traditional lending made up three-quarters of the gross funding for small and medium businesses in 2014, but the net amount fell £3bn to leave £167bn outstanding at the end of the year.

Peer-to-peer lending grew £400m to £770m in the year to October, according to the bank. Equity crowdfunding was negligible. Mr Morgan said many smaller businesses were "discouraged" from applying to banks by previous rejections or the cost of loans.

Digitally-inspired alternative sources of funding are an attractive and dynamic space. By all means turn to them, but you are advised to stay bang up-to-date with what is going on in the market.

Appendix D: An example business plan

**The Dart Valley Guest House
and Oriental Spa**
Business Plan

April 2015

THIS EXAMPLE BUSINESS PLAN INCLUDES
BOXES SUCH AS THIS WITH BRIEF GUIDELINE
INSTRUCTIONS ON HOW TO SET OUT YOUR
PLAN AND WHAT TO INCLUDE IN IT

Introduction

The Dart Valley is a distinctive destination, operates profitably and seeks co-funding to expand and become a leading player in spa services in South Devon.

➤ The Dart Valley Guest House and Oriental Spa (the 'Dart Valley') is a destination with a difference: it is set overlooking the stunning valley of the River Dart in South Devon and yet offers visitors a touch of the Orient in its room decor, cuisine and spa.

➤ It has 17 rooms for hire, most with views over the canyon, with spa and restaurant facilities offering a menu of Western and Oriental selections to both overnight and day visitors. It turned over £513k in 2014, with an operating margin of 18%.

➤ Phase II expansion is poised to start, costing £1.05m for a new building with 16 rooms and an outside, heated swimming pool.

➤ Revenues are forecast to almost double by 2019 and operating margin reach 34%, making the Dart Valley a leading player in spa services in South Devon.

➤ This business plan aims to secure a financial partner who shares the owners' vision.

Contents

Executive summary

1. The Dart Valley will become a leading player after the Phase II project, with sales doubling, profitability enhanced and opportunities outshining risks.

2. *The business:* The Dart Valley has progressed rapidly and above plan since opening in 2011.

3. *Market demand:* Market demand for travel to South Devon is forecast to be flat in visitor nights but growing at 2–3%/year in average spend.

4. *Industry competition:* Competitive intensity is medium to high, with the main risks being a copycat entrant or spas going the way of a fad.

5. *Strategy:* The Dart Valley is already a credible competitor to the Palace in local spa services and will become a regional leader after the Phase II project.

6. *Resources:* The resource implications of the Dart Valley's strategy are in line with past experience and under control.

7. *Financials:* The Dart Valley is forecast to grow revenues to over £1m and operating margin to 34% by 2019.

8. *Risk:* Risks of fad, copycat and slower build-up are outshone by opportunities such as the proven concept, spa profitability and replication at another site.

3

Executive summary   USE THIS SUMMARY PAGE AS A CHAPTER DIVIDER

1. The Dart Valley will become a leading player after the Phase II project, with sales doubling, profitability enhanced and opportunities outshining risks.

2. *The business:* The Dart Valley has progressed rapidly and above plan since opening in 2011.

3. *Market demand:* Market demand for travel to South Devon is forecast to be flat in visitor nights but growing at 2–3%/year in average spend.

4. *Industry competition:* Competitive intensity is medium to high, with the main risks being a copycat entrant or spas going the way of a fad.

5. *Strategy:* The Dart Valley is already a credible competitor to the Palace in local spa services and will become a regional leader after the Phase II project.

6. *Resources:* The resource implications of the Dart Valley's strategy are in line with past experience and under control.

7. *Financials:* The Dart Valley is forecast to grow revenues to over £1m and operating margin to 34% by 2019.

8. *Risk:* Risks of fad, copycat and slower build-up are outshone by opportunities such as the proven concept, spa profitability and replication at another site.

4

The business Background

The Dart Valley has progressed rapidly and above plan since opening in 2011.

➤ The Dart Valley is a destination with a difference:
- It is set overlooking the stunning Dart Valley in South Devon and yet offers visitors a touch of the Orient in its room decor, cuisine and spa (see offering and gallery in Appendix A).
- It has 17 rooms for hire, most with views over the valley, with spa and restaurant facilities offering a menu of Western and Oriental selections to both overnight and day visitors.

➤ *Goals and objectives*: our main goal is to give visitors a distinctive, treasured stay, thereby boosting the return rate, aimed to rise from 21% to 33% by 2019.

➤ *Strategy*: the early strategy of maximising occupancy rates at the expense of average room price will be resumed following completion of the Phase II extension.

➤ *Resources and key dates*: following 15 Aug 2012, our 1st day at 100% occupancy, marketing resources have been scaled down, but will need restoring in Phase II.

➤ *Financials*: Phase I work in 2010–11 turned out 17% over budget due to problems with the old building, but P&L growth has exceeded plan, with sales in 2014 reaching £513k (up 17% on plan) and operating margin 18% (14% in plan).

5

The business Segments

The Dart Valley's revenues derive mainly from accommodation services, followed by spa and catering, and primarily from leisure visitors.

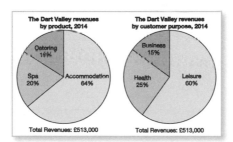

The Dart Valley revenues by product, 2014

Catering 16%
Spa 20%
Accommodation 64%

Total Revenues: £513,000

The Dart Valley revenues by customer purpose, 2014

Business 15%
Health 25%
Leisure 60%

Total Revenues: £513,000

➤ Further product/market segmentation (to, for example, revenues from business visitors on spa services) would add unnecessary complexity for this business.

6

Executive summary

1. The Dart Valley will become a leading player after the Phase II project, with sales doubling, profitability enhanced and opportunities outshining risks.

2. *The business:* The Dart Valley has progressed rapidly and above plan since opening in 2011.

3. *Market demand:* Market demand for travel to South Devon is forecast to be flat in visitor nights but growing at 2–3%/year in average spend.

4. Industry competition: Competitive intensity is medium to high, with the main risks being a copycat entrant or spas going the way of a fad.

5. *Strategy:* The Dart Valley is already a credible competitor to the Palace in local spa services and will become a regional leader after the Phase II project.

6. *Resources:* The resource implications of the Dart Valley's strategy are in line with past experience and under control.

7. Financials: The Dart Valley is forecast to grow revenues to over £1m and operating margin to 34% by 2019.

8. *Risk:* Risks of fad, copycat and slower build-up are outshone by opportunities such as the proven concept, spa profitability and replication at another site.

7

Market demand prospects ⬡ 3

Market demand for travel to South Devon is forecast to be flat in visitor nights but growing at 2–3%/year in average spend.

► The Dart Valley's addressed travel market in the Torbay and South Hams areas of South Devon is estimated at £225 million in 2014 (see methodology in Appendix B).

► The Dart Valley's broader travel market, that of the West Country as a whole, was valued by VisitBritain at £3.1 billion in 2013.

► Main long-term drivers have been per capita income growth, the growing propensity to take multiple short breaks, the steadily improving range of visitor facilities and attractions in the area.

► These drivers are expected to remain positive over the next few years.

► The main short-term driver was the 2009 recession induced by the financial crisis, which boosted domestic tourism through the 'staycation' effect, and has since returned to the *status quo ante* (see statistics in Appendix B).

8

Appendix D: An example business plan **247**

Market demand prospects ⬡ 3

Market demand for travel to South Devon is forecast to be flat in visitor nights but growing at 2–3%/year in average spend (continued)

➤ The market is forecast to remain flat in volume terms but grow in prices at 2–3%/year (see Appendix B).

➤ Larger and higher star hotels should fare better than the average over the next few years as visitors reverse their trading down behaviour during the recession.

➤ Hotels offering special premium or niche facilities such as spas should fare likewise.

➤ The main risk faced by South Devon hoteliers was the staycation rebound, but that seems to have now worked its way through and further contraction in the market seems unlikely.

9

Executive summary

1. The Dart Valley will become a leading player after the Phase II project, with sales doubling, profitability enhanced and opportunities outshining risks.

2. *The business:* The Dart Valley has progressed rapidly and above plan since opening in 2011.

3. *Market demand:* Market demand for travel to South Devon is forecast to be flat in visitor nights but growing at 2–3%/year in average spend.

4. *Industry competition:* Competitive intensity is medium to high, with the main risks being a copycat entrant or spas going the way of a fad.

5. *Strategy:* The Dart Valley is already a credible competitor to the Palace in local spa services and will become a regional leader after the Phase II project.

6. *Resources:* The resource implications of the Dart Valley's strategy are in line with past experience and under control.

7. *Financials:* The Dart Valley is forecast to grow revenues to over £1m and operating margin to 34% by 2019.

8. *Risk:* Risks of fad, copycat and slower build-up are outshone by opportunities such as the proven concept, spa profitability and replication at another site.

10

Industry competition Competitors

The Dart Valley faces an array of competitors, from luxury resorts to excellent B&Bs and Plymouth spas.

➤ Competitors are many (see details of offering and scale in Appendix C) and include:
  - Seven hotels in Torquay and four in South Hams, mainly four-star, offering full spa facilities, including swimming pool, spa pool, sauna and treatment rooms.
  - Two fitness clubs in Torquay offering full spa facilities.
  - Five hotels (one of which is a five-star) and three fitness clubs offering limited spa facilities, typically just a treatment room or two.
  - Half a dozen first class spas-cum-wellness centres in Plymouth, two in particular with an Oriental influence.

➤ All offer serious direct or indirect competition, but none mirrors the distinctiveness of the Dart Valley Guest House and Oriental Spa.

➤ West Country bedspace occupancy rates rose steadily from 47% in 2011 to 49% in 2014, though rates at seaside or countryside establishments, guest houses and B&Bs tend to be lower than for hotels in towns (Source: VisitBritain – see Appendix C).

➤ Average achieved room rates (AAGR) improved slightly in 2013:
  - 1%/year up since 2009 at English country hotels to £86 (Source: Hotel Britain 2014, BDO)
  - £69 for all English hotels outside London, flat since 2009 – see Appendix C.

11

Industry competition Intensity

Competitive intensity is medium to high, with the main risks being a copycat entrant or spas going the way of a fad.

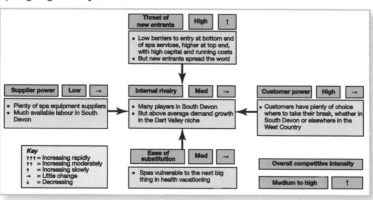

Source: Based on Michael Porter, *Competitive Strategy: Techniques for Analyzing Industries and Competitors*, The Free Press, 1980

12

Executive summary

1. **The Dart Valley will become a leading player after the Phase II project, with sales doubling, profitability enhanced and opportunities outshining risks.**

2. *The business:* The Dart Valley has progressed rapidly and above plan since opening in 2011.

3. *Market demand:* Market demand for travel to South Devon is forecast to be flat in visitor nights but growing at 2–3%/year in average spend.

4. *Industry competition:* Competitive intensity is medium to high, with the main risks being a copycat entrant or spas going the way of a fad.

5. *Strategy:* The Dart Valley is already a credible competitor to the Palace in local spa services and will become a regional leader after the Phase II project.

6. *Resources:* The resource implications of the Dart Valley's strategy are in line with past experience and under control.

7. *Financials:* The Dart Valley is forecast to grow revenues to over £1m and operating margin to 34% by 2019.

8. *Risk:* Risks of fad, copycat and slower build-up are outshone by opportunities such as the proven concept, spa profitability and replication at another site.

13

Strategy Customer purchasing criteria *Spa services* ⬡ 5

The main purchasing criteria in spa services are the effectiveness of the treatment, the standard of the premises and price.

Spa customer purchasing criteria		Importance	Change
Effectiveness	• Therapist capabilities • Understanding of benefits • Confidence in process	*High* *Low/Med* *Med*	→ → →
Efficiency	• Effort • Timeliness	*Low/Med* *Low*	→ →
Relationship	• Rapport • Enthusiasm	*Med* *Med/High*	↑ →
Range	• Facilities • Treatments	*Med/High* *Low/Med*	→ ↑↑
Premises	• Cleanliness, hygiene • Space, décor	*High*	↑
Price		*Med/High*	↑

YOU MAY PREFER TO PLACE THIS SLIDE IN APPENDIX D

14

Strategy Key success factors *Spa services*　　　　　　　　　　　　　　　　　**5**

The winning provider of spa services will have highly skilled and experienced therapists, quality premises, a positive, upbeat culture and tight control of costs.

Spa customer purchasing criteria		Importance	Change	Associated key success factors
Effectiveness	• Therapist capabilities • Understanding of benefits • Confidence in process	High Low/Med Med	→ → →	• Therapist skills • Qualification • Track record
Efficiency	• Effort • Timeliness	Low/Med Low	→ →	• Availability • Work ethic • Delivery
Relationship	• Rapport • Enthusiasm	Med Med/High	↑ →	• People skills (communication) • Positive, upbeat culture
Range	• Facilities • Treatments	Med/High Low/Med	→ ↑↑	• Range of facilities • Range of treatments
Premises	• Cleanliness, hygiene • Space, decor	High	↑	• Spa quality premises
Price		Med/High	↑	• Cost competitiveness

> YOU MAY PREFER TO PLACE THIS SLIDE IN APPENDIX D

Strategy The Dart Valley's competitive position *Spa services*　　　　　　　　**5**

The Dart Valley is already a credible competitor to The Palace in local spa services and could become a leader with the Phase II project.

Key success factors	Weighting	Dart Valley	The Palace	Fit4U	Smugglers' Cove	Dart Valley Phase II
Market Share	15%	2	4	3	2	3
Cost factors: Overhead control, Scale economies	25%	3	4	4	1	3.5
Management factors: Marketing	10%	2	5	4	4	4
Differentiation factors: Effectiveness—Standard of therapists	10%	5	4	4	5	5
Efficiency—Work ethic, Delivery	5%	5	3	4	5	5
Relationship—Communication, Attitude	10%	5	4	4	5	5
Range—Facilities, Treatments	10%	2	5	4	1	4
Premises—Hygiene, Décor, Space	15%	5	3	4	5	5
Competitive position	*100%*	3.5	4.0	3.9	3.1	4.1

Key to Rating: 1 = weak, 2 = tenable, 3 = favourable, 4 = strong, 5 = very strong

Note on selected competitors: Dart Valley Guest House & Spa, Torbay; The Palace Hotel & Spa, Torquay; Fit4U Fitness Club & Spa, Torquay; Smugglers' Cove Hotel & Spa, South Hams

> YOU MAY PREFER TO PLACE THIS SLIDE IN APPENDIX D

The Dart Valley is already a credible competitor to The Palace in local spa services and could become a leader with the Phase II project *(continued)*.

➤ XXXX
- XXX
- XXX
- XXX

> INSERT BULLETS JUSTIFYING YOUR RATINGS OF THE PRECEDING SLIDE AGAINST EACH KEY SUCCESS FACTOR, WITH SUB-BULLETS INCLUDING FACTS AND QUOTES WHICH CAN BE TAKEN AS SUPORTING EVIDENCE FROM:
> - MANAGEMENT.
> - CUSTOMER AND OTHER INTERVIEWS.
> - THIRD PARTY REPORTS OR MEDIA CLIPPINGS.
>
> THIS IS A KEY PART OF THE REPORT AND MAY RUN TO 2, 3 OR EVEN 4 SLIDES, EACH DISPLAYING THE SAME CONCLUSIVE HEADLINE.

> REPEAT THIS AND THE PREVIOUS SLIDE ON RATING COMPETITIVE POSITION FOR THE OTHER MAIN SEGMENTS – ACCOMMODATION AND CATERING IN THE CASE OF THE DART VALLEY.

17

The Dart Valley is poised to exploit strategic success to date with the Phase II project.

➤ The Dart Valley has come from nowhere to be a credible player in its niche by:
- Offering the overnight visitor an experience somewhat out of the ordinary – clean, crisp, comfortable accommodation spiced with a hint of the Orient, with stunning views over Devon's exquisite Dart Valley
- Offering the diner the choice of traditional European fare or home-cooked, delicately spiced Oriental cuisine, with the same lovely views
- Creating a spacious, relaxing environment, a high quality of therapy, and a culture of service and enthusiasm in its spa services, factors which counterbalance the limited range of facilities offered compared to leading local competitors
- And, on the other hand, by keeping a tight control over overheads.

➤ The Dart Valley's occupancy rates provide evidence of this:
- Average room occupancy by Year 3 of operations of 71%, well above the area average.

➤ Phase II will make it one of the leading providers of spa services in South Devon, not in scale or market share, but of competitive position, *hence profitability.*

➤ Strategic risks are low:
- The Dart Valley will offer in Phase II more of the same successful formula of Phase I.
- This concept, so successful so far, is unlikely to become dated over the next five years.

18

Executive summary

1. **The Dart Valley will become a leading player after the Phase II project, with sales doubling, profitability enhanced and opportunities outshining risks.**

2. *The business:* The Dart Valley has progressed rapidly and above plan since opening in 2011.

3. *Market demand:* Market demand for travel to South Devon is forecast to be flat in visitor nights but growing at 2–3%/year in average spend.

4. *Industry competition:* Competitive intensity is medium to high, with the main risks being a copycat entrant or spas going the way of a fad.

5. *Strategy:* The Dart Valley is already a credible competitor to the Palace in local spa services and will become a regional leader after the Phase II project.

6. *Resources:* The resource implications of the Dart Valley's strategy are in line with past experience and under control.

7. *Financials:* The Dart Valley is forecast to grow revenues to over £1m and operating margin to 34% by 2019.

8. *Risk:* Risks of fad, copycat and slower build-up are outshone by opportunities such as the proven concept, spa profitability and replication at another site.

19

Resources

The resource implications of the Dart Valley's strategy are in line with past experience and under control.

➤ Management – now proven in guest house and spa services.
  - Dick and Kay Jones now established, unlike three years earlier (see summary bios in Appendix E).
  - With Kay's connections, we envisage no difficulties in recruiting a spa manager with an Oriental heritage.

➤ Marketing – more of the same, but for 33 rather than 17 rooms (see Appendix F).
  - Local and regional advertising.
  - Attendance at regional promotions.
  - Competitive pricing off-season and other special packages, such as during weddings.
  - A new initiative is to partner with successful spa hotels elsewhere, giving them a cut on business referrals and offering the customer variety in where to stay next time.

➤ Operations – no serious constraints (see Appendix G).
  - Same supplies, purchasing process, provision of services, IT, reservation system (which has worked well after the inevitable teething problems), controls, compliance.
  - Planning permission now secured and using same building contractor for Phase II as for Phase I.
  - Environment, health and safety systems in place and record good so far (see Appendix H).

➤ Resource risk – under control.
  - Slippage or construction cost inflation – two months' delay and 10% contingency already in plan.
  - Health of owner managers – insurance taken, but in worst case the business is now highly saleable.

20

Executive summary

1. **The Dart Valley will become a leading player after the Phase II project, with sales doubling, profitability enhanced and opportunities outshining risks.**

2. *The business:* The Dart Valley has progressed rapidly and above plan since opening in 2011.

3. *Market demand:* Market demand for travel to South Devon is forecast to be flat in visitor nights but growing at 2–3%/year in average spend.

4. *Industry competition:* Competitive intensity is medium to high, with the main risks being a copycat entrant or spas going the way of a fad.

5. *Strategy:* The Dart Valley is already a credible competitor to the Palace in local spa services and will become a regional leader after the Phase II project.

6. *Resources:* The resource implications of the Dart Valley's strategy are in line with past experience and under control.

7. *Financials:* The Dart Valley is forecast to grow revenues to over £1m and operating margin to 34% by 2019.

8. *Risk:* Risks of fad, copycat and slower build-up are outshone by opportunities such as the proven concept, spa profitability and replication at another site.

21

Financials and forecasts Historics ⬡**7**

The Dart Valley has achieved satisfactory profitability since its launch in late 2011.

The Dart Valley P&L and key trading parameters, 2012–15

£000	2012 Actual	2013 Actual	2014 Actual	2015 Budget
Average no. of rooms available	17	17	17	17
Average achieved room rate (£)	64.1	69.5	73.9	79.5
Average room occupancy	39.2%	55.4%	71.1%	75.0%
Revenues – Accommodation	155	240	326	354
– Catering	45	65	82	87
– Spa	76	92	105	109
– Total revenues	276	397	513	550
EBITDA	−16	111	194	220
Operating profit	−117	10	93	119
Operating margin (%)	−42.4%	2.5%	18.1%	21.6%
Profit before tax	−152	−25	58	84

Source: Appendix I

22

Financials and forecasts Historics

The Dart Valley has achieved satisfactory profitability since its launch in late 2011 *(continued).*

► Occupancy of 39% in 2012 outperformed the planned 25–30% and has since grown to 71%, with 2015 forecast to reach 75%.

► AARR has been nudged up by 7.5%/year since 2012, with budget 2015 showing a further 3% increase to almost £80 and revenues reaching £550k.

► Breakeven at operating margin was achieved in early 2013 and at the bottom line towards the end of the year, both ahead of plan; operating margin grew to 18% by 2014 and should reach 22% in 2015.

► Following financing of £500k mortgage and £550k owner equity, no further cash has been injected; the business has been operationally cash positive since 2013.

► By end-2014, the book value of owner equity reached £431k and seems set to exceed the £550k invested by 2016; this takes no account of the enhancement in the value of the property since purchase and renovation.

23

Financials and forecasts Forecasts

The Dart Valley is forecast to grow revenues to over £1m and operating margin to 34% by 2019.

The Dart Valley P&L forecasts, 2014–19

£000	2014 Actual	2015 Budget	2016 Forecast	2017 Forecast	2018 Forecast	2019 Forecast
Average number of rooms available	*17*	*17*	*17*	*33*	*33*	*33*
Average achieved room rate (£)	*73.9*	*79.5*	*79*	*70*	*72*	*74*
Average room occupancy	*71.4%*	*75.0%*	*75%*	*60%*	*65%*	*71%*
Revenues – Accommodation	326	*354*	*368*	*506*	*564*	*633*
– Catering	82	*87*	*87*	*135*	*145*	*159*
– Spa	105	*109*	*109*	*263*	*273*	*284*
– Total revenues	**513**	*550*	*564*	*904*	*982*	*1076*
EBITDA	194	*220*	*214*	*397*	*466*	*546*
Operating profit	93	*119*	*113*	*212*	*281*	*361*
Operating margin (%)	**18.1%**	*21.6%*	*20.0%*	*23.5%*	*28.7%*	*33.6%*
Profit before tax	58	*84*	*78*	*107*	*176*	*256*

Source: Appendix I

24

Financials and forecasts Forecasts

The Dart Valley is forecast to grow revenues to over £1m and operating margin to 34% by 2019 *(continued)*.

➤ The Dart Valley revenues are forecast to double over 2014–19, despite some conservative assumptions.
  ▪ An assumed 10% drop in average achieved room rate and a 20% drop in occupancy rate once the new accommodation capacity comes onstream in 2016; given how full the guest house has been in recent months and the healthy forward bookings for this year and next, these assumptions seem reasonable.

➤ Operating margin is forecast to rise from 2014's 18% to 33%, likewise with conservative assumptions.
  ▪ An assumed doubling in staff costs, spread across room cleaning, waiting, cooking and spa services, with no increase in the bar, reception, accounts or gardens.
  ▪ A major marketing campaign planned for both 2016 and 2018.
  ▪ 100% debt finance assumed for the £1 million to be raised.

➤ The enhanced profitability reflects the impact of doubled revenues spread across an overhead base increasing more slowly, reflecting a more productive use of the existing and Phase II asset base.

25

Financials and forecasts Forecasts

The Dart Valley is set to outpace the market, with or without Phase II.

The Dart Valley market contextual revenue forecasts, 2014–19

Business segments	Revenues (£000)	Market demand growth (%/year)	Company competitive position (0-5)	Likely revenue growth (%/year)	Top-down revenues (£000)	Phase II-derived revenues (£000)	Total revenues (£000)
	2014	2014–19	2014–19	2014–19	2019	2019	2019
1	2	3	4	5	6	7	8
Accommodation	326	3–4%	3.6 to 3.9	5%	416	217	633
Catering	82	2–3%	3.3 to 3.5	3%	95	64	159
Spa	105	4–5%	3.5 to 4.1	7.5%	151	133	284
Total	513			5.2%	662	414	1,076

Source: Appendix I

Financials and forecasts Forecasts

The Dart Valley is set to outpace the market, with or without Phase II *(continued)*.

➤ When placed in a market context, the Dart Valley is well placed to beat the market even in the absence of the Phase II building programme.

➤ It would do so in two main ways:
  ▪ Growing accommodation revenues faster than the market, due to its strong competitive position – this would be done more by nudging up room rates than through higher occupancy, since the Dart Valley already enjoys high occupancy.
  ▪ Deriving a higher share of revenues from spa services, for both overnight and outside guests, even in the absence of the Phase II facilities, as the Dart Valley's range of services continues to develop and becomes better known.

➤ Over three-fifths of revenues by 2019 would be derived from the existing business, with the balance from the Phase II development.

Financials and forecasts Forecasts

The Dart Valley is forecast to generate an average of £300k cash each year following Phase II development.

The Dart Valley cash flow forecasts, 2014–19

£000	2014 Actual	2015 Budget	2016 Forecast	2017 Forecast	2018 Forecast	2019 Forecast
Profit before tax	58	84	78	107	176	256
Depreciation	101	101	101	185	185	185
Operating cash flow	159	185	163	269	324	387
Change in working capital	-9	-3	0	-23	-6	-8
Cash flow from operations	**150**	**182**	**162**	**246**	**318**	**380**
Capital expenditure	-4	-9	-1,045	-2	-10	-5
Cash flow pre-financing	146	173	-883	244	308	375
Mortgage	0	0	1,000	0	0	0
Cash surplus for year	**146**	**173**	**117**	**244**	**308**	**375**
Cash surplus (cum)	157	331	448	692	1,000	1,375

Source: Appendix I

Financials and forecasts Forecasts **7**

The Dart Valley's owner equity should exceed £1m by 2019.

The Dart Valley balance sheet forecasts, 2014–19

£000	2014 Actual	2015 Budget	2016 Forecast	2017 Forecast	2018 Forecast	2019 Forecast
Current assets – cash	157	331	448	692	1,000	1,375
Current assets – total	201	378	496	769	1,084	1,466
Capital assets	742	650	1,594	1,412	1,237	1,058
Total assets	943	1,028	2,090	2,181	2,321	2,524
Current liabilities	12	13	13	19	20	20
Long term liabilities	500	500	1,500	1,500	1,500	1,500
Owner equity	431	515	577	662	801	1,004
Total liabilities	943	1,028	2,090	2,181	2,321	2,524

Source: Appendix I

29

Executive summary

1. The Dart Valley will become a leading player after the Phase II project, with sales doubling, profitability enhanced and opportunities outshining risks.

2. *The business:* The Dart Valley has progressed rapidly and above plan since opening in 2011.

3. *Market demand:* Market demand for travel to South Devon is forecast to be flat in visitor nights but growing at 2–3%/year in average spend.

4. *Industry competition:* Competitive intensity is medium to high, with the main risks being a copycat entrant or spas going the way of a fad.

5. *Strategy:* The Dart Valley is already a credible competitor to the Palace in local spa services and will become a regional leader after the Phase II project.

6. *Resources:* The resource implications of the Dart Valley's strategy are in line with past experience and under control.

7. *Financials:* The Dart Valley is forecast to grow revenues to over £1m and operating margin to 34% by 2019.

8. *Risk:* Risks of fad, copycat and slower build-up are outshone by opportunities such as the proven concept, spa profitability and replication at another site.

30

Risk, opportunity and sensitivity

Risks of fad, copycat and slower build-up are outshone by opportunities such as the proven concept, spa profitability and replication at another site.

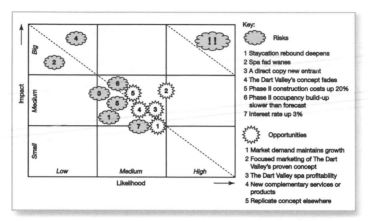

Key:

Risks

1 Staycation rebound deepens
2 Spa fad wanes
3 A direct copy new entrant
4 The Dart Valley's concept fades
5 Phase II construction costs up 20%
6 Phase II occupancy build-up
  slower than forecast
7 Interest rate up 3%

Opportunities

1 Market demand maintains growth
2 Focused marketing of The Dart
  Valley's proven concept
3 The Dart Valley spa profitability
4 New complementary services or
  products
5 Replicate concept elsewhere

Risk, opportunity and sensitivity

Risks of fad, copycat and slower build-up are outshone by opportunities such as the proven concept, spa profitability and replication at another site *(continued)*.

➤ The major risk is a slower build-up in occupancy than forecast (Cloud 6), but:
  - The forecast has built in a 15% hit in occupancy between 2016 and 2017, dropping from 75% to 60% . . .
  - . . . which is little higher than Year 2's 55% . . .
  - . . . and despite an assumed drop in AARR of 11% from £79 to £70.

➤ And the Dart Valley is no start-up – it is now a proven concept (Sun 2).

➤ Other promising opportunities stand out:
  - The transformation of the Dart Valley's spa services to a profitable segment in their own right (Sun 3), rather than a loss leader for the accommodation segment.
  - The introduction of complementary services and products (Sun 4), such as day trips, sporting trips, aromatherapy products.

➤ Finally, there is the opportunity (Sun 5) to replicate the Dart Valley's success:
  - A large B&B business in the Fal estuary in Cornwall has been identified which would be ideal and whose owners are planning to retire in a couple of years.
  - Even if the timing of that deal doesn't work out, there will be other suitably scenic properties on the market when the time is right.

Risk, opportunity and sensitivity

The plan is reasonably sensitive to lower occupancy rates, but such rates are considered most unlikely.

➤ We understand that this business is operationally highly geared, so have conducted appropriate sensitivity tests.
- The impact on profit before tax from inflated Phase II construction costs of 20% seems limited and containable – and there is only a minor cash flow impact in later years resulting from higher depreciation and lower tax.
- If occupancy rates turn out to be 15% below plan – for example, 51% in 2017 instead of the forecast 60% - the impact is greater; the income statement in 2017 drops into the red and the profit forecast for 2019 is halved; cash flow, however, remains positive, if shrunken.
- Such a drop is most unlikely; a 51% overall occupancy rate in 2017 would imply a level of just 23% in the new rooms of Phase II (compared to a forecast 44% in the business plan) and the Dart Valley managed to achieve 39% occupancy in 2012, its first year of operations.

The Dart Valley business plan sensitivity tests, 2017 & 2019

£000	Profit before tax		Cash flow	
	2017	2019	2017	2019
Business plan	107	256	244	375
Sensitivity tests				
Construction costs up 20%	94	243	247	377
Occupancy rates down 15%	−6	113	164	273
Both of the above	−19	100	167	276

33

Conclusion

END WITH A FINAL REPEAT OF THE HEADLINE
TO THE EXECUTIVE SUMMARY

The Dart Valley Guest House and Oriental Spa
will become a leading player in South Devon
after the Phase II project,
with sales doubling,
profitability enhanced
and opportunities outshining risks.

34

Appendices

A. The Dart Valley offering and image gallery

B. Market research and analysis

C. Competitor, utilisation and pricing data

D. Competitive position data

E. Management bios

F. Marketing plan

G. Operations data

H. Environment, health and safety data

I. Financial data

NOT SHOWN IN THIS BOOK, SINCE THE LEVEL OF DETAIL WOULD NOT BE PERTINENT TO THE READER'S BUSINESS PLAN

35

Appendix E: Further reading

Here are your top 10 books to read next:

Vaughan Evans, *The FT Essential Guide to Developing a Business Strategy: How to Use Strategic Planning to Start Up or Grow Your Business,* FT Publishing, 2013 – the companion to this book, taking the reader step by step through the process, summarised in Chapter 5 of this book, of creating a winning business strategy.

Vaughan Evans, *25 Need-to-Know Strategy Tools,* FT Publishing, 2014 – the 25 most important arrows in the quiver of the business strategist, each illustrated by a lively and topical case study.

Vaughan Evans, *Backing U!: A Business-Oriented Guide to Backing Your Passion and Achieving Career Success,* Business and Careers Press, 2009 – how to apply the tools of business analysis to your own prospects for career development or change, including starting UCo, your own company.

Vaughan Evans, *Stand, Speak, Deliver! 37 Short Speeches on How to Survive – and Thrive – in Public Speaking and Presenting,* Little Brown, for publication in late 2015 – 37 pithy, lively, entertaining speeches on each of the most important aspects of the art, as summarised for pitching your business plan in Chapter 10 of this book.

Jules Goddard and Tony Eccles, *Uncommon Sense, Common Nonsense: Why Some Organisations Consistently Outperform Others,* Profile, 2012 – one of the most readable and stimulating books on strategy (for example, what did BMW spot in the Mini that previous owners hadn't?).

Robert M. Grant, *Contemporary Strategy Analysis,* Blackwell, 8th edition, 2012 – the textbook bible since the 1980s for business students of strategy analysis.

John Mullins, *The New Business Road Test: What Entrepreneurs and Executives Should Do Before Writing a Business Plan*, FT Prentice Hall, 3rd edition, 2010 – strategy made real for business start-ups.

Alexander Osterwalder and Yves Pigneur, *Value Proposition Design: How to Create Products and Services Customers Want,* John Wiley, 2014 – the authors of *Business Model Generation* again offer a stimulating, visual, right-side-of-the-brain approach to business.

Doug Richard, *How to Start a Creative Business: The Jargon-free Guide for Creative Entrepreneurs,* David & Charles, 2013 – oodles of hot tips on what and what not to do in starting a business, from an entrepreneur who has seen and done it all many times over.

Sara Williams, *The Financial Times Guide to Business Start Up 2016,* FT Publishing, 2015 – the comprehensive, annually updated guide on the practicalities of getting a business going.

What did you think of this book?

We're really keen to hear from you about this book, so that we can make our publishing even better.

Please log on to the following website and leave us your feedback.

It will only take a few minutes and your thoughts are invaluable to us.

www.pearsoned.co.uk/bookfeedback

Index